LEGAL FRAMEWORK OF
THE SINGLE EUROPEAN CURRENCY

Legal Framework of the Single European Currency

EDITED BY

PAUL BEAUMONT AND NEIL WALKER
Professors of Law, University of Aberdeen

HART PUBLISHING
OXFORD – PORTLAND
1999

Hart Publishing
Oxford and Portland, Oregon

Published in North America (US and Canada) by
Hart Publishing
c/o International Specialized Book Services
5804 NE Hassalo Street
Portland, Oregon
97213-3644
USA

Distributed in Netherlands, Belgium and Luxembourg by
Intersentia, Churchillaan 108
B2900 Schoten
Antwerpen
Belgium

Distributed in Australia and New Zealand by
Federation Press
John St
Leichhardt
NSW 2000

Hart Publishing is a specialist legal publisher based in Oxford, England. To order
further copies of this book or to request a list of other publications please write to:

Hart Publishing, 19 Whitehouse Road, Oxford, OX1 4PA
Telephone: +44 (0)1865 434459 Fax: +44 (0) 1865 794882
email: hartpub@janep.demon.co.uk

British Library Cataloguing in Publication Data
Data Available

ISBN   1-84113-001-X (cloth)

Typeset in Sabon
by John Saunders Design & Production, Reading
Printed in Great Britain on acid-free paper
by Biddles Ltd, Guildford and Kings Lynn.

Contents

PART FOUR
Prospects

Notes on Contributors

Paul Beaumont is professor of European Union law and private international law, University of Aberdeen.

Paul Craig is professor of English law, St John's College, Oxford.

Alistair Darling is a member of the British Cabinet. He was Chief Secretary to the Treasury (1997–8), and is now Secretary of State for Social Services.

Michelle Everson is a Research Fellow, European University Institute, Florence.

Ian Harden is professor of public law, University of Sheffield. Since 1996 he has been on special leave, working as Head of Secretariat of the European Ombudsman.

Andrew Scott is senior lecturer, Europa Institute, University of Edinburgh.

Joanne Scott is senior lecturer in European Community law, Queen Maryand Westfield College, London and Jean Monnet Fellow (1998/9), European University Institute, Florence.

John Usher is Salveson Professor of European Institutions, Europa Institute, University of Edinburgh.

Stephen Vousden is a researcher, European University Institute, Florence.

Neil Walker is professor of legal and constitutional theory, University of Aberdeen.

Table of Cases

Table of Treaties

Table of Secondary Legislation

Table of National Legislation

Introduction

NEIL WALKER and PAUL BEAUMONT

THE introduction of the euro in January 1999 is a crucial landmark in the history of European integration. Indeed, so enormous are its ramifications for the economic, political and regulatory frameworks within which we live that it would be no exaggeration to announce the single currency as one of the most important developments of this fading European century. Yet, its significance notwithstanding, as events built up towards the crucial decisions about the identity of the participants in the first wave of the euro, we became struck by how little serious public debate and scholarly analysis there was in the United Kingdom about this development, most notably its legal dimension.

We can speculate on the reasons for this silence. The long shadow cast by British political and cultural ambivalence about participation would be one contributory factor, echoing similar scenarios in the earlier history of European Union. A more general economic illiteracy amongst all but economists, and thus an apprehension about thinking through the consequences, however profound, of shifts in our macro-economic foundations, would be another part of the explanation. Whatever the reasons, we determined that there was a need to begin to fill this gap. From that determination was born a major conference at Aberdeen Law Faculty on 6–8 May 1998 and this book, based on the conference proceedings.

At the weekend immediately preceding the conference, the decision had been taken that a group of eleven countries, which did not include the UK, would join the single currency on 1 January 1999 and that the European Central Bank (ECB), headed by its new President, Wim Duisenberg, would assume responsibility for the monetary policy that same day. Our event, therefore, could not have been more timely. Alongside a group of prominent academics—European lawyers, public lawyers and economists, we secured the participation of Alistair Darling, then Chief Secretary to the Treasury, member of the Cabinet, and second most important economic minister in the New Labour administration, to deliver a keynote address. His lecture, which is reproduced here with only minor editorial amendments, thus represents a fascinating archive—a first authoritative statement of the Government's strategic attitude towards the euro in the wake of confirmation that it would not be a founding member of the club. As we had hoped, the combination of wide-ranging scholarly analysis and political insight attracted a healthy regional, national and international audience of academics, professionals and public servants. Not only did the lively sessions that followed contribute to the type and quality of public debate which had been lacking, but they were also helpful to the speakers in refining their thoughts with a mind to the present publication.

The structure of the book is self-explanatory. Its direction is both (roughly) chronological and thematic. The first section seeks to set out the formative context of the euro along the three major axes of law (John Usher), economics (Andrew Scott), and politics (Alistair Darling). The second section concentrates upon the constitutional framework which governs the operation of the European Union (EU). "Constitutional" in this context is accorded a specialist meaning as well as its more traditional one. Ian Harden considers the issues of economic constitutionalism at the heart of the euro, in particular whether the regime of legal controls of the various economic variables associated with currency union is sufficiently comprehensive and coherent. Paul Craig concentrates on the more familiar but just as important ground of judicial constitutionalism, drawing upon the broader European case-law on judicial review to envisage its use, value and direction in the context of the workings of the ECB. In the third section we consider the relationship between the euro and the broader picture of European governance. Michelle Everson offers a general analysis of the types of regulatory problems and tensions which arise from subjecting such an intricate area of economic activity to legal and political control, and relates these problems to the accountability of the ECB. Joanne Scott and Stephen Vousden highlight the limited nature of Community programmes to tackle poverty and to redistribute wealth to the poorer countries and regions of the EU. In doing so they point up one of the weaknesses of economic and monetary union (EMU); that relatively little money is available for fiscal transfers to help economies, or parts of economies, within the euro-zone which are hard pressed. The last chapter was written after the euro's birth on 1 January 1999 and is able to take account of the UK Prime Minister's important statements, in late February 1999, on the UK's attitude to the euro. It attempts to deal with the relationship between economics, law and politics; the independence of the ECB; and whether or not the euro will be a lasting species of variable geometry in the EU.[1] Overall the book is both descriptive and analytical, informative and critical. It is about the fine detail of the law, but also places that law in historical, political and economic context.

---

[1] The Treaty of Amsterdam came into force on 1 May 1999 and therefore the book refers to the post-Amsterdam numbers in the European Community (EC) Treaty and in the Treaty on European Union (TEU) with the pre-Amsterdam numbers in brackets prefixed by 'ex'.

The Conference in May 1998, and therefore the book, would not have materialised without the financial assistance of the European Commission in the UK. We are particularly grateful to Caroline Boyle of the Commission's office in Edinburgh for helping with the idea of the conference and with securing funding for it. The conference was also financially supported by the Principal of the University of Aberdeen, Professor Duncan Rice; by the Dean of the Faculty of Law, Professor Christopher Gane; and by Ledingham Chalmers, Solicitors, particularly their managing partner—David Laing. The last mentioned sponsor has consistently supported the Faculty's annual European Law lecture, which on this occasion was of outstanding quality and given in the middle of the conference by Professor Joseph Weiler of Harvard University.[2]

The conference officer was Irene Veelenturf and she did a lot of much appreciated and excellent work to make the conference a reality and enable us as conference organisers to concentrate on building relationships and dealing with issues of policy. The conference benefited from the expert chairmanship of two distinguished contributors to European integration: Professor Trevor Hartley of the London School of Economics and the late Dr Allan Macartney MEP, Rector of the University of Aberdeen. Grateful thanks are also due to Eileen Carr, Administrative Assistant in the Faculty of Law, to Maureen Mercer and Amanda Walton, secretaries in the Faculty of Law, and to several undergraduate and postgraduate law students at the University of Aberdeen who assisted us with the conference organisation. Jessie Keuneman, Tim Johnson, and Jacob Nell, civil servants working for Alistair Darling, all helped us in the task of getting the Minister to Aberdeen with an appropriately worded speech and in transforming that speech into a chapter in this book.

Lastly we would like to thank our families, Gillian, Ross and Lewis and Marion, David and Anna, for the patience they show in allowing us to spend so much time writing and editing. Your love and support is invaluable.

1 March 1999
Faculty of Law,
University of Aberdeen

---

[2] Now published as J. Weiler, "The Constitution of the Common Market Place: Text and Context in the Evolution of the Free Movement of Goods" in Craig and de Burca (eds.), *The Evolution of EU Law* (Oxford, Oxford University Press, 1999), pp. 349–76.

PART ONE

The Birth of the Euro:
Legal, Economic and Political
Perspectives

1

Legal Background of the Euro

JOHN USHER

1. Introduction

THE decisions of the Heads of State and of Government of the member states of the European Union in May 1998 that 11 member states would go ahead to form an Economic and Monetary Union on 1 January 1999[1] meant that the euro would move from the realm of legal theory to market reality. The main aim of this paper is to examine the genesis of the euro and the legal consequences of its introduction as the currency of Austria, Belgium, Finland, France, Germany, Ireland, Italy, Luxembourg, the Netherlands, Portugal and Spain. A recurring sub-theme however will be the legal issues arising in this area from the fact that the euro will not be the currency of Denmark, Greece, Sweden or the United Kingdom.

2. The Legal History of Economic and Monetary Union

The original version of the European Community Treaty (EC Treaty) stated in Article 3 that the activities of the Community should include "the application of procedures by which the economic policies of the member states can be coordinated and disequilibria in their balances of payments remedied". This was reflected in the original Article 104, requiring each member state to pursue the economic policy needed to ensure the equilibrium of its overall balance of payments and to maintain confidence in its currency; and under the original Article 105(1), member states were to co-ordinate their economic policies so as to facilitate the attainment of those objectives. Those obligations can hardly be said to have been universally observed, and, indeed, in the context of the Common Agricultural Policy the European Court held in the late 1970s that the floating of exchange rates and the underlying failure to co-ordinate divergent monetary policies

---

[1] Council Decision 98/317 of 3 May 1998 (in accordance with Art. 121 (ex 109j(4)) EC), OJ 1998 L139/30.

constituted a breach of the obligation set out in Article 105(1).[2] To these provisions the Single European Act, which entered into force in July 1987, added a new Article 102a (itself replaced by a new version as Article 109m introduced by the Maastricht Treaty, now renumbered as Article 124 by the Amsterdam Treaty), which provided for the convergence of economic and monetary policies "necessary for the further development of the Community", and further added a new Chapter heading, "Co-operation in Economic and Monetary Policy".

The effect of all this came to be considered by the European Court in 1991, when it was asked to give its Opinion under Article 300 (ex 228) of the EC Treaty on the compatibility with that Treaty of an agreement with the EFTA countries creating the European Economic Area. The Court gave its *Opinion 1/91* in December 1991,[3] the same month as the Maastricht Treaty was concluded. In that Opinion, it found it necessary to analyse the nature and objectives of the EC Treaty and, *inter alia*, it concluded that the European Community already had the objective of achieving Economic and Monetary Union (EMU) under the terms of the version of the Treaty then in force. This may in fact have continuing relevance in so far as the UK is by virtue of its Protocol[4] not bound by the express Treaty objective flowing from the Maastricht Treaty in Article 4 (ex 3a) of the EC Treaty of introducing a single currency once it has given notice that it will not participate.[5] By way of example, although it was adopted before the UK gave its notice, Council Regulation 1103/97 on certain provisions relating to the introduction of the euro,[6] is concerned in particular with the change from the ECU to the euro which, as will be explained later in this paper, is a matter not envisaged expressly in the EC Treaty. It was however adopted at a Council meeting attended by ministers from all the member states under Article 308 (ex 235) of the EC Treaty, which allows action to attain "one of the objectives of the Community" where the Treaty has not provided the necessary powers. It is not inconceivable that there may be future occasions where use is made of Article 308 (ex 235) in the general area of economic and monetary union.

To a certain extent *Opinion 1/91* merely confirmed what had already happened in the political and legislative spheres. In December 1969, at the end of the original transitional period, a meeting of Heads of State or of Government (i.e. what is now known as the European Council) decided that a plan should be drawn up with a view to the creation of an economic

---

[2] See for example Cases 80–81/77 *Ramel* v. *Receveur des Douanes* [1978] ECR 927.

[3] *Opinion 1/91* [1991] ECR I–6079; the Court in fact held that version of the agreement not to be compatible with the EC Treaty, largely because of its institutional structure, but approved a revised version in April 1992 in *Opinion 1/92* [1992] ECR I–2821.

[4] Protocol 11 paras. 2 and 5.

[5] Notice given 3 November 1997.

[6] OJ 1997 L162/1.

and monetary union,[7] and in March 1970 a committee was set up under the chairmanship of the Luxembourg Prime Minister, M. Werner, to draw up a report on the basic issues by the end of May. This Report[8] reached the fundamental conclusion, repeated by the Delors Committee in 1989[9] that in an economic and monetary union:

> the Community currencies will be assured of total and irreversible mutual convertibility free from fluctuations in rates and with immutable parity rates, or preferably they will be replaced by a sole Community currency.

The Werner Committee also pointed out that monetary and credit policy would have to be centralised; that external monetary policy would fall within Community competence; that essential features of public budgets would be decided at the Community level; that regional and structural policies would no longer fall under exclusive national competence; and that there would need to be systematic and continuous consultation between the social partners. They observed that in the long run economic and monetary union could not do without the development of political union, and that it would be necessary to develop a centre of decision for economic policy and a Community system for the central banks. All of this may seem remarkably familiar in the context of the Maastricht debates. The Maastricht provisions on economic and monetary union find their genesis in the Report of a Committee chaired by Jacques Delors, the President of the Commission, which was set up following a meeting of the European Council in Hanover in June 1988 and which reported back in April 1989.[10]

The Delors Committee took as a starting point the view that the development of the single market necessitated a more effective co-ordination of economic policy between national authorities, pointing out that with full freedom of capital movements and integrated financial markets, incompatible national policies would quickly translate into exchange rate tensions and put an increasing and undue burden on monetary policy[11]—a prediction which appears subsequently to have been proved correct. They did, however, point out that EMU would be a quantum leap, implying far more than the single market programme.[12]

The Report briefly suggested that EMU would imply complete freedom of movement for persons, goods, services and capital, as well as irrevocably fixed exchange rates and, finally, a single currency.[13] It was also expressly pointed out that it would require a transfer of decision-making power from

---

[7] Compendium of Community Monetary Texts 1974, p.13 at p.15.

[8] EC Bulletin 1970 Supplement 11.

[9] 1989 Report para. 22.

[10] Agence Europe Documents No.1550/1551, 20 April 1989.

[11] Paras. 10–12.   [12] Para. 14.   [13] Para. 16.

member states to the Community as a whole, particularly in the fields of monetary policy and macro-economic management.[14] With regard to the monetary union, the Delors Report expressly referred to the Werner Committee Report,[15] and it was suggested that if there was an irrevocable locking of exchange rate parities, a single currency would be a natural and desirable further development, demonstrating that the move was irreversible and avoiding the transaction costs of converting currency.[16]

With regard to the mechanisms for achieving EMU, the Delors Committee recommended a three-stage process. The first stage did not require any Treaty amendments, and in fact the European Council meeting in Madrid in June 1989 decided that it should start on 1 July 1990.[17]

In stage two, which the Maastricht Treaty defined as beginning on 1 January 1994,[18] the fundamental recommendation was that the institutional structure should be established.[19] This was not wholly followed in the Maastricht Treaty, which provided for the creation of a transitional European Monetary Institute (EMI)[20] able to exercise some, but not all, of the powers to be enjoyed by the European Central Bank (ECB) in the third stage. The reason for this may be found in the structure of the ECB. By virtue of Articles 112 and 121(4) (ex 109a and 109j(4)) EC, the Governing Council of the Central Bank comprises the Executive Board of the ECB and the Governors of the central banks of the member states without a derogation (i.e. the "ins"). Article 112 (ex 109a) EC further provides that the Executive Board of the ECB shall comprise the President, the Vice-President and *four* other members. The President, the Vice-President and the other members of the Executive Board are to be appointed from among persons of recognised standing and professional experience in monetary or banking matters by common accord of the governments of the member states without a derogation at the level of Heads of State or of Government. It is therefore clear that the Executive Board of the ECB need not be representative even of all the participating member states. Indeed, it is provided that if there are member states with a derogation, the number of members of the Executive Board may be smaller than provided for in Article 11.1 of the Statute of the ESCB (European System of Central Banks) (a President, a Vice-President, and four others), but in no circumstances may it be less than four. On this basis it would be difficult to envisage all member states being involved during the second stage, only for some of them to drop out because they could not participate in the third stage; hence the European Monetary Institute.

---

[14] Para. 19.   [15] See *supra* n. 8.   [16] Para. 23.

[17] See for example, the recitals to Council Decision 90/141 on the progressive convergence of economic policies and performance during stage one of economic and monetary union, OJ 1990 L78/23.

[18] EC Treaty Art. 116 (ex 109e(1)) EC.

[19] Para. 57.   [20] Art. 117 (ex 109f) EC.

Finally, in the third stage, the date for the start of which was fixed under the Maastricht provisions as no later than 1 January 1999, the irrevocably locked exchange rates would begin, to be replaced by a single currency, and the relevant monetary and economic competences would be transferred to Community institutions. These institutions would have to have authority to impose constraints on national budgets to the extent to which this was necessary to prevent imbalances that might threaten monetary stability.[21] Presumably this is the source of Article 104 (ex 104c) EC, requiring member states[22] to avoid excessive government deficits and laying down procedures to enforce that obligation.

Since the first stage of EMU began on 1 July 1990, the provisions introduced by the Maastricht Treaty are largely relevant to the second and third stages. Article 116 (ex 109e) EC defined the second stage as beginning on 1 January 1994. Each member state was by then required to have adopted, *inter alia*, appropriate measures to comply with the prohibitions laid down in the new provisions on capital movements and payments, which will be considered later in this paper. Institutionally, Article 117 (ex 109f) EC provided for the establishment of the EMI at the start of the second stage. However, perhaps the most important feature of the second stage was the establishment of the criteria determining whether progress may be made towards the third stage, in Article 121 (ex 109j) EC.

3. Convergence Criteria

The determination of which member states are to participate in the third stage of EMU was based on a system of reports by the Commission and the EMI to the Council on the progress made in the fulfilment by the member states of their obligations regarding the achievement of EMU. These reports included an examination of the compatibility between each member state's national legislation, including the statutes of its national central bank, and Articles 108 and 109 (ex 107 and 108) EC on the independence of the ECB and of national central banks, and the Statute of the ESCB. The reports were also required to examine the achievement of a high degree of sustainable convergence by reference to the fulfilment by each member state of criteria which make reference very largely to factual situations and soft law, with the result that their nature could be regarded as having changed during the period between the signature of the Maastricht Treaty in February 1992 and the assessment which was made in May 1998. The criteria are as follows:

---

[21] Para. 59.

[22] With an exception for the UK under its Protocol. However, by virtue of a reference to Art. 116(4) (ex 109e(4)) EC, the UK must "endeavour" to avoid excessive government deficits.

(i) the achievement of a high degree of price stability
This is stated to be apparent from a rate of inflation which is close to that of, at most, the three best performing member states in terms of price stability. The Protocol on Convergence Criteria defines closeness in terms of not exceeding the rates of the three best states by more than 1.5 per cent, which in 1992 may have seemed a tight target. However, in the year ending in January 1998, the arithmetic average of the three best performing member states was 1.2 per cent,[23] and to exceed that by 1.5 per cent gives a range of error of more than one hundred per cent. The figure used was in fact 2.7 per cent.

(ii) the sustainability of the government financial position
This is stated to be apparent from having achieved a government budgetary position without a deficit that is excessive as determined in accordance with Article 104(6) (ex 104c(6)) EC. Under Article 104(2) (ex 104c(2)) EC, the relevant criteria relate to the ratio of the planned or actual government deficit to Gross Domestic Product (GDP) and to the ratio of government debt to GDP. These criteria are further refined in the Protocol on the Excessive Deficit Procedure, according to which government deficit must not exceed three per cent of GDP, and government debt must not exceed sixty per cent of GDP, but they are not absolute. A member state which breaches the deficit ratio will not be regarded as having an excessive government deficit if the ratio has declined "substantially and continuously" and reached a level that comes close to the reference value, or, alternatively, the excess over the reference value is only "exceptional and temporary" and the ratio remains close to the reference value.[24] Furthermore, a higher ratio of government debt will not be regarded as excessive if the ratio is "sufficiently diminishing" and approaching the reference value "at a satisfactory pace".[25] Thus both Belgium and Italy both had a ratio of government debt to GDP above one hundred and twenty per cent when the assessment of compliance with the convergence criteria was made[26] yet were not regarded as having an excessive deficit. However, this is not just a hurdle to be jumped over to gain admission to the third stage of EMU: the obligation to avoid an excessive government deficit remains in perpetuity,[27] and its enforcement is the subject of the Stability and Growth Pact discussed elsewhere in this volume.[28]

[23] Commission Recommendation of 25 March 1998, recital 6.

[24] Art. 104(2)(a) (ex 104c(2)(a)) EC.

[25] Art. 104(2)(b) (ex 104c(2)(b)) EC.

[26] Commission Report of 25 March 1998 on Progress towards Convergence, 1.3.1 and 1.3.7.

[27] See Hahn, "The Stability Pact for European Monetary Union: Compliance with Deficit Limit as a Constant Legal Duty", (1998) *CMLRev.* 77.

[28] See Ch. 4 *infra* by I. Harden. The two hard law components of the Stability and Growth Pact are Council Regulation 1466/97 on the strengthening of the surveillance of budgetary positions and of the surveillance and co-ordination of economic policies, OJ 1997 L209/1; Council Regulation 1467/97 on speeding up and clarifying the implementation of the excessive deficit procedure , OJ 1997 L209/6.

(iii) the observance of the normal fluctuation margins provided for by the Exchange Rate Mechanism (ERM) of the European Monetary System, for at least two years, without devaluing against the currency of any other member state

(iv) the durability of convergence achieved by the member state and of its participation in the Exchange Rate Mechanism of the European Monetary System being reflected in the long-term interest rate levels.

Before turning to the broader issues raised by these references to the European Monetary System, it may be observed that under the Protocol on Convergence Criteria it is stated that average nominal long-term interest rates should not exceed those of the three best states by more than two per cent. By the time the assessment was made, the figure derived from the three best states was 5.8 per cent,[29] so that again a margin of two per cent allows for a wide margin of error in relation to that norm, whatever may have been the situation in 1992.

So far as the European Monetary System (EMS) itself is concerned, its structure was laid down in a Resolution of the European Council of 5 December 1978,[30] backed up by an Agreement between the central banks of the member states of 13 March 1979 laying down the operating procedures for the EMS (hereinafter the 1979 Agreement).[31] A resolution is a type of act nowhere defined in the Treaties, whose legal consequences therefore are not laid down anywhere in the Treaties, though that does not mean that it has no legal consequences. However, the EMS constituted only what was meant to be its initial phase;[32] it was, for example, intended to create a European Monetary Fund within two years, but that never happened. Although its aim was to create a "zone of monetary stability in Europe", this should be seen in the context of a world of floating exchange rates. It did not create a fixed exchange rate system: it allowed margins of fluctuation, anticipated realignments of central rates against the ECU, and envisaged that the definition of the ECU itself could be changed. Indeed, between 1979 and 1986 there were on average nearly two realignments a year.[33] On the other hand, from then until the Autumn of 1992, the system remained relatively stable; dare it be suggested that in the late 1980s the participant states had similar economic goals, whereas by 1992 the priorities of some of them had become somewhat divergent, leading to the market pressures which drove the UK and Italy out of the ERM.

In this context it should be observed that the criterion with regard to the

[29] Commission Recommendation of 25 March 1998, recital 9.

[30] EC Bulletin 1978 No.12, point 1.1.11.

[31] Revised version printed in *Compendium of Community Monetary Texts* (1989), p.50.

[32] 1978 Resolution Art. 1.4.

[33] Coffey, Peter, *The European Monetary System: Past Present and Future* (2nd ed. 1987, Nijhoff, Amsterdam) pp.126–127.

ERM refers to the "normal" fluctuation margins and not to the "narrow" margins. Until 1993 it was the case, as is well known, that the normal margin was 2.25 per cent, with an exceptional band of six per cent. The decision taken on the night of 1–2 August 1993 by Ministers and Central Bank Governors adopted on a "temporary" basis a general margin of fluctuation of fifteen per cent, subject to a bilateral arrangement between Germany and the Netherlands to maintain a 2.25 per cent margin between their currencies.[34] Leaving on one side the view that such a wide band hardly represents a margin at all, it may be submitted that the fifteen per cent band became the "normal" margin of fluctuation. However, whether or not this interpretation is correct, it shows very clearly how the content of a binding Treaty provision which refers to "soft" law may effectively be amended by a change in that soft law. The attitude taken by the Commission in its Report and Recommendation of 25 March 1998 was on the one hand to say in its Recommendation[35] that the widening of the margins of fluctuation "modified the framework" for assessing exchange rate stability, while stating in its Report that it had used the margin of 2.25 per cent as the basis for its assessment, and seems to have been satisfied if a currency had "almost always" traded within that margin.[36]

The Treaty, however, refers to staying within the normal margin for two years, which gave rise to particular issues in relation to Finland, Italy and Sweden. Italy was one of the original participants in the ERM, albeit initially with a wider band of fluctuation of 6.25 per cent. However, like the UK, it found itself having to leave the system in September 1992, and did not rejoin until November 1996, less than two years before the assessment was made. However, in its Report,[37] the Commission stated that:

> although the lira has participated in the ERM only since November 1996, it has not experienced severe tensions during the review period and has thus . . . displayed sufficient stability in the last two years.

Finland, which only joined the Community in 1995, entered the ERM in October 1996, and in its Report[38] the Commission used wording virtually identical to that used in relation to Italy. However, Sweden, which also joined the Community in 1995, had not participated at all in the ERM, and was known politically not to wish to participate in stage three of EMU, but did not have the benefit (if such it be)[39] of a special protocol like

---

[34] See Agence Europe 23 August 1993 No.6034, pp. 3–4.

[35] Recital 8.

[36] See for example, Commission Report 1.3.11 in relation to Portugal.

[37] Para. 1.3.7.

[38] Para. 1.3.12.

[39] Given the difference between the rate of interest declared by the ECB for operations in the euro is 2.5%, and the UK bank rate is 5.25%, the present author is not inclined to regard the UK's position as a benefit.

the UK or Denmark. There is no mention of this last point in the Commission's Report, which instead observes that the Swedish crown had never participated in the ERM, and that during the relevant two years it had fluctuated against the ERM currencies, "reflecting, among other things, the absence of an exchange rate target", and the formal Council Decision[40] uses very similar wording. Both then conclude that Sweden did not fulfil the third convergence criterion. The conclusion may therefore be drawn that while this criterion has not been interpreted literally, a member state which does not participate at all in the ERM will not be regarded as meeting the criterion, at least if it has suffered currency fluctuation (which is highly likely to be the case). The practical consequence therefore may be said to be that to the extent that membership of the ERM is voluntary, participation in the third stage of EMU is also voluntary, even if no new member states are offered the special treatment given to the UK and Denmark.

In this context, it must be emphasised that the convergence criteria are not simply a set of tests which were applied once in 1998; they remain relevant so long as there are non-participant member states, and in the context of any future enlargement of the Community. The status of a member state with a derogation is envisaged as being transitional rather than permanent. Indeed the responsible Commissioner, M de Silguy, has taken to referring to member states with a derogation as "pre-ins".[41] Under Article 122(2) (ex 109k(2)) EC, at least once every two years, or at the request of a member state with a derogation, the Commission and the ECB must report to the Council in accordance with the procedure laid down in Article 120(1) (ex 109j(1)) EC. After consulting the European Parliament and after discussion in the Council, meeting in the composition of the Heads of State or of Government, the Council shall, acting by a qualified majority on a proposal from the Commission, decide which member states with a derogation fulfil the necessary conditions on the basis of the convergence criteria set out in Article 121(1) (ex 109j(1)) EC, and abrogate the derogations of the member states concerned. It may be submitted that this reference to Article 121(1) (ex 109j(1)) EC may create problems, because, as has been discussed above, two of the criteria for convergence laid down in that provision relate to the ERM of the EMS, and if the ECU had in fact by then become the single currency of a number of member states, that exchange rate mechanism simply could not operate; rather, it would appear that the currency of a member state with a derogation would have to stay in a defined relationship with the ECU as a foreign currency in order to qualify for admission to the third stage. However, the Treaty fails to deal with the question of an exchange-rate mechanism in

[40] Council Decision 98/317, OJ 1998 L139/30.

[41] Speech to Vienna Stock Exchange, 25 September 1998 (RAPID Documents Speech 98/182).

relations between member states which participate in EMU and those which do not.

The EMI prepared a draft framework for that relationship (a European Monetary System Mark II),[42] and this formed the basis of an agreement in principle on its structure at the Dublin European Council in December 1996. This framework was adopted in a European Council Resolution of 16 June 1997[43], following exactly the same pattern as the 1978 Resolution of the European Council on the original EMS.[44] It is thus an undefined act of an institution of the European Union, even though monetary policy is clearly and expressly an exclusive Community competence—at least for the participants in stage three;[45] by way of contrast, in the context of the convergence criteria, Articles 121 and 122 (ex 109j and 109k) EC are very careful to refer to the "Council meeting in the composition of Heads of State or of Government" rather than to the European Council.

The main features of the European Monetary System Mark II include the fact that, like the first version, participation in the ERM is voluntary for the member states outside the euro area, so that the Swedish precedent appears to remain valid. Nevertheless, it is stated that "Member States with a derogation can be expected to join the mechanism".[46] The ERM is based on central rates against the euro. The standard fluctuation band is plus or minus fifteen per cent around the central rates,[47] as in the original system after 1993, but "on a case-by-case basis, formally agreed fluctuation bands narrower than the standard one and backed up in principle by automatic intervention and financing may be set at the request of the non-euro area Member State concerned."[48] In fact, Greece has entered the standard band, but Denmark is participating in ERM II within a narrow band of fluctuation plus and minus 2.25%.[48a] However, it is also stated that "the standard and narrower bands shall not prejudice the interpretation of the third indent of Article 109j(1) [now 121(1)] of the EC Treaty",[49] a singularly unhelpful provision given the doubts discussed above. It may be suggested, following the language of the Commission Recommendation of 25 March 1998 and the Council Decision of 3 May 1998, that what will really matter is whether the currency has suffered "severe tensions".

For the sake of completeness, it may also be observed that the convergence reports of the Commission and the EMI were required also to take

[42] Report of the EMI to the informal Ecofin Council, Verona, 12–13 April 1996.

[43] OJ 1997 C236/5.

[44] European Council Resolution of 5 December 1978 (EC Bulletin 1978 No.12, point 1.1.11).

[45] See Louis, "A legal and institutional approach for building a Monetary Union" (1998) CMLRev. 33 at p. 70.

[46] European Council Resolution of 16 June 1997, para.1.6.

[47] Para. 2.1.   [48] Para. 2.4.

[48a] Bulletin Quotidien Europe No. 7310, 28 ord 29 September 1998.

[49] Para. 2.5.

account of the development of the ECU, the results of the integration of markets, the situation and development of the balances of payments on current account and an examination of the development of unit labour costs and other price indices.

4. The Euro

As from 1 January 1999, the currency of the participating states became the euro.[50] The euro replaced the EC's own unit of account, the ECU.[51] However, euro notes and coins will only be introduced after a transitional period of three years.[52] The aim of this section is to analyse the legislation adopted by the EC to deal with the legal problems arising from the replacement of the ECU by the euro, the replacement of the national currencies of the participants by the euro, and the continued use of national banknotes and coins until 2002.

A. replacement of the ECU by the euro

The replacement of the ECU by the euro is a matter which was not foreseen by the Maastricht Treaty, since it was only decided at the meeting of the European Council in December 1995 that the name to be given to the European currency should be the "euro" rather than the term "ECU" used in the Treaty. As recorded in the recitals to Council Regulations 1103/97[53] and 974/98,[54] at the meeting of the European Council in Madrid on 15 and 16 December 1995, the decision was taken that the term "ecu" used by the Treaty to refer to the European currency unit was a generic term, and the Governments of the fifteen member states reached the common agreement that this decision was "the agreed and definitive inter-pretation of the relevant Treaty provisions"and that the name given to the European currency should be the "euro". Thus, without changing the Treaty, the Treaty term was changed. The use of the term "euro" was in fact judicially challenged by a member of the European Parliament,[55] but his first action was held inadmissible since he attempted to challenge the proposal which eventually became Regulation 1103/97 rather than a binding legal act, and his second action was held inadmissible because the Regulation was not of direct and individual concern to him.

So far as the origins of the ECU itself are concerned, the European

---

[50] Council Regulation 974/98, OJ 1998 L139/1, Art. 2.
[51] Council Regulation 1103/97, OJ 1997 L162/1, Art. 2.
[52] Council Regulation 974/98, OJ 1998 L139/1, Art. 10.
[53] OJ 1997 L162/1.   [54] OJ 1998 L139/1.
[55] Case T–175/96 *Berthu* v. *Commission* [1997] ECR II–811; Case T–207/97 *Berthu* v. *Council* [1998] ECR II–509

Communities have from the outset required their own accounting unit. The problem was recognised in the old Coal and Steel High Authority's Decision No.2 of 13 December 1952[56] dealing with the levy payable under that Treaty. Article 50(2) of the Coal and Steel Treaty provided that the levies should be assessed annually on the relevant products according to their average value, and what the High Authority decided to do was in fact to fix a levy in units of account, these being units of account of the European Payments Union established in 1950. The effect, at least in theory, of using the unit of account was that the High Authority could fix a flat rate levy which should be the same in real terms irrespective of where in the Community the products originated, and irrespective of the currency used in any actual transaction. The levy under Article 50(2) of the Coal and Steel Treaty was, of course, intended as the "own resource" of the Coal and Steel budget, and the modern budget of the European Communities (which in fact excludes the Coal and Steel operational budget)[57] is itself always drafted in terms of units of account.[58] The aim, of course, was to avoid using the currency of any one member state, but one result of the introduction of the euro will be that the Community will be using the currency of eleven of its member states for its own accounting purposes.

Units of account are used not only in the budget itself, but also in relation to funds falling outside the scope of the budget as such. So, for example, successive European Development Funds, created originally for the benefit of those countries associated with the Community under Article 131 of the EEC Treaty, with subsequent European Development Funds being created for the purposes of the 1963 and 1969 Yaoundé Conventions and for the purposes of the subsequent Lomé Conventions, have been denominated in units of account, even though these funds have been financed through fixed contributions from the member states. Indeed, it was in the context of the fourth European Development Fund, established pursuant to the 1975 Lomé Convention,[59] that the modern unit of account calculated from the current values of a basket of currencies was used for the first time.

Turning to the greatest source of Community expenditure, the Common Agricultural Policy, the major common organisations are based on a common price policy,[60] in which the prices are all fixed in units of account.[61] Leaving aside the sad history of monetary compensation introduced when currencies first floated in 1971, the theory was that there are single prices at

[56] JO 1952 No.1, p.3.

[57] Art. 20 of the Merger Treaty 1965 provides for the ECSC *administrative* expenditure to be shown in the general budget of the European Communities, and limits the amount of that expenditure to be met from the ECSC levy.

[58] European Currency Units (ECUs) have been used in the general EC budget since the entry into force of the 1980 Financial Regulation, OJ 1980 L345/23.

[59] Council Decision 76/568, OJ L176/8.

[60] See Usher, *The Law of Agriculture in the EEC* (Oxford, Clarendon Press, 1988).

[61] Originally defined in Council Regulation 129/62, JO 1962, p. 2553.

the Community level, and exchange risks are borne at the national level.[62] However, the introduction of the euro means that the Community prices are set in the currency of eleven of the member states, and there are exchange risks only for the member states which do not participate.[63]

It has already been mentioned that the unit of account chosen by the Coal and Steel Community in 1952 was the unit of account of the European Payments Union, which happened to correspond to the gold value of the US dollar. At the end of 1958 the European Payments Union was replaced by the European Monetary Agreement, and the identical European Monetary Agreement unit of account became the unit of account used for Community purposes. When the first common agricultural legislation was enacted in 1962, Regulation 129/62[64] again defined the agricultural unit of account at the official value of the US dollar, that is a value of 0.88867088 grammes of fine gold. It was also there provided that where sums given in one currency were required to be expressed in another currency, the exchange rate to be applied should be that which corresponded to the par value communicated to and recognised by the International Monetary Fund.

The demise of the European Monetary Agreement at the end of 1972 did not in fact lead to an immediate change in the definition of the unit of account. Indeed, the 1973 Financial Regulation[65] expressly retained the gold parity unit of account for budgetary purposes, despite the fact that currencies had by then been floating for two years.

The modern basket-type unit of account was first created, under the name of the European Unit of Account (EUA) in April 1975[66] as a method of calculating the amount of aid payable under the first Lomé Convention. The external value of the EUA was derived from the value in June 1974 of the "Special Drawing Rights" (SDR) of the International Monetary Fund,[67] based on a basket of currencies which gave a heavy weighting to the US dollar. The original value of the SDR was, in turn, based on the gold value of the US dollar.[68] Hence, a link can be traced between the original unit of account and the modern ECU, and indeed between the dollar and the euro. The name of the EUA was changed to the European Currency Unit (ECU) in December 1978,[69] when this basket unit found a

---

[62] Following the entry into force of Council Regulation 3813/92, OJ 1992 L387/1, as amended by Council Regulation 150/95, OJ 1995 L22/1, but see Council Regulation 942/98 amending Regulation 724/97 on compensation for revaluations affecting farm incomes, OJ 1998 L132/1.

[63] See Commission Proposal for a Council Regulation 2799/98 establishing agrimonetary arrangements for the euro, OJ 1998 L 349/1.

[64] JO 1962, p. 2553.   [65] OJ 1973 L116/1.

[66] Council Decision 75/250, OJ 1975 L104/35.

[67] As stated in the recitals to Decision 75/250 itself.

[68] See note 64 above.

[69] Council Regulation 3180/78, OJ 1978 L379/1.

new role as the core of the EMS, but the definition remained exactly the same, although it was subsequently changed in September 1984[70] and again in September 1989[71] (a definition consolidated in 1994).[72]

The fundamental characteristic of the EC's basket unit was that it comprised fixed sums of national currencies, not fixed percentages of national currencies. These fixed sums did not change automatically when central rates were altered in an EMS realignment or when market values fluctuated, so that the percentage composition of the unit in terms of national currencies might, and indeed did, change. The percentage share of a currency which rose in value increased, since the EUA and later ECU comprised a fixed element of that currency, and the percentage share of a currency whose value diminished would inevitably decrease, since there was still the same nominal sum in that currency represented in the unit. For example, during the period 1975 to 1983, when the definition of the EUA/ECU remained unchanged, the percentage of the unit represented by the same fixed sum of German currency rose from about twenty-seven per cent to about thirty-seven per cent.[73] By way of comparison, in the most recent definition in 1989, its share was set at 30.1 per cent.[74]

When the ECU was created in the context of the EMS, the European Council's Resolution of 5 December 1978[75] expressly provided that the value and composition of the ECU would be identical with the value of the EUA at the outset of the system, so that Council Regulation 3180/78,[76] changing the value of the unit of account used by the European Monetary Cooperation Fund,[77] defined the ECU as the sum of exactly the same currency elements as the EUA. Under the 1978 Resolution, the weightings of the currencies used in the definition of the ECU could be revised within six months after the entry into force of the EMS and thereafter every five years, although a revision could be requested at any other time if the weight of any currency had changed by twenty-five per cent or more.[78]

It must, however, be emphasised, that just as the 1975 EUA reflected the overall value of the SDR, and the 1978 ECU reflected the external value of the EUA, so also the 1978 Resolution of the European Council states categorically that "revisions must not in themselves modify the external value of the unit of account".[79] Hence, a revision in itself could have no immediate effect on the value of the unit of account, although obviously the future development of the unit might well be affected by its new composition.

---

[70] Council Regulation 2626/84, OJ 1984 L247/1.
[71] Pursuant to Council Regulation 1971/89, OJ 1989 L189/1.
[72] Council Regulation 3320/94, OJ 1994 L350/27.
[73] Commission of the EC, *The ECU* (1984), p.12.
[74] Council Regulation 1971/89, OJ 1989 L189/1, Art. 1.
[75] EC Bulletin 1978 No.12, point 1.1.11.
[76] OJ 1978 L379/1.
[77] Created by Council Regulation 907/73, OJ 1973 L89/2.
[78] Art. 2(3).   [79] Art. 2(3).

Whereas one of the basic characteristics of the ECU was that its composition could be changed, even if in principle only every five years, Article 118 (ex 109g) EC introduced by the Maastricht Treaty states categorically that the currency composition of the ECU basket shall not be changed, no doubt with the intention of building confidence in the international money markets. The result of this was that the September 1989 definition remained in force and could not be altered, since it could not in principle be revised until September 1994 under the previous rules, and this date was after the entry into force of Article 118 (ex 109g) EC. This meant that the definition of the ECU could not reflect an element of the currencies of the member states which joined since that date: Austria, Finland and Sweden.

Article 121 (ex 109g) EC further provided that from the start of the third stage, the value of the ECU should be irrevocably fixed in accordance with Article 123 (ex 109l(4)) EC, which in turn required that from that date, the Council should, acting with the unanimity of the member states which are able and willing to participate, adopt the conversion rates at which their currencies should be irrevocably fixed and at which irrevocably fixed rate the ECU should be substituted for these currencies, the ECU thereby becoming a currency in its own right, as the "euro". These conversion rates were fixed by Council Regulation 2866/98.[79a] It was nevertheless still provided, in terms redolent of the 1978 Resolution, that this measure should by itself not modify the external value of the ECU. The irrevocable fixing of the value of the ECU relates only to those currencies which it replaces, but the fundamental consequence is, that from the start of the third stage of EMU, the ECU no longer is a basket in which the currencies of all member states are represented but rather the currency of the participating member states. If non-participating member states wish to maintain a fixed relationship with it or maintain a narrow range of floating against it within the context of the European Monetary System Mark II, they will find themselves pursuing something over which they have no direct influence—unless they actually join the single currency system.[80]

Following the decision at the Madrid European Council to use the term "euro", however, Regulation 1103/97[81] was adopted in June 1997 under Article 308 (ex 235) of the EC Treaty to deal with the problems of conversion; it was adopted therefore contemporaneously with the Amsterdam Treaty, even if that Treaty did not make any formal amendment to introduce the term "euro". Under Article 2 of this Regulation, every reference in a legal instrument to the ECU as defined under Community law is to be replaced by a reference to the euro at a rate of one euro to one ECU, and in an effort to cover the private sector use of the ECU, references in a legal instrument to the ECU are deemed to be references to the ECU as defined in

---

[79a] OJ 1998 L359/1.
[80] Art. 122(3), (4) and (5) (ex 109k(3), (4) and (5)) EC.
[81] OJ 1997 L162/1.

Community law, subject to the intentions of the parties. It is further declared, in Article 3, which is just as relevant to the replacement of national currencies by the euro as it is to the replacement of the ECU by the euro, that the introduction of the euro is not to have the effect of altering any term of a legal instrument or of discharging or excusing performance under any legal instrument, nor of giving a party the right unilaterally to alter or terminate such an instrument. No doubt this provision was adopted in response to worries about the possible frustration of contracts following the introduction of the euro. It is however subject to anything which parties may have agreed between themselves, although it is highly unlikely that any contract entered into before the Madrid European Council in December 1995 will have contemplated the introduction of the euro.

It might finally be observed in this context that under Article 4(4), monetary amounts to be converted from one national currency unit into another are first to be converted into a monetary amount expressed in the euro unit, and are then to be converted into the other national currency unit. This reflects the fact that even during the transitional period before euro notes and coins are introduced, the currency unit is the euro,[82] as will be explained below, so that there are no bilateral exchange rates between the former national currencies except as a consequence of the conversion rate against the euro. It is further provided in Article 4(1), presumably for the same reason, that the conversion rates shall be adopted as one euro expressed in terms of each of the national currencies of the participating member states.

B. replacement of national currencies by the euro

In order to give the markets maximum notice as to legal rules applicable on the replacement of national currencies by the euro, even though no formal legislation could be issued until the decision had been taken on which countries should participate in the third stage of EMU,[83] the Council published a Resolution in July 1997[84] setting out what it expected to be the text of the legislation. Following the decision to move to the third stage of EMU, a formal Regulation was adopted on 3 May 1998[85] which, apart from filling in the blanks, is virtually identical to the text published in the Resolution. This Regulation declares unequivocally in Article 2, that as from 1 January 1999 the currency of the participating member states is the euro, that the currency unit is one euro, and that one euro shall be divided into one hundred cents (which again is a matter with which the Treaty does

---

[82] Council Regulation 974/98, Art. 2.

[83] EC Treaty Art. 123 (ex 109l).

[84] European Council Resolution of 7 July 1997 on the legal framework for the introduction of the euro, OJ 1997 C236/7.

[85] Council Regulation 974/98 of 3 May 1998 on the introduction of the euro, OJ 1998 L139/1.

not expressly deal). The euro was to be substituted for the currency of each participating member state at the conversion rate[86] set at the start of the third stage under Article 123(4) (ex 109l(4)) of the EC Treaty,[86a] and it is the unit of account of the ECB and of the central banks of the participating member states.[87]

While the euro may have become the currency of the participating member states in 1999, euro banknotes and coins will not be introduced until January 2002.[88] During the intervening period, and for up to six months thereafter, national notes and coins will remain in use, but their legal nature will change: under Article 6 of the Regulation they have become divisions of the euro rather than continuing as currencies in their own right. They are only legal tender, however, within their territorial limits as of the day before the commencement of EMU.[89] The Regulation provides that where in a legal instrument reference is made to a national currency unit, "this reference shall be as valid as if reference were made to the euro unit according to the conversion rates."[90] Furthermore, the substitution of the euro for the currency of each participating member state does not in itself have the effect of altering the denomination of legal instruments in existence on the date of substitution.[91]

In principle, and subject to anything the parties may have agreed, acts to be performed under legal instruments stipulating the use of or denominated in a national currency unit are to be performed in that national currency unit, and acts to be performed under legal instruments stipulating the use of or denominated in the euro unit are to be performed in the euro unit.[92] However, any amount denominated either in the euro unit or in the national currency unit of a given participating member state, and payable within that member state by crediting an account of the creditor, can be paid by the debtor either in the euro unit or in that national currency unit. The amount is to be credited to the account of the creditor in the denomination of his account, with any conversion being effected at the conversion rates.

The Regulation also empowers member states under Article 8(4) to take measures to redenominate in the euro unit outstanding debt issued by that member state's general government, and to enable the euro unit to be used as a unit of account by security and commodity markets and in systems for the regular exchange, clearing and settlement of payments.

Banknotes denominated in euros, and coins denominated in euros or in cents are to be put in circulation in the participating member states as from 1 January 2002[93] and, subject to a changeover period of up to six months,[94] will be the only banknotes and coins which have the status of legal tender in all these member states. Nevertheless, issuers of national

---

[86] Art. 3.
[86a] The conversion rate was set by Council Regulation 2866/98 (OJ 1998 L359/1).
[87] Art. 4.   [88] Art. 10.   [89] Art. 9.   [90] Art. 6(2).   [91] Art. 7.   [92] Art. 8.
[93] Art. 10.   [94] Art. 15.

banknotes and coins are required to continue to accept the banknotes and coins previously issued by them against euros at the conversion rate.[95] Authority to issue notes and coins stems from Article 106 (ex 105a) of the EC Treaty. Article 106(1) (ex 105a(1)) EC sets out what would perhaps be the most important monetary function of the ECB, going to the heart of what has been traditionally regarded as a function of the state:[96] for the participating member states, the ECB has the exclusive right to authorise the issue of banknotes within the Community. The ECB and the national central banks may issue such notes, and the bank notes issued by the ECB and the national central banks are the only such notes to have the status of legal tender within the Community. With regard to coins, Article 106(2) (ex 105a(2)) EC permits participating member states to issue coins subject to approval by the ECB of the volume of the issue. The Council may, acting in accordance with the cooperation procedure[97] and after consulting the ECB, adopt measures to harmonise the denominations and technical specifications of all coins intended for circulation to the extent necessary to permit their smooth circulation within the Community, resulting in the enactment of Council Regulation 975/98 of 3 May 1998 on the denomination and technical specifications of euro coins intended for circulation.[98]

C. practical problems

The coexistence for three years of the euro as the currency of the participating member states with national banknotes and coins gives rise to a number of possible difficulties which the Commission has endeavoured to address in three non-binding recommendations. The first[99] sets out a standard of good practice on banking charges. This provides that banks should not charge for the following:

- the conversion of incoming and outgoing payments denominated in the euro unit or in the national currency unit during the transitional period;
- the conversion of accounts from the national currency unit to the euro unit both during and at the end of the transitional period;
- the exchange for their customers of "household amounts" of national banknotes and coins for euro banknotes and coins in 2002.

In addition, banks should not charge a different fee for services in the euro unit than that for otherwise identical services in the national currency unit.

---

[95] Art. 16.

[96] See the judgment of the European Court in Case 7/78 R. v. *Thompson* [1978] ECR 2247.

[97] Art. 252 (ex 189c) EC. The failure of the Amsterdam Treaty to amend any of the provisions relating to EMU means that this is the only sector where the co-operation procedure is encountered after the entry into force of that Treaty.

[98] OJ 1998 L139/6.

[99] Commission Recommendation 98/286 of 23 April 1998, OJ 1998 L130/22.

The second recommendation[100] sets out a standard of good practice with regard to dual display of prices which would require:

- a clear indication from retailers on whether they will accept payments in euro units in the transitional period;
- clear distinction between, on the one hand, the unit in which the price is set and in which amounts to be paid are to be calculated and, on the other hand, the counter-value which is displayed for information purposes only.

This recommendation also calls for agreements, where possible, on common formats and designs for dual displays, and suggests that as a general rule dual displays can be limited to the final price which consumers have to pay and to the total on financial statements or receipts.

The third recommendation[101] is largely concerned with monitoring and information, but suggests that given that the changeover to the euro may pose particular challenges for small enterprises, businesses, individually or through representative organisations, should agree on principles which would help small enterprises with the changeover. In particular, it recommends that firms should give a period of notice before issuing or asking for invoices in euros in order to allow their customers and suppliers time to prepare themselves properly. In addition, where a small firm requests a supplier to continue showing prices in national currency alongside prices in euros on invoices, the supplier should accept.

It remains to be seen how effective these recommendations will be. It might merely be observed that in the area of financial services, there are numerous examples of non-binding recommendations being replaced by binding legislation. Thus, Commission Recommendation 87/63[102] was eventually replaced by Directive 94/19 of the European Parliament and of the Council on deposit guarantee schemes,[103] and Commission Recommendation 90/109 on transparency of banking conditions[104] has given way to Directive 97/5 of the European Parliament and Council on cross-border credit transfers.[105] However, the three recommendations at issue here are transitional in their nature, and it may be suggested that they are likely to retain their current status.

5. Wider Legal Effects - Monetary Movements and Taxation

A single currency implies a single currency area, and it may be wondered how far the restrictions normally associated with a Treaty "freedom" are

---

[100] Commission Recommendation 98/287 of 23 April 1998, OJ 1998 L130/26.
[101] Commission Recommendation 98/288 of 23 April 1998, OJ 1998 L130/29.
[102] OJ 1987 L33/16.   [103] OJ 1994 L135/5.   [104] OJ 1990 L67/39.
[105] OJ 1997 L43/25.

appropriate in a single currency area. On the other hand, the single currency area is not a single taxation area, and the Treaty rules on monetary movements have to apply not just within a single currency area but also within the four other currency areas of the non-participating member states. However, one result of the move to the euro is that the freedom of capital movements is the only Treaty "freedom" where the basic rules have been changed, with new rules coming into force in January 1994 at the start of the second stage of EMU.[106]

The original Treaty provisions had the distinction of constituting the only Treaty "freedom" not to have been capable of giving rise to rights enforceable by individuals.[107] However, there is a long history of secondary legislation: the first Council Directive under Article 67 was enacted during the first stage of the original transitional period on 11 May 1960, but it, and the later Directives which amended it, liberalised only a defined list of capital movements. A new approach was followed by Council Directive 88/361,[108] which finally established the basic principle of free movement of capital as a matter of Community law with effect, for most member states, from 1 July 1990. Subject to its other provisions, Article 1(1) provided that "Member States shall abolish restrictions on movements of capital taking place between persons resident in Member States", and although there was still a nomenclature of capital movements annexed to the Directive, it was stated to be to facilitate its application, rather than to introduce distinctions in treatment. Annex I itself stated that the nomenclature was not intended to be an exhaustive list of the notion of capital movements, and it should not be interpreted as restricting the scope of the principle of full liberalisation of capital movements in Article 1. However, in the absence of a Treaty definition, the headings of the nomenclature (which in reality owe much to the previous lists) indicate the concept of capital underlying the Directive: direct investments, investments in real estate, operations in securities normally dealt in on the capital market, operations in units of collective investment undertakings, operations in securities and other instruments normally dealt in on the money market, operations in current and deposit accounts with financial institutions, credits related to commercial transactions or to the provision of services in which a resident is participating, financial loans and credits, sureties, other guarantees and rights of pledge, transfers in performance of insurance contracts, personal capital movements, physical import and export of financial assets, and "other capital movements" (defined to include transfers of the moneys required for the provision of services).

The introduction to the Annex further states that the capital movements mentioned are taken to cover all the operations necessary for the purposes

---

[106] EC Treaty Art. 73a (repealed by the Treaty of Amsterdam).
[107] Case 203/80 *Casati* [1981] ECR 2595.
[108] OJ 1988 L178/5.

of capital movements, i.e. the conclusion and performance of the transaction and related transfers, and should also include access for the economic operator to all the financial techniques available on the market approached for the purpose of carrying out the operation in question.

Two particular comments may be made about this nomenclature. The first is that in the continued silence of the Treaty it may remain a useful source of illustration of the principle of the free movement of capital even after the entry into force of Articles 56 to 60 (ex 73b to 73g) EC.[108a] The second is that many of the movements listed are clearly current payments under Article 73h(1) (what was then Article106(1) EEC and has now been repealed by the Treaty of Amsterdam), even though the Court had held in Cases 286/82 and 26/83 *Luisi and Carbone* v. *Ministero del Tesoro*[109] that Article106(1) EEC was directly effective. At first sight it might seem that to include such movements in the Directive was superfluous. However, it might be suggested that the difficulties in distinguishing clearly between capital movements and current payments, and the narrow way in which the Court read Article106 in Case 308/86 *Lambert*,[110] holding that it was not relevant to the way an **exporter** received payment, instead merely being concerned to ensure that the **importer** was able to make the payment, and that it entitled the exporter only to payment in his own currency, meant that there was some practical advantage in including what were possibly current payments in the concept of liberalised capital movements. It may, nevertheless, be observed that the 1988 Directive purported to be made under Articles 69 and 70(1) EEC, which related only to capital movements. It is now clear that borrowing money from a bank in another member state to buy a house fell within the scope of the Directive, see Case C–484/93 *Svensson and Gustavsson* v. *Ministre du Logement*,[111] though it has subsequently been suggested by AG Tesauro in his Opinion in Case C–118/96 *Safir* v. *Skattemyndigheten i Dalarnas Län*[112] that a narrower concept of capital movements should be adopted.

As has already been indicated, the Maastricht Treaty introduced new provisions on "capital and payments" with effect from 1 January 1994, the date set for the start of the second stage of EMU. The fundamental rules are set out in Article 56 (ex 73b) EC, paragraph 1 of which states that within the framework of the provisions set out in that Chapter, all restrictions on the movement of capital between member states and between member states and third countries shall be prohibited, and paragraph 2 of which states that

---

[108a] As has now been held by the European Court in Case C–222/97 *Trummer and Meyer* (16 March 1999).

[109] [1984] ECR 377.   [110] [1988] ECR 4369.   [111] [1995] ECR I–3955.

[112] [1998] ECR I–1897, 1905–7. The Court dealt with the case as an unlawful restriction on the freedom to provide services and did not regard it as necessary to comment on the questions concerning free movement of capital, including the matters of scope discussed by the Advocate-General, see paras. 34–35 of the judgment.

within the same framework, all restrictions on payments between member states and between member states and third countries shall be prohibited.

At first sight a fundamental distinction between these provisions and the original provisions—and indeed from the situation reached under the 1988 Directive—is that it appears that movements to and from third countries are to be treated in the same way as movements between member states. With hindsight, this can be seen as anticipating the need to ensure the external movement and availability of the new single currency. However, in reality there are differences which remain. Under Article 57 (ex 73c) EC, the provisions of Article 56 (ex 73b) EC are stated to be without prejudice to the application to third countries of any restrictions which existed on 31 December 1993 under national or Community law adopted in respect of the movement of capital to or from third countries involving direct investment (including investment in real estate), establishment, the provision of financial services or the admission of securities to capital markets; in other words, they do not require existing lawful restrictions to be abolished in these (admittedly limited) areas. Furthermore, the second paragraph of Article 57 (ex 73c) EC, empowering the Council to legislate on those capital movements, makes reference to "endeavouring" to achieve the objective of free movement of capital between member states and third countries to the "greatest extent possible", language redolent of the original capital movement provisions in relation to movements between member states. Under Article 59 (ex 73f) EC, where, in exceptional circumstances, movements of capital to or from third countries cause, or threaten to cause, serious difficulties for the operation of EMU, the Council, acting by a qualified majority on a proposal from the Commission and after consulting the ECB, may take safeguard measures with regard to third countries for a period not exceeding six months if such measures are strictly necessary. Finally, by virtue of Article 60 (ex 73g) EC, the Council may take urgent measures under Article 301 (ex 228a) EC, where Community action to interrupt or reduce economic relations with one or more third countries is required by a common position or in a joint action adopted under the EU provisions on a common foreign and security policy, in relation to the movement of capital and on payments as regards the third countries concerned; indeed, pending such measures, member states themselves may, under the second paragraph of Article 60 (ex 73g) EC, take unilateral measures against a third country with regard to capital movements and payments "for serious political reasons". The freedom is therefore not absolute. Be that as it may, to the extent that a payment or capital movement is not excluded, Article 56 (ex 73b) EC has been held to be directly effective even with regard to capital movements to third countries such as Switzerland and Turkey.[113]

---

[113] Cases C–163, 165 and 250/94 *Sanz de Lera* [1995] ECR I–4821.

This in itself is an interesting development given the Court's reluctance in earlier case-law automatically to extend concepts developed in the context of the internal market to situations governed by similar language in relations with third countries. So, for example, in Case 270/80 *Polydor v. Harlequin*[114] in the context of the free movement of goods, it was held that even where a free trade agreement does expressly prohibit not only quantitative restrictions but also measures having effects equivalent to quantitative restrictions, the same interpretation of that phrase need not be given in the context of trade with a non-member state as will be given in the context of trade between states, since there is no intention to create a single market under free trade agreements.

A synthesis of the approach to the direct effect of provisions of international agreements was given in the context of an agreement between the Community and Portugal in the *Kupferberg* case.[115] The Court started from the principle that it is open to the Community and the third country to agree what effect the provisions of the agreement are to have in the internal legal order of the contracting parties, and that the matter fell to be decided by the Court only in the absence of express agreement on the point, emphasising however that it was open to the courts of one contracting party to consider that certain provisions were directly effective even if that view was not shared by courts of the other contracting party. It then went on to consider whether the provision at issue could be regarded as unconditional and sufficiently precise to have direct effect in the light of the object and purpose of the agreement, concluding that the provision at issue imposed an unconditional rule against discrimination in matters of taxation, dependent only on a finding that the products affected were of like nature, so that it could be applied by a court and produce direct effects throughout the Community. The Court did, however, emphasise that, despite the fact that the provision at issue had the same object as Article 90 (ex 95) of the EC Treaty, each of these provisions should be interpreted in its own context, and that the interpretation given to Article 90 (ex 95) EC could not be applied by way of simple analogy to the corresponding provision of an agreement on free trade. However, in *Sanz de Lera* the judgment does not discuss these issues, and simply holds Article 56 (ex 73b) EC to be directly effective in itself and on its own terms.

While, like other Treaty freedoms, the new capital movement provisions do allow member states on certain defined and limited grounds to take measures which may restrict movements both within the Community and outside it, these provisions do not really seem to make allowance for the existence of a single currency area which does not include all the member states. The safeguard clause which may be used by the Community as

---

[114] [1982] ECR 379.
[115] Case 104/81 *Hauptzollamt Mainz v. C. A. Kupferberg & Cie KG* [1982] ECR 3641, [1983] 1 CMLR 1.

opposed to its member states in Article 59 (ex 73f) EC relates only to third countries, stating that where, in exceptional circumstances, movements of capital to or from third countries cause, or threaten to cause, serious difficulties for the operation of EMU, the Council, acting by a qualified majority on a proposal from the Commission and after consulting the ECB, may take safeguard measures with regard to third countries for a period not exceeding six months if such measures are strictly necessary. There is no provision for parallel measures in relation to non-participant member states, even though such states may remain entitled to take or be authorised to take measures even with regard to movements to or from other member states to protect their balance of payments under Articles 119 and 120 (ex 109h and 109i) EC. However, while as a matter of legal theory there may be an imbalance between these provisions, it may be wondered how likely it is that an EMU of eleven member states would need to invoke safeguard measures against the other four.

Turning to the movement of capital and payments between member states as such, it may be wondered why, given that the 1988 Directive already laid down the basic principle of unrestricted free movement of capital between persons resident in member states, it was felt necessary to draft new Treaty provisions apparently to the same effect. One substantive difference is that by treating payments between member states in the same way as capital movements, the new Treaty provisions remove any lingering doubts as to the precise scope of the freedom to make current payments. A more fundamental reason, no doubt, is that as secondary legislation, a Directive could relatively easily be amended, and progress to EMU could hardly be envisaged unless monetary movements between member states rested on the same legal basis as the other fundamental features of that Union, i.e. provisions of the EC Treaty itself.

It has nevertheless been held that both Article 1 of the 1988 Directive, in Cases C-358 and C-416/93 *Bordessa and Mellado*[116] and Article 56(1) and (2) (ex 73b(1) and (2)) of the EC Treaty, in Cases C–163, 165 and 250/94 *Sanz de Lera*,[117] are drafted in a manner sufficiently clear, precise and unconditional to be directly effective, and therefore give rise to rights enforceable by individuals before their national courts from their respective dates for implementation (1 July 1990 and 1 January 1994 respectively). However, the direct effect of a Directive is a residual concept, only relevant where a member state has failed to comply with its obligations under the Directive in time,[118] and only available against the member state on which that obligation is imposed,[119] although the concept of the member state may

---

[116] [1995] ECR I–361.

[117] [1995] ECR I–4821.

[118] Case 148/78 *Ratti* [1979] ECR 1629.

[119] Case 152/84 *Marshall* v. *Southampton Area Health Authority* [1986] ECR 723.

extend to local authorities[120] or to utilities and other undertakings given special powers by the public authorities[121]—which in the present context could perhaps include banking authorities and regulators. On the other hand, the direct effect of a clear, precise and unconditional provision of the Treaty may be invoked against any subject of the law on which it imposes obligations,[122] which raises the question whether Article 56 (ex 73b) EC imposes obligations on subjects of the law other than the state itself.

Neither paragraph of Article 56 (ex 73b) EC is addressed to member states as such; they simply state, in absolute terms, that all restrictions on the movement of capital and on payments between member states shall be prohibited. In this area analogies may be drawn not only with the free movement of goods, but also with the freedom to provide services where it has long been established that the relevant Treaty rules may be invoked against private sector employers, trade unions and professional associations,[123] and that Article 56 (ex 73b) EC may therefore be invoked against operators in the private sector with regard to transactions between member states. It is not difficult to envisage a situation in which the unilateral conduct of a financial institution, for example with regard to the terms and conditions under which it will effect monetary transfers to other member states, may be regarded as restricting payments between member states. Indeed, with regard to the competition rules of the Treaty, it has long been accepted that the charges levied for transferring money from one member state to another may affect trade between member states.[124]

Like all the other Treaty freedoms, the freedom of capital movements and payments between member states is subject to permitted restrictions, set out in Article 58 (ex 73d) EC, which resembles the drafting of Article 30 (ex 36) of the EC Treaty in relation to the free movement of goods, in that it requires that such restrictions should not constitute "a means of arbitrary discrimination or a disguised restriction" on the free movement of capital and payments as defined in Article 56 (ex 73b) EC. A point of particular interest here is the question of permitted tax discrimination. Article 58(1)(a) (ex 73d(1)(a)) EC provides quite simply that in the context of free movement of capital, the prohibition of restrictions on capital movements is without prejudice to the right of member states to apply provisions of their tax law which distinguish between taxpayers who are not in the same situation with regard to their place of residence or with regard to the place where their capital is invested.

---

[120] Case 103/88 *Costanzo* v. *City of Milan* [1989] ECR 1839.

[121] Case C–188/89 *Foster* v. *British Gas* [1990] ECR I–3313.

[122] A concept most frequently encountered in the area of competition law, see e.g. Case 127/73 *BRT* v. *SABAM* [1974] ECR 313.

[123] See e.g. Case 36/74 *Walrave and Koch* v. *Union Cycliste Internationale* [1974] ECR 1405, where it was held that the rules on free movement of workers and those on freedom to provide services could be invoked against a professional cycling association.

[124] Case 172/80 *Züchner* v. *Bayerische Vereinsbank* [1981] ECR 2021.

At first sight this might be taken as a clear authorisation to discriminate in the tax system between residents and non-residents. Most of the discussion has centred on the question whether this provision allows discrimination *against* non-residents, which could clearly conflict with the fundamental Treaty freedoms relating to establishment, provision of services, and movement of workers, although the conclusion may be reached that this provision does not in fact override the basic Treaty freedoms, which clearly do prohibit adverse discrimination within the scope of their application.[125] Be that as it may, in the more recent decision in Case C-118/96 *Safir* v. *Skattemyndigheten i Dalarnas Län*,[126] where it was held to be a breach of Article 49 (ex 59) EC for Sweden to impose a different tax regime for insurance policies purchased from providers outside Sweden, which would have the effect of deterring Swedish residents from taking out such policies despite the fact that it was intended to achieve tax neutrality between policies purchased inside and outside Sweden, it was stated that the decision on this point made it unnecessary to determine whether the legislation was also incompatible with Articles 56 and 58 (ex 73b and 73d) EC—even though under the express terms of Article 50 (ex 60) EC, services are only services within the meaning of the Treaty to the extent that they do not fall under one of the other Treaty freedoms.

On the other hand, it has been suggested that the aim of Article 58(1)(a) (ex 73d(1)(a)) EC was to permit discrimination *in favour of* non-residents. The provision must, however, be taken in its context: in effect it is drafted as a permission to take measures which might interfere with the free movement of capital and payments, rather than *carte blanche* to discriminate. In other words, the fact that a measure may be justifiable as a restriction on the movement of capital and payments does not necessarily make it acceptable as a state aid. In any event Article 58(1)(a) (ex 73d(1)(a)) EC is subject both to the caveat that such measures "shall not constitute a means of arbitrary discrimination or a disguised restriction on the free movement of capital and payments as defined in Article 56 [ex 73b]", and to a Declaration made by the member states when the Maastricht Treaty was signed stating that:

> The Conference affirms that the right of Member States to apply the relevant provisions of their tax law as referred to in Article 58(1)(a) [ex 73d(1)(a)] of this Treaty will apply only with respect to the relevant provisions which exist at the end of 1993. However, this Declaration shall apply only to capital movements between Member States and to payments effected between Member States.

This at the least amounts to a political commitment not to introduce any new measures of the type at issue. It may be suggested that one reason

---

[125] See Usher, "Tax discrimination under the new capital movement provisions and the basic Treaty freedoms" in Rudanko and Timonen (eds.), *European Financial Area* (Helsinki, University of Helsinki, 1998), pp.259–75.

[126] [1998] ECR I–1897, see *supra* n. 112.

for the presence of Article 58(1)(a) (ex 73d(1)(a)) EC was the failure to deal with the question of tax *evasion* when capital movements were originally liberalised under the original Treaty rules by Council Directive 88/361,[127] which finally established the basic principle of free movement of capital as a matter of Community law with effect, for most member states, from 1 July 1990, as mentioned in the annexed paper. Directive 88/361 expressly envisaged in its Article 6(5) that the Commission would submit to the Council by 31 December 1988 proposals aimed at eliminating or reducing risks of distortion, tax evasion and tax avoidance "linked to the diversity of national systems for the taxation of savings and for controlling the application of these systems", and the Council was to take a position by 30 June 1989. The Commission did in fact put forward a proposal,[128] albeit slightly late, for a Directive on a common system of withholding tax on interest income, requiring the payer of interest to deduct from the amount of interest due a withholding tax at a rate of at least fifteen per cent, so as at least to ensure the payment of a "minimum taxation of interest". However, under Article 6(5) of the Directive, the Council was required "in accordance with the Treaty" to act unanimously, and it failed to approve the proposal (largely, it would appear, as the result of opposition from the UK and Luxembourg), with the result that the capital movements Directive entered into full effect with no corresponding Community tax legislation, with all the possibilities for tax evasion to which that might give rise.

Nevertheless, as the single market has become more of a reality, and in particular as exchange risks (and artificial interference with interest rates at the national level) have been eliminated for those member states participating in EMU, the market effects of differential tax systems have become more obvious. In the area of the free movements of goods the Community did indeed take steps to limit the range of variation in rates of VAT.[129] However, there is now clearly a political impetus in this area, exemplified by an Ecofin meeting on 1 December 1997 which adopted a Code of Conduct for Business Taxation,[130] and reached political agreement on the need for legislation on withholding tax. The Commission has now put forward a new proposal for a Directive "to ensure a minimum of effective taxation of savings income in the form of interest payments within the Community".[131] This is based on the "coexistence" model under which member states can apply a withholding tax at source (of which the suggested level is twenty per cent) or provide information on income from savings to other member states, and its scope is limited to interest paid in each member state to individuals resident in another member state.

So far as the Code of Conduct for Business Taxation is concerned, it is

[127] OJ 1988 L178/5.   [128] OJ 1989 C141/5.
[129] Directive 92/77, OJ 1992 L316/1, on rates of VAT.
[130] OJ 1998 C2/3.
[131] COM(1998) 295 final (20 May 1998).

emphatically stated to be "a political commitment" concerning those measures which affect, or may affect, in a significant way the location of business activity in the Community. Within that scope, it is stated that tax measures which provide for a significantly lower effective level of taxation, including zero taxation, than that which generally applies in the member state in question are to be regarded as potentially harmful and therefore covered by the Code. The Code further provides that when assessing whether such measures are harmful, account should be taken of, *inter alia*:

(i) whether advantages are accorded only to non-residents or in respect of transactions carried out with non-residents, or

(ii) whether advantages are ring-fenced from the domestic market, so they do not affect the national tax base, or

(iii) whether advantages are granted without any real economic activity or substantial economic presence within the member state offering such tax advantages, or

(iv) whether the basis of profit determination in respect of activities within a multinational group of companies departs from internationally accepted principles, notably those agreed upon within the OECD, or

(v) whether the tax measures lack transparency, including where statutory rules are relaxed at administrative level in a non-transparent way.

The commitments of the member states under the Code are divided into "standstill" and "rollback". With regard to the former, they commit themselves not to introduce new tax measures which are harmful within the meaning of the Code, and with regard to the latter, they commit themselves to re-examining their existing laws and established practices, having regard to the principles underlying the Code and to the review process set out in the Code. Member states undertake to amend such laws and practices as necessary with a view to eliminating any harmful measures as soon as possible, taking into account the Council's discussions following the review process.

The review process requires member states to inform each other of existing and proposed tax measures which may fall within the scope of the Code. In particular, member states are called upon to provide at the request of another member state, information on any tax measure which appears to fall within the scope of the Code. It also involves an element of assessment. Any member state may request the opportunity to discuss and comment on a tax measure of another member state that may fall within the scope of the Code, so as to permit an assessment to be made of whether the tax measures in question are harmful, in the light of the effects that they may have within the Community. That assessment will take into account all the factors identified above. In reviewing tax measures, the Council also emphasises the need to assess carefully the effects which they have on other member states, *inter alia*, in the light of how the activities concerned are effectively taxed throughout the Community.

6. Conclusions

The fact that there is now open discussion at the Community level of such previously "no-go" areas as taxation illustrates how far the achievement of EMU has shifted the focus of debate. It also illustrates the fundamental underlying issue, which is whether there can really be a long-lasting dichotomy between monetary policy and economic and fiscal policy. In the meantime, for the academic lawyer, the introduction of the euro shows a fascinating intermingling of hard law, soft law and political commitment, and a test-bed for theories of differential integration.

2

The Macro-economic Context of the Euro

ANDREW SCOTT

1.Introduction

IN May 1998 the European Union Heads of Government and State decided that eleven of the fifteen European Union (EU) member states should proceed to the third stage of economic and monetary union (EMU) from 1 January 1999. This decision, based on reports prepared by both the European Commission and the European Monetary Institute in accordance with Article 121(1) (ex109j(1)) EC,[1] testified to the fact that these member states had met the so-called convergence criteria set out in the European Community Treaty (EC Treaty). The EC Treaty stipulated that four convergence criteria had to be met before a member state would be deemed eligible to participate in the single currency area. These involved convergence of the inflation rate towards the average recorded by the best performing member states, exchange rate stability, interest rate convergence, and the avoidance of "excessive deficits".[2] In the event, only Greece was adjudged to have failed to meet these criteria. Both Denmark and the UK had secured opt-outs from the monetary union provisions of the EC Treaty, and therefore were not candidates for progressing to the third stage, while Sweden did not want to join at that time and deliberately failed to meet the convergence criteria.[3]

In this chapter I will focus on three issues. First, I will review, briefly, the economic implications of EMU, and consider the problems which theoretical and empirical economic studies indicate are likely to accompany the

---

[1] See European Commission, *Convergence Report 1998*, (Brussels, 1998) and European Monetary Institute, *Convergence Report* (Frankfurt, 1998).

[2] An excessive deficit was said to exist if (a) the budget deficit to GDP ratio was above 3%, unless temporary and exceptional or (b) the debt to GDP ratio exceeded 60% or was making sufficient progress towards this level. See Arts. 104(2) and 121(1) (ex 104c(2) and 109j(1)) EC, and Protocols 5 (Excessive Deficit Procedure) and 6 (On the Convergence Criteria).

[3] See Chs. 1 and 8 by J. Usher and by P. Beaumont and N. Walker.

introduction of the euro—the EU's single currency. Second, I will examine the role of the European Central Bank (ECB) in the EU economic policy process, and consider how its actions may, or may not, contribute to a resolution of these difficulties. Finally, I will focus on the problem of unemployment within the EU, which the shift to monetary union can be expected to influence, and comment on this in the light of the changes to the EC Treaty made by the Treaty of Amsterdam agreed upon at the June 1997 Amsterdam meeting of the European Council.

Two broad propositions are being advanced in this chapter. The first is that the effect of *this* monetary union may be to undermine economic and social cohesion within the EU.[4] This follows from the fact that EMU will weaken fundamentally the ability of individual member states to pursue macro-economic policies which presently are used to combat particular economic problems within national economies. In many cases it is this, rather than the direct effects of EMU, that represents the principal source of the "costs" of European monetary union, costs that may be politically damaging and therefore unacceptable over the longer term. The second proposition is that the absence of an institutional mechanism capable of reconciling the very narrowly defined remit of the ECB (i.e. achieving price stability), with the general expectation that closer European integration will deliver material economic benefits across the EU, will lead to a further erosion in the legitimacy of the EU. This leads me to argue that supplementary mechanisms to buttress EMU may well be needed if this arrangement is to be both politically and economically stable. The difficulty is not in identifying these additional mechanisms, but in securing the political commitment necessary for their development. The chapter focuses principally on the macro-economics of EMU. Whilst recognising that the transition to EMU has important implications at the micro-economic level—indeed the identifiable gains from EMU are, primarily, micro-economic in character[5]—I will not consider these in this chapter.

2. The Macro-Economic Issues

Following the decision that the third stage of EMU is to begin on schedule with eleven member states adopting the euro on 1 January 1999, we can expect the attention of national policy-makers to switch from addressing

[4] It is important to stress that it makes little intellectual sense to be for or against the principle of EMU. At that level we simply observe that monetary unions exist across the world and tend, on balance, to be reasonably stable. However, it is legitimate to point to defects in specific formulations of a monetary union. The comments that follow represent a critique of the EC Treaty version of EMU, and cannot be applied to the principle of EMU.

[5] The principal gains are elimination of transactions costs, removal of the risk of unexpected exchange rate changes, and seigniorage. For a comprehensive analysis of this see P. De Grauwe, *The Economics of Monetary Integration* (OUP, 1997).

the question "how to meet the convergence criteria in order to join the third stage of EMU" to "how to live with the consequences of participating in the third stage of EMU". This is particularly true for those countries that still fail to meet a strict definition of the excessive deficit criteria stipulated in the EC Treaty and its Protocols. This is the case in Belgium and Italy, both of whom have a ratio of public debt to Gross Domestic Product (GDP) of more than double the sixty per cent upper limit.[6] Of course, participation in EMU itself may assist these countries to lower this ratio. In so far as the common, euro-zone wide rate of interest is below that previously prevailing in these two highly indebted countries,[7] the annual cost arising from servicing the outstanding stock of debt will fall. This will reduce the burden of debt servicing on annual government expenditure, leaving greater scope to eliminate some part of the outstanding stock of debt. Moreover, to the extent that lower interest rates lead to an expansion of the level of economic activity in these countries, the level of GDP will rise and the debt-to-GDP ratio will decline further. What is clear, however, is that no EMU member state has the option of non-observance of the excessive budget convergence criteria following the introduction of the euro. This follows from the adoption of the Stability and Growth Pact (SGP) at the Amsterdam European Council in June 1997.[8] The SGP not only commits all EMU countries to remain bound by the three per cent and sixty per cent ceilings on domestic fiscal policy criteria, but it also defines a scale of financial sanctions to be imposed on any EMU member state which breaches these criteria.[9] Only where a country can demonstrate that "exceptional" circumstances exist, as defined by the SGP, may it incur an annual budget deficit in excess of three per cent of GDP, or allow the stock of debt to exceed sixty per cent of GDP.[10]

Member states that still have to satisfy the EC Treaty convergence criteria may experience economic problems of transition to EMU. There may be local costs of early accession to EMU in countries whose domestic

---

[6] In Belgium the debt-to-GDP ratio in 1997, the reference year, was 122.2% while in Italy it was 121.6%. A further seven countries recorded a debt-to-GDP ratio of between 60% and 80%.

[7] This has certainly been the case historically with respect to Italy, though less so in Belgium.

[8] See Council Regulation 1466/97, OJ 1997 L209/1; Council Regulation 1467/97, OJ 1997 L209/6 and European Council Resolution of 17 June 1997 OJ 1997 C236/5 for the text of the Stability and Growth Pact.

[9] EU member states not in the first wave of EMU continue to be bound by the relevant provisions of the EC Treaty.

[10] Art. 2 of Regulation 1467/97 defines an exceptional circumstance as ". . . an annual fall of real GDP of at least 2%", although an annual fall of less than 2% may be deemed to be exceptional and therefore permitted. The Resolution of the European Council OJ 1997 C236/5, established, at para. 7, that an annual fall of at least 0.75% in real GDP *may* be taken to be indicative of a severe recession, permitting an excessive deficit to emerge without penalty.

inflation rate is still above that recorded by the best performing EMU countries.[11] Given that inflation across the monetary union inevitably must fall to the rate prevailing in those member states with the lowest inflation rates, the shift to monetary union may produce a temporary increase in unemployment in the higher inflation economies. This is because nominal wage negotiations in those countries, as elsewhere, will reflect expectations of the future rate of inflation that are based on previous experience. If, however, the (post-EMU) actual rate of inflation is lower than the (historically based) expected rate of inflation, the result will be an increase in real wages which is likely to cause a rise in the level of unemployment. Higher unemployment will persist until nominal wage claims adjust (downwards) to reflect the lower rate of inflation, thereby returning real wages to their original level. Just how long this expectations-adaptation exercise will take is uncertain, although given that this problem has been well advertised one might expect expectations to adjust relatively quickly. But, of course, the speed at which expectations of the future rate of inflation adjusts to the new regime is critically dependent on economic agents' judgement regarding the credibility of the anti-inflation policy adopted by the new monetary authority (i.e. the ECB), as well as by the stability of the economic relationships upon which these policies rest. If economic agents regard the ECB as lacking in conviction to maintain—for example—a restrictive monetary policy against a background of high (or rising) unemployment, or if they expect a higher rate of inflation to result from that policy, high nominal wage claims may persist and the adjustment costs of EMU in terms of increased unemployment will be all the greater. If, on the other hand, ECB credibility is high, then these adjustment costs are likely to be correspondingly lower. I will return to the matter of credibility and accountability with respect to the ECB later in the chapter.

Notwithstanding the debate concerning the institutional structure of, and policy process within, the ECB, it is clear from the EC Treaty that its principal objective is to maintain price stability.[12] And while ECB "credibility" is a crucial element in shaping the adjustment of expectations and, ultimately, the *short run* employment costs of EMU, the ECB has still to resolve the difficult technical question of deciding which variable it will target in order to deliver price stability. Two alternative monetary policy strategies are available to the ECB.[13] The first is to target the rate of inflation directly, with the rate of interest being pegged at the level necessary to

---

[11] This was not a significant problem in the first wave of euro countries because the gap between the best performing and worst performing state in terms of inflation was only 0.7%.

[12] Art. 105(1) EC.

[13] See the statement delivered by the ECB President, Dr Duisenberg, to the European Parliament's Subcommittee on Monetary Affairs, 22 September 1998.

secure price stability. Under this arrangement, interest rates can be expected to change in response to current inflationary trends. This is the approach that the Bank of England has followed since September 1992, when sterling was forced out of the original Exchange Rate Mechanism (ERM I). The appeal in the inflation-targeting approach is that it is transparent and is widely understood. The difficulty, however, is that empirical studies indicate that changes in rates of interest (effected by changing the supply of money) only influence the underlying rate of inflation after a time lag—which may be as much as two years. Consequently, if the current rate of inflation exceeds its target—or target band—this will reflect policy decisions made many months in the past. The second approach is for the ECB to control inflation by regulating the quantity of money in circulation (i.e. the money supply). This involves selecting an appropriate aggregate measure of the supply of money in circulation, and restricting the growth of money supply to the underlying rate of economic growth for the EU in general.[14] Targeting the growth of the money supply is the approach preferred by the German Central Bank (the Bundesbank), arguably the most successful post-war central bank in terms of the control of inflation. Monetary aggregates have an advantage in that they are readily measurable, and differences between the targeted and the actual rate of monetary growth can be quickly detected and corrected. The disadvantage with this method, however, is that very little is known at present about the transmission mechanism that links changes in money supply to subsequent changes in the inflation rate at the level of the euro-zone. In particular, the (monetarist) model that predicts a given change in the supply of money will produce a particular change in the rate of inflation, is based on the assumption that the underlying demand for money is basically stable, or that it changes only slowly over relatively long periods. While many studies have been conducted into the demand-for-money function within individual economies, we have very little empirical knowledge about the stability of the demand-for-money function at the level of the euro-zone. Consequently, the technique of achieving EU price stability by targeting some measure of euro-zone money supply is somewhat risky.

Leaving aside the technical problems that remain to be resolved by the ECB, the most frequently studied problems associated with EMU involve the consequences for national economies of the loss of domestic competence over monetary policy. In particular, the literature is dominated by contributions which focus on the impact of EMU on the process of economic adjustment when individual economies no longer have the ability to adjust domestic monetary policy (interest rates and the exchange rate) in order to stabilise the economy in the event of an unexpected economic

---

[14] The conventional "monetarist" wisdom is that inflation is directly, and proportionately, attributable to the rate of growth of the money supply exceeding the economy-wide rate of economic growth.

shock.[15] Under EMU, intra-EU exchange rates will disappear, and a
common interest rate will apply across the area as a whole. The question
arises: what are individual countries to do if their economies are experi-
encing real economic difficulties in the form of falling output and rising
unemployment where the government has no scope to lower interest rates or
devalue the exchange rate in order to stabilise the economy? This is a
scenario most commonly associated with the consequences of an
asymmetric economic shock.[16] It is true that the government concerned will
still have recourse to fiscal policies to address this problem. However, as we
noted above, the conditions of the SGP curtail significantly the effective
freedom of action on the part of individual governments to respond through
offsetting fiscal policy activism in such a situation.[17] If, on the other hand,
the external economic shock impacts evenly across the monetary union, the
stabilisation problem may become more manageable. On the assumption
that inflationary pressures in the economy generally will subside as the level
of economic activity declines following a shock, it is likely that the ECB
would be able to lower the common interest rate without fear of inflation.
This would tend to boost domestic investment and consumption (and
possibly exports), thereby countering the employment and output impact of
the economic shock on the euro-zone economy, and diminishing accordingly the stabilisation role required of national fiscal policies. However, in
the case of asymmetric shocks, where only a few member states are
adversely affected, it is unlikely that the ECB would adjust the prevailing
monetary policy. In that case, the entire burden of the stabilisation and
adjustment effort would be borne by (domestic) fiscal policy in the
"shocked" member states. Four adjustment routes are available at that level:

(i) A reduction of money wages in the shocked economy thereby widening
the differential between wages in that economy, and the euro-zone average.
To the extent that businesses locate capital expenditure in response to
lower wages, an inflow of investment capital can be expected to restore
some part of economic activity to the shocked economy. The problem is—
as seen in the German re-unification episode—nominal wages within a
single currency area tend towards equality rather than greater inequality. If
we are to rely on widening national—or regional—nominal wage differen-

---

[15] For a recent review of this issue, see M. Feldstein, "The Political Economy of the
European Economic and Monetary Union: Political Sources of an Economic Liability", *The
Journal of Economic Perspectives*, 11(4) at 23. See also De Grauwe *supra* n.5 for a compre-
hensive review of these matters.

[16] This is where an external disturbance impacts substantially on one economy in a
monetary union, but only slightly or not at all on the other economies. It may take the form
of a sector-specific shock, or a country-specific shock.

[17] It is important to note that an "expansionary" fiscal policy is, in part, an automatic
response to recession given the increase in transfer payments (especially unemployment
benefits) this triggers and the decline in government revenue from taxation as the level of
economic activity falls.

tials as a mechanism for offsetting unfavourable shocks, then we must have some idea of the specific mechanics whereby this will occur. One might suggest that the very experience of unemployment is just such a device, but it is equally likely that this experience will provoke a political crisis instead. The risk for the stability of the monetary union is that an adverse political reaction will result long before the necessary wage adjustment occurs, and this could lead to a much broader type of (political) instability which carries with it deeper problems for business.

(ii) Labour made unemployed by the shock could move to countries or regions of greater economic prosperity and so better employment opportunities. The problem is that labour mobility is not particularly well developed even within the nation state, far less between nation states characterised by different languages and cultures. And even were it to occur, what would be the economic and political consequences of labour mobility on a large scale from the perspective of the prosperous areas of the monetary union? Would they really welcome this? Again, what type of environment would this create for business—even if we are to ignore the broader social consequences?

(iii) A third adjustment route is to have an enhanced element of automatic and discretionary fiscal transfers both within the individual countries themselves (but subject to SGP deficit ceilings), so that national governments can respond appropriately to the economic shock affecting output and employment, and between countries within EMU, so that resources are transferred from the more prosperous countries to those affected by the economic shock. This latter solution would involve developing common fiscal modalities to facilitate discrete transfers of resources between national governments, or the development of common (and centralised) EU fiscal instruments, such as a common unemployment insurance scheme, that operate as "automatic" stabilisers in the event of an asymmetric shock. It is clear, however, that the SGP restricts the capability of individual governments to conduct stabilisation policies individually. Consequently only limited stabilisation can be achieved by the operation of national fiscal policies. Moreover, there are no common fiscal measures operating at the level of the EU to effect an inter-country transfer of resources with a view to stabilising the shocked economy. Indeed, it is the non-existence of a common fiscal policy that distinguishes the EU model of monetary union from virtually every other example of a functioning monetary union and which is, arguably, its most significant weakness. It is true that EU structural (regional) policies provide for some element of cross-border fiscal transfers to support economic development in the economically disadvantaged regions of the Union.[18] However, both in terms of scale and orientation, this

---

[18] See Ch. 7 *infra* by J. Scott and S. Vousden.

is wholly insufficient to address the type of regional or national economic problems that are likely to accompany an asymmetric shock.

(iv) Finally, the adjustment route of protectionism could be adopted. After all, if we go back to the experiences of the 1970s we find that a typical response on the part of the EC member states in the face of the oil price rise-induced recession was a turning inwards and the general spread of "new protectionism". And while such a response would be considerably more difficult in the current environment—principally because of the Single European Market (SEM) rules and the enforcement of these by the European Court of Justice—the point remains that political pressures to restrict freedom of trade are likely to intensify if domestic employment and output are falling while economic conditions elsewhere in the euro-zone remain relatively buoyant. I would argue that there is a risk—presently not considerable but nonetheless present—of protectionist pressures within the euro-zone increasing should ill-judged policy shifts be undertaken. Any tendency towards a re-fragmentation of the single European market would be a high price to pay for monetary union.

The foregoing analysis of economic adjustment under EMU raises the possibility that individual member states are set to experience significant economic and political tensions should the fears of the EMU-pessimists be realised. In the absence of greater national wage flexibility or labour mobility, and assuming that a common euro-zone fiscal policy will not be forthcoming, the outcome could be a euro-zone characterised by even higher levels of long-term unemployment as the deflationary effects of a restrictive fiscal policy and the inability to adjust to unexpected external shocks combine to lower the level of economic activity. Inevitably, of course, there is a risk of overstating the severity of the potential problems under EMU. There are three important qualifications that can be offered to the preceding analysis.

First, there has been some fine tuning of euro-zone fiscal policy. As noted, adherence to the SGP will obviously constrain the role of national fiscal policy under EMU. Members must not breach the upper ceilings of three per cent of GDP for the budget deficit, or sixty per cent of GDP for the total volume of debt. If they do, they are liable to pay a penalty; if they are allowed to avoid the penalty then they jeopardise the credibility of the single currency arrangement. Under the SGP rules, only under "exceptional circumstances" will an EMU member be permitted to breach these fiscal ceilings—i.e. definitely where output has fallen by two per cent or more over a period of four quarters, and possibly where the annual fall in output lies between three-quarters of one per cent and two per cent.[19]

---

[19] Over the period 1961–96, and for fifteen EU member states (giving 525 observations), there were only forty-five occasions during which real GDP within an EU country fell. On

Advocates of the SGP insist that its fiscal rules simply define a framework for sound economic policies; policies that prudent fiscal authorities should, in any event, be following. This argument gains force since, in the post-EMU situation, member states are prohibited from "printing" currency with the result that budget deficits can be financed only from higher (and unpopular) domestic taxation and/or increased government borrowing. But government borrowing post-EMU involves the issue of euro-denominated debt instruments. In the absence of a limit to the scope for an individual government to borrow, any tendency on the part of one government to over-borrow would affect the terms on which all other governments could borrow.[20] By this logic, the fiscal rules of the SGP will be associated with lower interest rates and a higher level of economic activity throughout the euro-zone area than otherwise would be the case. It is also worth emphasising that an expansionary fiscal policy is not necessarily the appropriate response to an asymmetric economic shock. This will depend very much on the nature of the shock. The case for fiscal stabilisation is greatest where the effect of the shock is temporary—for instance, the consequences of a cyclical downturn in a country's major export market. If the effect of the shock is permanent, on the other hand, this will require an adjustment to the real economy through a change in relative prices. In this case, stabilisation policy through deficit expenditure may simply delay the required adjustment and make it more difficult to achieve subsequently.

Despite accepting the general proposition that fiscal policy should be conducted prudently, significant doubts remain concerning the specific terms of the SGP. These relate to the strong likelihood that a temporary economic downturn (possibly cyclical, but not necessarily so) may occur in one country which, although not "exceptional" in the SGP definition, nonetheless triggers a significant fall in output and employment.[21] Rather than requiring annual deficits to remain within a three per cent ceiling, one solution would be to require that a particular fiscal outturn (e.g. a balanced budget) was achieved over the course of a business cycle thereby giving governments scope to finance stabilisation measures *as required* during the down-swing phase of the business cycle, and compensating through budget surpluses during the up-swing phase. As matters stand,

thirty occasions this fall exceeded 0.75%, but there were only seven instances where it exceeded 2% over one year, European Commission, *Economic Policy in EMU, Part B: Specific Topics* (Brussels, 1997). Thus the "exceptional" cases provided for in the SGP are, indeed, truly exceptional. Note that national budget deficits frequently have exceeded 3% despite the infrequency of falling real GDP.

[20] The bond market itself would not penalise excessive borrowing by one government on the grounds that, regardless of the volume of debt instruments in circulation, there was virtually no risk of default on the part of an EU member state.

[21] Adhering to the SGP conditions may well increase the volatility of output and employment beyond that caused by the initial shock. See Eichengreen, B. and Wyplosz, C., "The Stability Pact: more than a minor nuisance?", *Economic Policy*, No.26, at 65.

with the rules focusing on the unadjusted fiscal position, the possibility arises that temporary disturbances may instead have permanent effects simply because governments lack the fiscal capacity to address these while remaining within SGP ceilings. Undoubtedly the immediate pressure will be felt by those countries already close to, or exceeding, the SGP ceilings, and it is there that the deflationary bias of EMU may be most evident. Current developments are problematic in this respect. To the extent that the euro-zone economies now move into a phase of sustained and relatively rapid economic growth, we would expect budget deficits to fall and, possibly, surpluses to appear. However, and in the light of the profound economic crises afflicting the global economy at present (i.e. the financial and economic turmoil in South East Asia and parts of South America and the collapse of the Russian economy), there is no certainty that an upturn in euro-zone economic growth is imminent. The lack of a formal mechanism for co-ordinating the common euro-zone monetary policy with national fiscal policies appears to be a significant gap in the architecture of EMU. Given the extent of the dislocation to the euro-zone economies which may be triggered by external events, the euro-zone may find itself in a situation where monetary policy and fiscal policy are operating in opposing directions, rather than as two elements of one overall policy.

Secondly, EMU pessimists are often accused of underestimating the contribution that labour market flexibility can make to the adjustment of national economies to asymmetric shocks. There are three routes through which labour market changes will assist economic adjustment: greater geographic mobility of labour; greater money wage flexibility; and greater occupational mobility. Empirical evidence suggests that the geographic mobility of labour in the US constitutes a significant adjustment mechanism to asymmetric shocks that impact at a state level. As already noted, mobility across the euro-zone is much less and it is difficult to conceive of public policy that can increase this. Similarly, a significant increase in the degree of (downward) money wage flexibility on a national (or regional) basis is equally difficult to conceive, certainly if we consider the history of this in the EU. However, it may be that greater wage flexibility will arise following EMU as the employment costs of wage equalisation become apparent. Third, undoubtedly there is a role for occupational flexibility as an adjustment mechanism. This raises a host of complex problems, not the least of which is to identify—with any confidence—the nature of the specific rigidities in EU labour markets and to propose measures to rectify this.

The final qualification to the pessimistic view of the consequences of EMU is the possibility that monetary union will reduce the asymmetric element of any economic shocks. There are two reasons why this might occur. The first is that EMU will result in the elimination of multiple exchange rates as impediments to intra-EU trade flows. As trade intensifies, it is argued that the productive base (industry and services) of the economies of the euro-zone will become ever more diversified with the result that most conceivable external shocks will impact equally across the euro-zone. While it is easy to devise scenarios where patterns of economic specialisation throw up especially acute problems of asymmetric disturbances—where a sectoral disturbance in effect becomes a regional or national disturbance as a consequence of the prevailing distribution of economic activity across the area as a whole—the counter view is that specialisation will become less acute as integration proceeds thereby weakening this tendency. Should this transpire, the types of problems being addressed above would be much less severe. The second reason for a diminution of asymmetric shocks derives from the argument that the single largest source of economic shocks to impact on an economy are changes to national economic policies, especially to national monetary policy. Given that members of the euro-zone have a common monetary policy, the prevalence of asymmetric shocks, by definition, will be reduced. Unfortunately in relation to both reasons it is difficult to draw any firm conclusions from the empirical record. Some work that has been undertaken demonstrates that—rather than becoming less specialised following economic integration—economies in fact become more specialised thus increasing the possibility that an industry-specific shock will have asymmetric effects.[22] Moreover, there has been a resurgence of interest among economic geographers in the core-periphery analysis of the evolution of economic geography. Both these lines of argument would predict that economic structures across the euro-zone as a whole will diverge (though not equally) over time, making the problem of adjustment to asymmetric shocks all the more difficult.

3. The ECB, the Treaty and Policy Responses

In this section I turn to the implications that arise from the foregoing analysis on the assumption that EMU does impact negatively on the stabilisation function that national governments typically have played, both as a consequence of the loss of monetary policy as an independent instrument of domestic economic management and in the context of the constraints on fiscal policy enshrined within the SGP. In that event, the analysis of monetary union will move outside a strictly economic framework and engage directly in the political and governance aspects of European integration. In particular, to the extent that EMU is *seen to be* a cause of higher unemployment and lower output, and many EMU opponents argue this will be the case, it would seem likely that pressure will increase for a

---

[22] However, it is difficult to ignore the orthodox proposition which states that specialisation increases (rather than diminishes) as barriers to market integration are lowered.

response to be forthcoming at the level of the euro-zone, rather than at the level of the member state. Otherwise the legitimacy of integration is likely to be ever more contested, and the entire process jeopardised. In the first instance it is probable that popular dissatisfaction will focus on two issues in the current debate. The first is the operation, policy and accountability of the ECB. It is, after all, the ECB which is responsible for devising and implementing the common monetary policy, and it is likely that its actions in this respect will come under very close scrutiny. The second issue is the rate of unemployment across the EU and, in particular, the extent to which policies exist, or should be introduced, *at the level of the euro-zone or of the EU*, to counter high, or rising, levels of unemployment. The likelihood of employment policy becoming a matter of common EU concern and, ultimately, common action, has been enhanced by the agreements reached at the Amsterdam European Council which incorporated into the EC Treaty specific obligations in this field.[23]

In the period around the introduction of the single currency, the debate over the appropriate role of the new monetary authority has gathered momentum. A dominant feature of these discussions are concerns that the ECB will be pre-occupied with the anti-inflationary role ascribed to it by the EC Treaty, and that it will pay scant regard, if any at all, to other economic policy problems confronting Europe's policy-makers— particularly unemployment. The EC Treaty, of course, reinforces this view:

> When exercising the powers and carrying out the tasks and duties conferred upon them by this Treaty and the Statute of the ESCB, neither the ECB, nor a national central bank, nor any member of their decision-making bodies shall seek or take instructions from Community institutions or bodies, from any government of a Member State or from any other body. The Community institutions and bodies and the governments of the Member States undertake to respect this principle and not to seek to influence the members of the decision-making bodies of the ECB or of the national central banks in the performance of their tasks.[24]

Clearly this Article is intended to entrench the *political* independence of the ECB within the EC Treaty. Beyond this, the *policy* independence of the ECB too is guaranteed by the Treaty:

> Overdraft facilities or any other type of credit facility with the ECB or with the central banks of the Member States (hereinafter referred to as "national central banks") in favour of Community institutions or bodies, central governments, regional, local or other public authorities, other bodies governed by public law, or public undertakings of Member States *shall be prohibited, as shall the*

---

[23] The limited nature of the employment provisions introduced into the EC Treaty by the Treaty of Amsterdam is considered infra at notes 35–40 and in S. Weatherill and P. Beaumont, *EU Law* (Harmondsworth, Penguin,1999, 3rd ed.), Ch. 20.

[24] Art. 108 (ex 107) EC.

purchase directly from them by the ECB or national central banks of debt instruments.[25]

In short, the ECB is not permitted to "monetise" national debt instruments, thus avoiding the possibility of money supply targets being overshot by virtue of the actions of member states' fiscal authorities. That route to greater inflation is constitutionally precluded. The motives for establishing both political and effective policy independence for the ECB are well understood, and involve establishing immediately the credibility of the ECB as an institution capable of meeting its primary objective of price stability by virtue of its immunity from all sorts of political pressures that may be expected to arise from time to time. As an institution, the ECB will be able to formulate and implement monetary policy as is necessary for achieving price stability (however this may be defined) free from external political interference of any sort. Consequently, the expectations of economic actors (especially labour) should adjust very quickly to the edicts delivered by the new monetary authority, with the result that price stability can be attained without significant consequences for the level of employment. At the same time, of course, these arrangements describe the only type of common monetary system which the low inflation countries would countenance joining.

The independence of the ECB is enshrined by the EC Treaty, and is reinforced by judicial controls. This is significant. The powers of the ECB to act independently in monetary policy matters are not devolved or sanctioned by another authority—such as the European Council or the European Parliament—and cannot be altered by either institution. Instead the constitution of the ECB is set out in the Treaty itself, with the result that any attempt to alter the operating rules of the ECB would require the amendment of the Treaty and, therefore, the agreement of *all* member states—and not only members of the euro-zone. Whilst the EC Treaty does provide for considerable powers to be exercised by the EMU "ins" as distinct from the "outs", there is no opportunity for the operating rules of EMU, including the statutes relating to the ECB, to be changed other than by the unanimous consent of the Union acting in the forum of an inter-governmental conference. Again, the reasons for this are linked directly to the importance of maintaining over time the independence and the credibility of the ECB.

The gains associated with the carefully crafted independence of the ECB have been dealt with extensively in the literature.[26] Less often referred to is the accountability of the ECB.[27] The question of accountability arises

---

[25] Art. 101 (ex 104) EC, emphasis added.

[26] See, for example, M. Artis and B. Winkler, "The Stability Pact: Safeguarding the Credibility of the European Central Bank", *National Institute Economic Review*, No. 163, 1, at 87.

[27] For some discussion see Chs. 6 and 8 *infra* by M. Everson and by P. Beaumont and N. Walker

because the corollary of devising arrangements that maintain the independence of the ECB is that, necessarily, the ECB subsequently cannot be held to account for its actions. Were it to be accountable in a conventional sense to some national central banks, then it may well be—at least implicitly—susceptible to political interference with all the consequences that follow with respect to its anti-inflationary credibility. The authority of the ECB derives from its autonomy to act, and its autonomy to act is protected by a constitutional arrangement that immunises its actions from interference from within the explicitly political arena. The nature of, and lines for enforcing, ECB accountability is significant in two respects. The first is in the event of the ECB acting in an incompetent manner; the second is where it acts in an unpopular manner from the perspective either of a national government or popular opinion. Competence in this context is defined as the ability of the ECB to discharge efficiently its tasks and obligations as laid out in the EC Treaty. Popularity, on the other hand, refers to the standing of the ECB with regard to external judgement on its activities, including the views of member state governments with regard to the output consequences of the monetary policy that is being pursued in the context of the remit that national governments continue to hold in stabilising domestic employment and output levels. Assuming the standard tenets of democratic government prevail, an argument can easily be made that the ECB should be accountable (in that sanctions could be imposed or its policy stance adjusted) in both senses—that is, where it is either incompetent or unpopular.

I have already touched upon the competence aspect of ECB activities when discussing the technical problems that the ECB will face in devising specific policies that actually deliver price stability. It is by no means a foregone conclusion that the ECB will achieve price stability, or will do so other than at a cost in terms of associated output and employment losses should expectations take time to adjust, or the credibility of the policy be doubted. The problem of accountability in this context arises should the ECB fail to deliver price stability given that there is no political mechanism to dismiss the Executive Board or the Governors of the National Central Banks within the euro-zone either singly or collectively.[28] A more likely scenario, however, is where the political pressure on the ECB increases not because it is deemed to be incompetent, but rather as a response to what are regarded as inappropriate monetary policy decisions given prevailing

---

[28] In some Central Bank arrangements (e.g. New Zealand) the Governor has a formal contract with the national government under which sanctions may be imposed should the Central Bank fail to discharge its duties properly. No such provision exists with respect to the ECB. On the other hand, there is a judicial mechanism for dismissing an individual member of the Executive Board in Art. 11.4 of the Protocol on the Statute of the ESCB: "If a member of the Executive Board no longer fulfils the conditions required for the performance of his duties or if he has been guilty of serious misconduct, the Court of Justice may, on application by the Governing Council or the Executive Board, compulsorily retire him".

economic circumstances in one or more euro-zone states. This is not an unlikely situation. The ECB will be introducing a common monetary policy for which there is no precedent, and it must quickly establish a reputation for credibility if its actions and pronouncements are to be effective. For these reasons, delivering price stability may be extremely difficult to achieve in the first years of operation of the ECB. Consequently, there may be a temptation for the ECB to pursue price stability dogmatically, with scant regard to the impact on output or employment across the euro-zone. If the incentive structure of ECB policy contains no negative weighting to reflect the social undesirability of rising unemployment or falling output, then why should the ECB develop modalities for delivering price stability without unduly jeopardising employment objectives held by national governments? Why should not the ECB embark instead on a course of "shock therapy" by pursuing tight monetary policy in the first instance should it deem this to be necessary to establish credibility and lower the inflationary pressures in the economy?

If the monetary policy stance taken by the ECB meets with the disapproval, individually or collectively, of the member state governments, then how will this be dealt with? According to a strict reading of the EC Treaty, it cannot be addressed. As we have noted, the immunity of the ECB to political interference is fairly well entrenched. Moreover, the simple fact that membership of the ECB Board includes central bankers from the included countries is *unlikely* to lead to a significant measure of domestic political reflection in the formulation of common monetary-policy: indeed, any substantial measure of disagreement (political, geographical, economic) is likely only to empower technical experts, thereby shifting monetary policy even further distant from political debate. Here, it is not the legitimacy of the arrangements for formulating monetary policy *per se* that becomes the subject of political debate, but rather the legitimacy of the *non-existence* of any arrangements for modifying that policy under a particular set of circumstances—if you like, the absence of any policy feedback rule. It seems only realistic to assume that the non-existence of such arrangements may bring the activities of the ECB into conflict with public opinion from time to time, and that this will lead to a loss of public confidence in the underlying policy-making arrangements. This is all the more likely when one considers that there is a range of national inflation-unemployment trade-off points existing within the euro-zone—possibly a different one for each member state. Precisely these differences are likely to be the source of tension between member states and the ECB. Indeed, it may well be that a greater number of trade-off positions arise post-EMU than previously, as hitherto acquiescent small-nation monetary authorities try out their "voice" within the new arrangements. Ultimately the risk is that there is a rising tide of opinion against EMU, and that this undermines what has clearly been shown to be very fragile public support for European integration.

The appropriate solution to the above problem lies neither in changing the formal mandate of the ECB nor its political independence. Indeed, either course of action would simply introduce an alternative series of problems:

- it may lead the ECB to be less rigorous in delivering price stability, thus breaching the competence criterion,
- in a monetary union characterised by inter-governmental bargaining and where political cycles are not synchronised, it is unlikely that a single, Union-wide inflation-unemployment trade-off can be agreed upon, with the result that inter-governmental tensions as to the appropriate monetary policy are just as likely to emerge as are member state-ECB tensions, and may be more damaging,
- different national labour markets are likely to display different degrees of flexibility in the face of asymmetric shocks. Thus, even quite similar external disturbances (as well as asymmetric ones) will have different domestic economic and political consequences for which no single monetary policy response would be appropriate.

Consequently, it is difficult to argue that the rules governing the ECB activities, or the objective of these activities, should be altered in order to accommodate concerns over their implications for national stabilisation policy. Even a cursory consideration of the potential for conflict between individual member states that would arise should the ECB be so mandated, far less any discussion concerning the efficacy of macro-economic policy in tackling unemployment, should persuade us that there are significant factors militating against broadening the economic remit of the ECB. If we accept that it might be neither appropriate nor desirable for the ECB to give priority to employment or output considerations instead of price stability in formulating monetary policy, how might the types of difficulties and tensions discussed here be mediated? It is at this point that both the EC Treaty and Union-wide governmental pronouncements are less than helpful.

A first approach to the problem is to be found under the EC Treaty itself. Indeed, to some extent it anticipates this problem under the provisions of Article 105. This states that whilst the, ". . . primary objective of the ESCB shall be to maintain price stability"[29] nonetheless that:

> Without prejudice to the objective of price stability, the ESCB shall support the general economic policies in the Community with a view to contributing to the achievement of the objectives of the Community as laid down in Article 2.[30]

Article 2 of the EC Treaty in turn sets out the broad tasks of the Community, tasks that included promoting "a high level of employment . . ." However, the explicit task of promoting employment finds only limited

[29] Art. 105(1) EC.   [30] *Ibid.*

resonance elsewhere in the EC Treaty. Indeed, under Article 2 (ex B) TEU, promoting employment was not included as an "objective" of the Union, nor was it included under Article 3 EC—which details the specifics of Community policy objectives, until the Treaty of Amsterdam amendments. Thus although it is conventional to expect a central bank to pay some regard to the stabilisation function when determining monetary policy (e.g. as the Bundesbank does),[31] the EC Treaty as it stands does not provide a mechanism to insist upon the ECB taking account of stabilisation considerations when formulating its policy stance.[32] The autonomy of the ECB is secured by the absence of any effective route for its accountability. Consequently, the provisions of Article 105 are unlikely to persuade the ECB to intensify its stabilisation efforts whenever public opinion demands. A central feature of the EC Treaty approach to monetary union is that price stability takes precedence over any other objective that the Treaty stipulates for the ECB—a situation that is unlikely to change over the foreseeable future.

A second approach, echoed by Professor Rudiger Dornbusch in a letter to the *Financial Times*, is to appoint as President of the ECB a person who has "significant public relations skills". As Dornbusch rightly points out:

> Everybody has their view of what the ECB might accomplish, ranging from price stability to full employment. The room for frustration, and hence political interference with the independence of the ECB, is substantial. Hence the need to select a leader who has demonstrated communication skill.[33]

What Dornbusch is pointing to here is that public expectations of the role of the ECB must be tailored to its functions. This is, manifestly, not the situation at the present time. In so far as there are expectations that the ECB can contribute directly to stabilisation efforts at the national level, these expectations are liable to be frustrated and this may lead, in turn, to demands that the autonomy of the ECB be weakened. For many reasons, it is unreasonable to expect the leader of the ECB, regardless of whom this might be, to be able to massage potentially hostile public opinion across the diverse economic, political and social landscape of the euro-zone. The reality is that a conflict in policy is likely to arise, and the public relations attributes of Europe's central bankers seem to be a particularly slender thread on which to hang the future legitimacy of either the ECB or the EMU project.

A third option, and one that has been promoted since the Maastricht Treaty was signed, is to bolster the fiscal capacity at the Union-level, in order to permit it to play a stabilisation role. As we have already noted,

---

[31] See E. Kennedy, *The Bundesbank: Germany's Central Bank in the International Monetary System*, (Chatham House, 1991).

[32] However, for a consideration of how the other political institutions might influence the ECB to take seriously the requirement under Art. 105 EC to support the Community's economic policies, including high employment, see Chap. 8 *infra* by P. Beaumont and N. Walker.

[33] *Financial Times*, 13 November, 1997.

this is a powerful general conclusion derived from the fiscal federalist literature, albeit there are considerable differences of opinion as to the extent of the centralised fiscal capacity necessary to achieve an acceptable measure of stabilisation.[34] There is little, if any, likelihood of any movement in this direction over the foreseeable future. The main paymaster of the EU, Germany, wants to reduce its budgetary contributions and any future budget growth will be absorbed in the significant economic costs associated with the eastward enlargement of the EU.

It seems, therefore, that none of the above options represent a feasible mechanism for reconciling the constitutional requirements that the EC Treaty places upon the ECB on the one hand, with what may subsequently be expected from the ECB *as a para-public* monetary agency on the other hand. This is a consequence of what we might describe as a missing element in the new arrangements of EU macro-economic policy management. This policy-gap represents a potentially unstable position for the EU, in that it is the Union that properly will be confronted with—and held to be responsible for—any adverse shift in Union-wide public opinion over the conduct of the common monetary policy. In the face of adverse economic shocks, member state governments are likely to put pressure on the ECB to adjust its stance accordingly.

As noted, the concerns set out above can be represented as arising from the emergence of a policy-gap (or competence-gap) in the EU macro-economic policy framework. Moreover, it is likely that this gap has widened further as a consequence of the Amsterdam Treaty; a text that may well be a cause of even greater intra-Union tension in the future. This is because the reforms to the EC Treaty agreed upon at the Amsterdam European Council in June 1997 may well further raise the expectations of EU citizens that economic instruments are to be developed at the level of supranational governance to tackle the economic problems of the EU, particularly the high level of unemployment.

In the period since the ratification of the Maastricht Treaty, much has been written about the crisis of legitimacy of EU governance. Indeed, from the outset the InterGovernmental Conference (IGC) that convened in 1996 was explicitly charged with considering reforms of the Treaty that would enhance the direct relevance of the Union, and hence its legitimacy, to the individual citizen. Despite the promises that closer economic and political integration would generate material economic benefits across the Union, a promise that was particularly associated with the earlier single European market programme, unemployment rates across the EU in the mid-1990s stood at over twelve per cent and showed no sign of falling. For political

---

[34] For a fuller debate on this issue, see T. Bayoumi and P. Masson "Fiscal Flows in the United States and Canada: lessons for monetary union in Europe", *European Economic Review*, Vol.39 at 253 and A. Italianer and M. Vanheukelen "Proposals for Community stabilization mechanisms: some historical applications", *European Economy*, No.5, at 493.

reasons at least, the view gained broad support that the project of European integration should have some basic Treaty objective to create higher levels of employment.[35] The outcome was that the Amsterdam text introduced an entirely new Title in the EC Treaty (Title VIII) on Employment, and ensures that a new emphasis is to be given to job creation and preservation in the scope of common, EC, activities. This is evident in the revised Article 2 (ex B) TEU and reflected forcefully in the revised Article 3(i) EC which states that the activities of Community shall include:

> the promotion of co-ordination between employment policies of the Member States with a view to enhancing their effectiveness by developing a co-ordinated strategy for employment[36]

The new Title VIII Employment (Articles 125-130 EC) pronounces that Member States ". . . shall regard promoting employment as a matter of common concern . . ."[37] and that, crucially "The objective of a high level of employment shall be taken into consideration in the formulation and implementation of Community policies and activities".[38] The Amsterdam text also provides for the creation of an Employment Committee to have an advisory capacity and to ". . . monitor the employment situation and employment policies in the Member States and the Community".[39]

It is very clear from the Amsterdam text that the nature of the employment policy envisaged by the Council in adopting this text is essentially micro-economic in focus. That is, the types of policies over which intra-Union co-ordination is to be encouraged relate to ". . . promoting a skilled, trained and adaptable workforce and labour markets responsive to economic change . . ."[40]

In other words, there is in this text no explicit expectation that member state macro-economic policies should be geared towards securing progress towards "full" employment, despite calls on the part of some member states that indeed this should have been the case. Nonetheless, when read in conjunction with other proposed revisions to the EC Treaty (see especially Article 127(2)), this discussion on measures to promote employment may well fuel expectations that the EU collectively is set to address the employment consequences over the entire range of its policy deliberations, *including* monetary policy.

Against the backdrop of the Amsterdam amendments to the EC Treaty, there are real dangers that the recipe set out in the EC Treaty for monetary union begins to lack credibility. There is, on a strict reading of the proposed

---

[35] Although the German and British Governments initially opposed proposals to introduce a formal statement on employment to the EC Treaty, arguing that this was a matter solely of national concern, the German Government ultimately yielded to pressure from France and from the Scandanavian countries that a high level of employment should be incorporated as an explicit policy of European integration.

[36] Art. 3(i) EC.   [37] Art. 126(2) EC.   [38] Art. 127(2) EC.

[39] Art. 130 EC, first indent.   [40] Art. 125 EC.

text, some grounds for arguing that the likely employment consequences arising from the stance proposed with respect to monetary policy should be taken into consideration by the ECB before the policy is implemented. However, it is clear from the EC Treaty that this interpretation conflicts with the general understanding of, and detailed provision for, the activities undertaken by the ECB. From the perspective offered in this chapter, the problematic issue arising from the Amsterdam amendments is that expectations once again have been raised that the EU will develop a policy response to the prevailing level of—and changes to the level of—unemployment within member states, and that included within this policy response will be an appropriate adjustment of monetary policy. Failure to do so—at least in the sense that individual member states might be critical of the monetary policy adopted by the ECB as being excessively restrictive—is likely to increase the level of public displeasure towards the ECB in particular, and the EU generally. This situation seems to have arisen as a consequence, firstly, of the need to increase the relevance of the EU to the ordinary citizen—which prompted member states to introduce an employment-related element into the Treaty—and, secondly, by what has been the essentially piecemeal nature of the response on this issue that has been forthcoming. However, the conclusion is that the Amsterdam amendments widen, rather than narrow, the expectations-capability gap relating to EU economic policy, and this is likely to increase hostility towards the ECB whenever a conflict arises between the policy mix appropriate for price stability and that required to stabilise (some part of) the economy of the Union.

By addressing the matter in this way, we can move on from the debate that has surrounded the credibility of European monetary union as an arrangement involving a number of distinctive economies, some of whom may "lose" from entering that arrangement, and discuss EMU more from the perspective of its impact upon the credibility of the EU. Following upon the conclusion of the IGC and the entry into force of the Amsterdam Treaty, the clear implication is that EMU increasingly will be regarded as an arrangement incapable of meeting the aspirations of its citizens. Consequently, post-Amsterdam the legitimacy crisis may be set to worsen with the EU becoming a more—rather than less—contested proposition. This is a danger not only at the level of the individual citizen, but equally at the level of the member state, leading to questions concerning the stability of the Union over the medium term.

4. Conclusions

The arguments set out here point to the need to develop a meaningful Union-wide capacity to respond to unemployment, especially in the post-EMU context in which national stabilisation measures have been constrained but where the problem of unemployment continues to worsen. Given that macro-economic policy is unlikely to fulfil this role, the necessary response will require to build upon labour market developments within individual member states. The significance of labour market flexibility thus becomes central in determining the success of EMU. To the extent that the geographic distribution of unemployment will change post-EMU as a consequence of the introduction of a single monetary policy, with asymmetric shocks (among other factors) accounting for this, countries characterised by "high" labour market flexibility will be better placed to respond. The opposite will also be true: labour market inflexibility will worsen the employment consequences of shocks post-EMU. What is much less clear is the mechanisms through which labour market flexibility is to be provided. There are significant differences between EU governments regarding the extent to which the relevant labour market policies can be expected to succeed. These differences need not reflect different political orientations of governments, nor differences in the willingness to embark upon the necessary policy. In fact, these differences may simply reflect different histories with regard to economic development. In that sense, therefore, they can be said to be path-dependent. Despite this, labour market flexibility is a matter of vital common concern, influencing as it will, the future prospects of monetary union and, indeed, of European integration more generally.

3

The Euro – Preparing for the Future

ALISTAIR DARLING

1. Introduction

I AM delighted to be back at the University of Aberdeen's Law Faculty, having graduated from here twenty three years ago. The subject of this conference reminds me of an examination question. "What is the legal framework of the European Single Currency? Discuss."

You will be pleased to know that you are not going to get a legal dissertation from me. There are others, far better qualified than I who will be doing that for you. I am here as a member of the Government, a politician, not a lawyer. I have not practised law for over ten years. But even though I have not practised, there is one aspect of my legal training that I shall not forget. And one particular legal principle, central to the profession, is never ever to give free legal advice. So what I have to say concentrates on the economic and political aspects of the single currency, which is what I think you would expect.

I do so because whilst clearly the euro is and has to be underpinned by a legal framework, it is impossible to divorce the law, the economics and the politics. The concept of the European Union (EU) itself is a political one. The adoption of a single currency is a political act with an economic purpose, underpinned by law. As in the single market the legal framework is delivering political and economic objectives—just as it should do. So I want to give you a political and economic overview. I want to set out how the Government sees developments in Europe as well as to set out our position so far as the United Kingdom is concerned.

2. The Government's Economic Approach

Let me, first of all, put the European single currency and single market in an economic context. The world has been transformed over the last few years. We do live in a global economy. As we know only too well, what happens on the other side of the world can affect us shortly thereafter.

Industries typically span geographical and political boundaries. No country can go it alone. It makes sense therefore to break down artificial barriers between us; to expand markets—to build a single European market in Europe in particular. That is why we have always made clear our determination to open markets and to engage constructively in Europe. This country was built on its willingness and ability to look outwards beyond its shores. And our future lies in continuing to do that. That is why this Government is outward-looking. We have to be, and that has driven our policy in Europe and elsewhere.

We are one of the most open economies in the world, trading twenty-five per cent of GDP compared with America's ten per cent. Nearly sixty per cent of our exports are on mainland Europe. An astonishingly high level of international investment into Europe—forty per cent of it—comes to the UK. Aberdeen is perhaps proof of not only the increasingly cosmopolitan nature of our society but the global nature of our trade—a city that has in the last quarter of a century been transformed into an internationally renowned centre. Our future lies in our ability to trade as freely as possible. The world must move towards breaking down barriers to trade. That is the way to increase growth and increase prosperity.

3. The Single Currency in Europe

After this weekend (2–3 May 1998), we now know that in just over seven months' time the single currency will become a reality. What is more, a German business selling products to France or the Netherlands, for example, will be able to do so without exchange rate risk, with lower transaction costs and with more transparent prices. This in itself will be a big challenge to a British competitor hoping to supply the same order.

Next year consumers in this country will start to see some retailers pricing goods both in euros and in sterling. The euro will affect us here in the UK. On any view this is an historic development—in economic terms and in political terms, one of the most dramatic of this century.

European monetary union (EMU) will mean we face more competition for trade and for future investment across Europe. The tragedy is that we should have been preparing for this years ago, but because of the paralysis that affected the last Government that simply did not happen. This Government is determined to make up the lost ground and substantial progress has been made already. It is encouraging that many companies are now preparing for the euro, although far more need to do so. Right across the country we need to face up to the new competition pressures.

We cannot afford to repeat the mistakes that the UK has made in the past. Too often as Europe developed we stood aside arguing amongst ourselves as to whether we should be in or out. That inevitably led to indecision, instability and loss of influence—and of course has denied us a national economic consensus and sense of direction.

These arguments are now behind us. We are part of the EU. Our future lies in Europe. Only a few months ago people said the single currency would never happen. Well now it has, and you can have a euro bank account, a euro credit card, and pay for some of your shopping in euros from next January.

We are part of the biggest single market in the world. That is a tremendous opportunity. So now is the time, more than ever before, for us to play a determined role in Europe; to show leadership to our country's advantage, as well as to that of our European partners. It is that determination and approach that has driven us during the course of our European Presidency.

4. European Presidency

The euro has been launched under the UK Presidency of the Council of the European Union in the first half of 1998, on a sound basis in accordance with the Treaty. We have taken the initiative in developing a "European third way" of economic reform, combining market efficiency with social justice. The Chancellor of the Exchequer's initiative on economic reform was widely welcomed at the York informal Ecofin in March, where member states committed themselves to concrete action on structural reform of Europe's labour, capital and product markets:

- agreement on the principle of open markets and free competition requiring reform of all markets;
- strong support for UK proposal from member states to maintain momentum on reforming their product and capital markets;
- Commission reviews of the impact of Community policies, a study of price differentials, impact of European capital markets legislation and cost of raising finance;
- Commission to produce a "scorecard" with indicators of effective market integration and track record in implementation of single market measures;
- measures to ensure that financial services legislation keeps up with rapidly evolving markets;
- measures to make it easier to raise capital across borders, especially for small and medium sized enterprises.

With the European Conference in March 1998, we have launched the accession process that will lead to the enlargement of the EU.

During our Presidency, the European Commission has launched its proposals for reform of EU policies—Agenda 2000—including proposals for reform of the Common Agricultural Policy, Structural Funds and future financing. Furthermore, we have launched initiatives and made progress across a wide range of other fronts: on combating crime and drugs, on the environment, on openness and transparency. This has been a successful Presidency for the UK, showing how we engage constructively in Europe, pushing our reform programme in Europe and at home.

5. Monetary Union

The euro will become a reality in eleven countries in January 1999. So let me set out our position.

In October 1997 we became the first British Government to declare that, in principle, a successful single currency, like the Single European Market, would be of benefit both to Europe and to the UK. We do not believe there is any constitutional bar to membership: the test for us is what is in Britain's best economic interest. That is an important point. We are the first Government to declare *in principle* support for the single currency.

The fact is of course that it would not be in our economic interests to join in January 1999 as there is not the necessary convergence with the rest of Europe. To join now would be to accept a monetary policy which suited other European economies but not our own. As of May 1998, our official interest rate is 7.25 per cent (base rate), while in Germany and France it is 3.3 per cent (repo rate), reflecting the different stage of the economic cycle we are at compared with them. We need a period of stability and settled convergence before we can join, and our policies here are designed to achieve that. And in order to ensure a genuine choice in the future we must also make the necessary practical preparations now. We are working closely with business to do just that.

In New Labour's 1997 election manifesto we made clear that the final decision would rest with the British people. That remains the case. But we need to be in a position to make a realistic choice, yes or no. At the moment it would be a theoretical choice. The practical preparations have not been made. So we aim to continue our economic strategy and make practical progress in order that a real and genuine choice can be made.

The vital test for us is not based on dogma—but on economics—whether it is good for business, jobs and prosperity. That is why we have said that, if a successful single currency can meet our economic tests, then Britain should join. In other words, we are, in principle, in favour of joining a successful single currency.

Clearly joining involves a pooling of economic sovereignty—as in the single market now. But we see no constitutional bar to joining. We will join if it is in Britain's economic interests to do so. We made it clear that in reaching our decisions we will apply five key economic tests. Sustainable convergence between Britain and the economies of the single currency; sufficient flexibility to cope with the economic change; its effect on investment; the impact on the financial services industry; and whether the single currency will be good for employment.

So our strategy is to prepare and then decide. To build a broad consensus, stretching across the country and in particular the world of business. I do not believe that we can postpone consideration without loss of influence for another ten years, as some suggest. It is common sense that the long period of indecision that has characterised the politics of this country should be brought to an end. After so many years of debate we should be able to resolve the question of principle and agree that the economic benefits will mark the decisive test.

It is practical common sense to say that, if the economic case is compelling, we should be prepared to join. Equally, it is very practical sense that when other countries have been preparing seriously since 1992, we should begin real preparations now.

6. Preparing for the Euro

We have now begun to put in place the preparations which will allow us to be ready for the euro when it comes in 1999, and give us the real choice to join early in the next Parliament. Government and business in particular must prepare intensively during the next few years. We are working with business to prepare for the introduction of the euro in 1999. After all it will affect business here and in Europe immediately.

This Government is doing as much as it can to facilitate the use of the euro in 1999. We are consulting business on amending the Companies Act to make it easier for British firms to issue shares in euros and to convert existing shares into euros. We are looking at other legislative steps the Government should take to make the euro easier for firms to use. Many will be pleased to learn that businesses and individuals will be able to pay their taxes to the Inland Revenue and VAT to Customs and Excise in euros from January 1999! Accounts can be held in euros and some EU grants will be available in euros as well.

My colleague David Simon[1] has a special responsibility in this area. He is holding a number of discussions across the whole country in order to see what else the Government can do in order to facilitate the single currency. And these discussions have been used by the Treasury's Euro Preparations Unit to design our efforts to help business prepare for the euro. Information is also being made available from banks, accountants and chambers of commerce. The Government is supporting and encouraging this.

[1] Lord Simon of Highbury; Minister for European Trade and Competitiveness.

We are also committed to helping British companies compete in world markets. Our Competitiveness White Paper[2] will outline our approach to structural reform to improve competition across UK industry. In short we are determined to ensure that when the single currency is introduced in eleven European countries next year, we are *all* in a position to benefit from it.

Businesses also have made it clear to us that if they are to plan properly they need to know as soon as possible what changes would be made if the UK were to join monetary union. Planning something on this scale requires time and good preparations. That is why we will publish, before the end of year, an outline changeover plan (see page 179 *infra*), a document which will explain to business and the general public what steps need to be followed if we adopt the single currency.

I make no apology for setting out, at some length, some of the practical preparations we are taking. Clearly it is only the Government that can make legislation in this country. Only the Government can set the macroeconomic framework within which we operate. But government also has a duty to help the country, both individuals and business, make the practical preparations that will make all the difference to the euro working well.

Let us now turn to where we are now.

7. The Brussels Summit

At the beginning of May 1998 it was agreed that eleven countries will join the single currency on 1 January 1999. The European Central Bank (ECB), headed by its new President, Wim Duisenberg, will assume responsibility for the monetary policy that day.

The Heads of Government also agreed nominations to the executive board of the ECB. They determined to agree bilateral conversion rates that will apply between participating countries from 1 January.[3] They also made a declaration on the importance of sustaining fiscal discipline and economic reform. These are both vital to ensuring the benefits of economic and monetary union (EMU) are maximised and I will return to them.

The Heads of Government acted with full respect for the Maastricht Treaty and for the independence of the Central Bank. The recommendation of the Finance Ministers as to which countries should be in the first wave of monetary union were based on criteria laid down in the Maastricht Treaty. The European Monetary Institute (EMI) stressed in their report that performance has been assessed over a period of years, taking account of relevant economic factors all in terms of the Treaty.[4]

[2] Published in November 1998 as *Our Competitive Future: Building the Knowledge Based Economy*, cm 4176.

[3] These conversion rates were finally agreed on 31 December 1998; see Regulation 2866/98, OJ 1998 L359/1.

[4] European Monetary Institute, *Convergence Report* (Frankfurt, 1998).

The EMI report, signed by all the EU Central Bank governors, concluded that "major improvements in terms of convergence have been made", but were correct to add that there was clear need for more structural reform. All the candidates have inflation below the 2.7 per cent reference level. All have achieved a high degree of exchange rate stability as required by the Maastricht Treaty. The Commission and the EMI also highlighted that considerable progress had been made in bringing budget deficits under control. On the sustainability of the fiscal position, both countries with high debt ratios have made commitments that they will run primary surpluses and that their debt is on a clear downward trend.

On their assessment of country performance against the convergence criteria, the Commission concluded that eleven member states had a sufficient degree of convergence to qualify them for the single currency.

8. The New Economic Discipline

Central to the success of the European currency is the need for the appropriate economic discipline. We need that discipline here and throughout the EU. At home, we have made clear our determination to modernise this country's economic approach. First and foremost it is essential that Government takes an unashamedly long-term view to end the damaging cycle of boom and bust that has caused so much damage to this country in particular. Economic stability is the key.

In the year since we took office we have begun to put in place the building blocks we need. We have set out to raise the rate of sustainable growth to increase prosperity so that everyone can share in higher living standards and greater job opportunities.

First, a commitment to low inflation has been made. We began the process of ensuring monetary stability straight away. Within days of entering office we gave the Bank of England operational independence to fix interest rates to meet the Government's inflation target.[5] This institutional change is designed to underpin our commitment to long-term price stability. Commitment to low inflation is absolutely essential for business, savers, and those on fixed incomes alike. And already long term interest rates are the lowest they have been for over thirty-three years.

Secondly, the Chancellor of the Exchequer has put in place a deficit reduction plan cutting the huge burden of debt left by the last Government. Last year the deficit was over £22 billion. It is now due to fall and to move into balance. We have inherited a situation where we were spending over £25 billion a year just to service that debt—more than we spend on education across the whole of the UK. So the deficit reduction plan, together with the significant degree of fiscal tightening put in place in the first two

---

[5] Formalised in the Bank of England Act 1999.

budgets, amounting to some two and a half per cent of national income, will make a significant contribution to achieving the stability we need. Long-term fiscal stability is a key to our future success.

Thirdly, the Comprehensive Spending Review will deliver sustainable public finances which set the spending priorities of this Government for the rest of this Parliament and beyond. And fourthly, we have set about removing barriers to growth, expanding our economic capacity by creating the right climate for high levels of investment. That is why we cut corporation tax in the last budget to the lowest level ever.

The Government is modernising the Welfare State, getting more people back into work and investing in school buildings and education. The New Deal for the long-term and young unemployed is already in operation. And our reforms to the tax and benefit system, the most radical reforms for a whole generation, will help break down the barriers to work. They will make work pay. The Government is determined to support policies which open markets and to engage constructively in Europe.

There is something more as well. Governments in the future have to be open about their economic policy. That is why we are enacting legislation that will enforce a Code for Fiscal Stability. The Government will set out its objectives and its assessment of current economic conditions. Openness brings credibility. Credibility brings confidence. Confidence is essential to economic well-being. We believe that approach is essential not just here but throughout Europe and throughout the world.

So too is the need to increase employability. As the Prime Minister and Chancellor of the Exchequer have made clear here and in Europe, in a world where capital is increasingly mobile it is the skills, training, adaptability and employability of the work force that will mark us out as a place to invest. That is the global economy in which we live.

That is why under our Presidency the Ecofin Discipline and Reform declaration made clear that it attached particular importance to increasing the degree to which growth can be translated into additional employment. Emphasis was put on structural reforms, on making product, labour and capital markets more efficient, and on improving the adaptability of labour markets in order to better reflect wage and productivity developments. Emphasis was also placed on ensuring that national education training systems are effective and relevant to employment, and on seeking to encourage entrepreneurship, notably by attacking the administrative obstacles business faces. Further, attention was paid to enabling easier access to capital and to venture capital funds, particularly for smaller medium sized enterprises; increasing tax efficiency by avoiding harmful tax competition, and on addressing all aspects of social security systems in the context of ageing population.

That is similar to the agenda we are following here. It is now being adopted across Europe.

9. New Discipline

So a new discipline is required. Not just the Government but our European partners attach great importance to discipline and stability, and also to the economic reform that will deliver the high levels of growth and employment that we all want to see. The Ecofin declaration re-emphasises the importance of fiscal disciplines so the full benefits of monetary union can be realised.

The Stability and Growth pact states that all member states have to commit themselves to policies that allow them to respect the three per cent deficit ceiling, even during an economic downturn. Surveillance procedures allow Ecofin to monitor progress of each member state. Prudence in Europe cannot be a one off commitment to meeting a target for a particular year. It has to be locked in as a continuing commitment for the whole European Union.

As the Prime Minister has already said, the decisions last weekend, despite the sometimes frustrating nature of the process, were in the end the right ones—right for Europe and right for Britain. And he emphasised that to ensure that the single currency was successful, member states had to continue to implement economic reforms of product, capital and labour markets and to promote employability and job creating entrepreneurship. That is during the course of our Presidency we intend to make further progress in these areas, particularly at the Cardiff European Council in June 1998.

10. The Law, Economics and Politics

It is clear that the legal basis of monetary union is secure. But it is also important to establish the political commitment to ensure a sound economic basis for the success of the single currency. That demands a change of attitude, a change of economic culture, and a recognition that the world has changed dramatically. The global economy is a reality. And if the single currency is to work then all European Governments and all political parties have to recognise the opportunities that can flow from the rigorous discipline we now need, and from a determined commitment to reform and modernisation of our economies.

It is that commitment to modernisation and reform that has driven us here in the UK. And it has to drive us all in Europe—a determined political approach to underpin long-term economic success.

PART TWO

Constitutional Framework
of the Euro

4

The Fiscal Constitution of EMU

IAN HARDEN*

1. Introduction

A. *constitutional dimensions of EMU*

IT is sometimes forgotten that "EMU" does not stand for "*European Monetary Union*", but for "*Economic* and Monetary Union". The confusion is understandable. The basic idea of a monetary union is easy to grasp: that is, separate national currencies are replaced by a single currency. It is not obvious what the words "*economic and*" add to this.

The main constitutional elements of monetary union also seem clear at first sight.[1] The first element consists of the allocation of powers between member states and the supranational level. In the case of member states participating in the single currency, there is a complete transfer of monetary policy competence to the supranational level. The second element consists of the institutional arrangements for deciding monetary policy. Monetary policy for the single currency is to be formulated by the European Central Bank (ECB). The Treaty requires the ECB's primary objective to be the maintenance of price stability. It also provides for the ECB to be independent, so as to prevent political pressures that might compromise price stability.[2]

It should be noted, however, that the binding principles of central bank independence and price stability are not contingent on adoption of the single currency. With one exception, the member states which do not participate in the single currency must also have an independent central bank to decide monetary policy at national level.[3] Furthermore, the requirement to make price stability the primary objective applies to the

---

* The author writes in a personal capacity.

[1] Unless otherwise stated, the paper deals with the position after the beginning of the third stage of EMU on 1 January 1999.

[2] Arts. 105 and 108 (ex 105 and 107) EC.

[3] Art. 108 (ex 107) EC; Art. 43.2 of the Statute of the ECB/ESCB. The exception is the UK: see Protocol on Certain Provisions Relating to the United Kingdom of Great Britain and Northern Ireland.

European System of Central Banks (ESCB), which consists of the ECB and the national central banks of all the member states, whether they participate in the single currency or not.

These provisions represent a third constitutional element, which concerns neither the exercise of competences at the supranational level, nor the division of competences between that level and the member states. Rather, it consists of binding principles and institutional requirements for the exercise of a competence that remains with the member states. In other words, Community law regulates the constitutional framework for the exercise of an important aspect of public authority at national level.

The economic aspect of EMU also involves regulation of what happens in the member states, but with two main differences from the constitutional regulation of monetary policy. First, instead of a prescribed institutional formula, there is limited regulation of the relevant national procedures. Second, the arrangements that have been put in place have a dynamic character, in that the Community level procedures are designed to interact with the national procedures and influence their outcomes.

This chapter describes and analyses these arrangements. It does not seek to judge their adequacy from an economic perspective. Nor does it try to predict what substantive policy choices may emerge from the process of interaction between Community procedures and national procedures. Naturally, however, the extent to which policy choices are left open rather than being pre-determined is an important part of the analysis.

B. monetary union and economic policy

Since the "monetary union" part of EMU appears to make sense by itself, it is tempting to think that the same must be true of "economic union". This would be a mistake. There is no event, separate from the adoption of the single currency, which could give the term "economic union" a distinct meaning of its own. The Treaties do not therefore refer to monetary *union* or economic *union* in isolation, although the EC Treaty has separate chapters for monetary *policy* and economic *policy*.[4] In fact, the reason why the Treaties present "economic and monetary union" as indissociable is probably to underline the fact that monetary union also has implications for *economic* policy. However, it is not clear exactly what these implications are. Three points should be noted at the outset.

First, there is no unambiguous attribution of economic policy competence to the Community level. The Treaty provides for the member states to regard their economic policies as a matter of common concern and to co-ordinate them in the Council. This co-ordination is to provide part of

---

[4] Title VII (ex VI) chapter 1 (economic policy) chapter 2 (monetary policy); Art. 2 (ex B) TEU and Art. 2 (ex 2) EC.

the basis for the adoption of *an* economic policy, as one of the activities of the member states and the Community.[5] These broad-brush provisions have little meaning separate from the concrete rules, principles and procedures which are discussed in section 4 below. Secondly, there is no economic policy counterpart of the ECB or ESCB. Formally at least, economic policy at the Community level is to be dealt with by existing institutions and bodies.[6]

Finally, the Treaty does not explicitly define "economic policy". In ordinary usage, the term covers a wide range of issues and can even embrace all government actions intended to affect the economy.[7] In this sense, the transfer of economic policy competences to the supranational level is essential to the whole enterprise of European Union (EU). In the context of monetary union, however, it is macro-economic policy that is of primary significance. The term "macro-economic policy" refers to efforts to steer the economy as a whole and in particular, to promote high levels of employment and growth, a low level of inflation and a favourable balance of external trade. It is normally understood to include monetary policy, exchange rate policy and fiscal policy. Many economists would also emphasise the importance of labour market (or employment) policies.[8] As already noted, the Treaty has a separate chapter for monetary policy. Furthermore, its rather incomplete provisions concerning exchange rate policy for the single currency are also contained in the monetary policy chapter. The Treaty of Amsterdam adds a new and separate Title on Employment to the EC Treaty Title VIII (ex Title VIa). The economic policy chapter of the Treaty is therefore concerned with matters of fiscal policy and hence with the government budgets of the member states.

The next section explains what a government budget is and the political and constitutional significance of the budget, as well as the meaning of the term "fiscal policy". Section 3 explains the principles that underlie the economic policy provisions of the Treaty and the tensions which are

[5] Art. 99(1) (ex 103(1)) EC and Art. 4 (ex 3a) EC. Art.105 (ex 105) EC also provides that, without prejudice to the objective of price stability, "the ESCB shall support the general economic policies in the Community . . .".

[6] However, it should be noted that the Monetary Committee will be replaced by the Economic and Financial Committee from the beginning of 1999. As regards Ecofin, see the Resolution of the Luxembourg European Council on Economic Policy Co-ordination in Stage 3 of EMU.

The Ministers of the states participating in the Euro area may meet informally among themselves to discuss issues connected with their shared specific responsibilities for the single currency. The Commission, and the European Central Bank when appropriate, will be invited to take part in the meetings.

See *infra* section 4 for the Ecofin decisions in which only participating member states are entitled to vote.

[7] See e.g. T. Daintith (ed.), *Law as an Instrument of Economic Policy: comparative and critical approaches* (Berlin, de Gruyter, 1988).

[8] See Ch. 2 *supra*.

reflected in the "Stability and Growth Pact". Sections 4 and 5 look in detail at the principles and procedures that have been established at Community level, as modified and supplemented by the Stability and Growth Pact.

2. Budgets, Public Finance and Fiscal Policy

The "budget" is a document containing a list of planned government revenues and expenditures for a certain time period, often one year. It is the central reference point in the procedures for planning, executing and accounting for public spending and for authorising taxation.

The budget is central to the business of government. There is little that governments can do without spending money and in order to spend they must also tax. Budgetary procedures are therefore fundamental to the control and accountability of government. Furthermore, the budget provides answers to three fundamental questions of public finance.[9]

The first of these questions is: how large should government be relative to the private sector and to what extent should government be involved in economic activities? The budgeting aspect of this question is the decision about total public expenditure.

The second question is: which specific activities should government be engaged in and which social groups should receive special attention and financial benefits from government? The budgeting aspect of this question is the allocation of total expenditure between different spending programmes and agencies.

The third question is: who should carry the burden of financing government activities? In budgeting, this is the decision about the distribution of the tax burden between different sources of public revenues. This question has a time dimension. By borrowing (i.e. having a budget deficit) part of the burden of taxation is shifted to the future. A budget surplus, on the other hand, reduces the stock of public debt which taxpayers will have to finance in the future. Since present and future taxpayers are not identical, the time dimension involves issues of fairness between them.

A. fiscal policy

Budget deficits and surpluses also have an effect on the economy as a whole. Tax revenues normally tend to fall in cyclical downswings (as companies earn less profits and fewer people are in employment), whilst public expenditure rises (more claimants for social security and welfare

---

[9] This section contains material from Jürgen von Hagen and Ian Harden, "National Budgetary Processes and Fiscal Performance", in *European Economy: Towards Greater Fiscal Discipline. Reports and Studies 1994 No.3* 311–418, (Luxembourg, Office for Official Publications of the European Communities, 1994).

benefits). The opposite effects are observed in cyclical upswings. The budget balance therefore tends to become more negative in a recession and more positive towards the high point of the economic cycle. These effects (sometimes labelled "automatic stabilisers") can help smooth cyclical movements of income and employment and maintain price stability. Governments may also act to change the levels of budget deficits or surpluses that would otherwise occur, in order to seek some desired combination of macro-economic targets. The operation of the automatic stabilisers and possible discretionary action to change the budget balance is usually referred to as a government's "fiscal policy".

Excessive budget deficits may stimulate inflation and threaten the soundness of the public finances, eventually leading to default or further inflation. However, what constitutes an appropriate level of budget deficit or surplus is a matter of economic and political dispute. The same is true for the level of accumulated public debt. These disputes are complicated by the already-mentioned fact that budget deficits and surpluses affect the distribution of the tax burden over time.

Earlier plans for monetary union, made in the 1970s, assumed that the Community budget would grow big enough to be the basis of a fiscal policy.[10] The Maastricht model of EMU, however, makes no assumption that the budget will increase beyond its present level of less than two percent of Community Gross Domestic Product (GDP), whereas the EU-average ratio of public spending to GDP for the member states is around fifty per cent.[11] It is clear, therefore, that a *Community* fiscal policy could only be possible indirectly, through co-ordination of member states' fiscal policies.

3. Autonomy, Discipline and Co-ordination

It should be clear from the previous section why the government budget is important. It is at one and the same time: a key instrument in the control and accountability of government; the forum for resolving the conflicts between different interests that are inherent in the three public finance questions; and the mechanism of fiscal policy. As a result, the budget in most countries is treated as a matter of high constitutional and political significance. The impact of EMU on the budgetary freedom of the member states is therefore a highly sensitive issue. According to the Commission's analysis, carried out before Maastricht, the public finance

[10] Report of the Study Group on the Role of Public Finance in European Integration, 2 Vols., (Brussels, 1977).

[11] 50.6% in 1996. In the same year, the highest public expenditure to GDP ratio was in Sweden (66.9%) and the lowest in Ireland (36.3%), 63 *European Economy, Annual Economic Report for 1997*, (OPOCE, 1997).

regime of EMU should provide for an appropriate mix of "autonomy, discipline and co-ordination".[12]

A. *autonomy*

As regards the *autonomy* of member states, the first point to note is that EMU does not prescribe answers to either of the first two questions of public finance that were identified above. That is to say, there are no limits on how big or how small the public sector can be in each member state, nor is there any regulation of the allocation of spending between different programmes. Member states also retain the right to decide their own fiscal policies, within the limits established by the disciplinary provisions discussed below and subject to the principle of co-ordination.

The counterpart of autonomy is limited responsibility for others. The so-called "no bail-out" provision of Article 103 (ex 104b) EC provides that the Community shall not be liable for or assume the commitments of governments, (central, regional or local) or of other public authorities, other bodies governed by public law, or public undertakings of any member state. Similarly, member states shall not be liable for or assume each other's commitments.[13]

The no-bail out provision means that there can be no Community guarantee against a member state defaulting on its debt, unlikely as such an event may be. It is not a bar on fiscal transfers to support the public spending of a member state, either through state-to-state or Community-to-state transfers. At present, however, the Union has no general mechanism for providing such transfers.[14] From the beginning of the third stage of EMU, Article 100 (ex 103a (2)) EC allows Community financial assistance to a state that is "in difficulties or is seriously threatened with *severe* difficulties caused by exceptional occurrences beyond its control". (emphasis added).

This provision applies to both participating and non-participating member states. For participating member states, it replaces Article 119 (ex 109h)) EC, which has been used as the basis for Community loans.[15]

---

[12] M. Emerson et al, *One Market, One Money* (Oxford, Oxford University Press, 1992) and 44 *European Economy* (1990) 5–437.

[13] See also Council Regulation 3603/93 of 13 December 1993, OJ 1993 L332/1.

[14] Both the Structural Funds and the Cohesion Fund are for defined purposes, although the aggregate amount received is an important component of the overall public finance position of some member states. The Protocol on Economic and Social Cohesion provides for Community financial contributions to projects in the fields of environment and trans-European networks in member states with a per capita GNP of less than 90% of the Community average. See also Council Regulation 1164/94, 1994 OJ L130/1. See further, Ch. 7 *infra*.

[15] See Council Regulation 1969/88 1988 OJ L178/1, establishing a single facility providing medium-term financial assistance for member states' balances of payments and e.g. Decision 93/67/EEC 18/1/93 OJ L22/121 (loan to Italy).

Article 119 (ex 109h) EC provides for mutual assistance to a state which is: "in difficulties or is seriously threatened with difficulties as regards its balance of payments . . ."

Although Article 100 (ex 103a) EC is not limited to balance of payments difficulties, it is more restrictive than Article 119 (ex 109h) in two ways. First, the threatened difficulties must be "severe", although this term is not defined. Second, whereas mutual assistance under Article 119 (ex 109h) EC requires a qualified majority, the Council must act unanimously under Article 100(2) (ex 103a(2)) EC unless the severe difficulties are caused by a natural disaster. In any event, the wording of the provision would clearly not authorise a general or automatic system of fiscal transfers to be established.

B. discipline and co-ordination

The "disciplinary" provisions of the Treaty concern government debt and deficits. There are rules about how deficits may be financed. In particular, direct government borrowing from a central bank (or the ECB) and privileged access to financial institutions are forbidden.[16] The reason is that such borrowing could threaten the principle that the primary objective of monetary policy is price stability.

As noted in section 2.A above, excessive budget deficits may stimulate inflation and threaten the soundness of the public finances, eventually leading to default or further inflation. The Treaty establishes the principle that member states must avoid "excessive government deficits" in the third stage of EMU.[17] However, there are no precise rules as to what constitutes an "excessive deficit". Instead, the Treaty lays down a procedure (the "excessive deficit procedure"), which may lead to a decision by Ecofin (i.e. the Council meeting in the composition of economic and finance ministers[18]) that an excessive deficit exists. The normal Article 226 (ex 169) EC procedure through which the Commission may bring an infringement of Community law by a member state before the Court of Justice is specifically excluded.[19]

The excessive deficit procedure has two different purposes. The first is

[16] Arts. 101 and 102 (ex 104 and 104a) EC. These rules apply to Community institutions and bodies as well as to public authorities of the member states. See also Regulation 3604/93 specifying definitions for the application of the prohibition of privileged access referred to in Art. 102 (ex 104a) EC of the Treaty. OJ L332/4.

[17] Art.104(1) (ex 104c(1)) EC. Unless and until the UK moves to the third stage it continues to have the second stage obligation to "endeavour to avoid" excessive deficits: see Protocol on the UK and Art. 116 (4) (ex 109e(4)) EC. Note also that Art. 4 (3) (ex 3a(3)) EC lists "sound public finances" as one of the guiding principles for the activities (adoption of an economic policy and introduction of a single currency) referred to in that Article.

[18] See Declaration No 3 attached to the EC Treaty.

[19] Art. (104 (10) (ex 104 c(10)) EC. Art. 227 (ex 170) EC (possibility for another member state to bring proceedings) is also excluded.

inherently temporary; the provisions form part of a test which member states must pass in order to join the single currency. In May 1998, eleven member states which submitted themselves to the test were deemed to have passed. The first purpose has therefore ceased to have any direct relevance to them.[20] The second purpose is to establish arrangements to operate durably from the beginning of the third and permanent stage of EMU, on 1 January 1999.

The original idea behind the Treaty appears to have been that whilst budget *discipline* would be made compulsory through the excessive deficit procedure, a separate procedure involving "multilateral surveillance" under Article 99 (ex 103) EC would allow for the voluntary *co-ordination* of member states' economic (i.e. fiscal) policies.[21] This neat division of labour has subsequently become blurred, because the "Stability and Growth Pact"(SGP) uses the possibilities provided by multilateral surveillance to re-inforce the excessive deficit procedure.

C. the stability and growth pact

In 1995, the then German finance minister, Theo Waigel, proposed a "Stability Pact" to supplement the provisions of the Treaty concerning budget deficits. After discussion at the European Councils held in Madrid (December 1995), Florence (June 1996) and Dublin (December 1996), the Pact (renamed the "Stability and Growth Pact") was agreed at the same time as the Treaty of Amsterdam. Subsequently, the Luxembourg meeting of the European Council in December 1997 adopted a "Resolution on Economic Policy Co-ordination in the third stage of EMU" and a "Stability Declaration", accompanied the May 1998 decision as to which member states would participate in the single currency from its outset, on 1 January 1999.[22]

The Stability and Growth Pact (SGP) consists of two Council Regulations and a Resolution of the European Council.[23] This mixture of elements makes it difficult to ascribe a precise legal status to the Pact as a

---

[20] The other four member states still have to pass the test before they could move to the single currency. In the case of the UK and Denmark this possibility is foreseen by separate opt-out protocols. Greece and Sweden have derogations which should be kept under review, with a view to eventual abrogation in accordance with Art. 122(2) (ex 109k(2)) EC.

[21] See Emerson, *infra* n.12.

[22] Declaration by the Council (Ecofin) and the Ministers meeting in that Council issued on 1 May OJ 1998 L139/28.

[23] Regulation 1466/97 of 7 July 1997 on the strengthening of the surveillance of budgetary positions and the surveillance and co-ordination of economic policies, OJ 1997 L209/1; Regulation 1467/97 of 7 July 1997 on speeding up and clarifying the implementation of the excessive deficit procedure, OJ 1997 L209/6; Resolution of the European Council on the Stability and Growth Pact, OJ 1997 C 236/1. Regulation 1466/97 came into force on 1 July 1998. Regulation 1467/97 enters into force on 1 January 1999.

whole. Obviously, the two Regulations are part of Community law. The Resolution states that it provides "firm political guidance"[24] but, as will be seen below, the guidance relates to the interpretation and implementation of legal provisions.

The substance of the SGP, like the provisions of the Treaty which it supplements, reflects a tension between advocates of binding rules to limit budget deficits and advocates of discretion. This is not just a question of how far the member states are subject to legally binding rules; the advocates of such rules also want a rule-governed enforcement process, with automatic sanctions and a strict timetable.

The next two sections of the chapter analyse respectively the excessive deficit procedure and the multilateral surveillance procedure, as supplemented by the SGP. As explained above, the SGP means that the conceptual distinction between "discipline" and "co-ordination" no longer maps neatly onto the two procedures. Separate treatment still seems justified, however, given that the two procedures are legally distinct and the special regime of sanctions applies only in the legal framework of the excessive deficit procedure. Except where otherwise stated, the provisions are described as they apply to the participating states after 1 January 1999.

4. The Excessive Deficit Procedure

A. introduction

The excessive deficit procedure (EDP) is established by Article 104 (ex 104c) EC and Protocol No 5 of the EC Treaty.[25] Regulation 3605/93 defines certain key terms and establishes a system of regular reporting of information from member states to the Commission.[26] Further provisions concerning the EDP are contained in Regulation 1467/97, which is one of the three elements of the SGP, and in the SGP Resolution.

It must be emphasised that, as used in the Treaty, the concept of an "excessive deficit" refers to a possible outcome of the EDP. A member state has an "excessive deficit" if Ecofin decides that it has "after an overall assessment".[27] There is no exhaustive list of the factors that may be taken

---

[24] Three grades of firmness can be identified in the language of the Resolution. In descending order, these are: (i) "commits itself to" (or "is committed to"), (ii) "is urged to" (iii) "is invited to".

[25] On the Treaty provisions and Protocol, see generally Alexander Italianer, "The excessive deficit procedure: a legal description" in M. Andenas, L. Gormley, C. Hadjiemmanuil and I. J. Harden (eds), *European Economic and Monetary Union: the Institutional Framework*, (Dordrecht, Kluwer, 1997).

[26] Council Regulation 3605/93 of 22 November 1993 on the application of the Protocol on the excessive deficit procedure annexed to the Treaty establishing the European Community 1993 OJ L332/7.

[27] Art. 104(6) (ex 104c(6)) EC.

into account in this assessment. Furthermore, even the more specific provisions of the Treaty leave room for interpretation and require the exercise of judgement. Nor are sanctions automatic since the Treaty provides that Ecofin "may" decide to apply one or more types of sanction.[28] Without entering into jurisprudential debate, it seems reasonable to say that Ecofin has a margin of discretion in identifying excessive deficits and imposing sanctions. The EDP involves other actors too, in particular the Commission and the Economic and Financial Committee (successor to the Monetary Committee),[29] whose roles also involve judgement and interpretation and hence a margin of discretion.

One of the purposes of the SGP is to speed up the operation of the EDP by establishing a precise timetable. According to recital 15 to Regulation 1467/97, an overall maximum period of ten months between the relevant reporting date and a decision by Ecofin to impose sanctions seems both feasible and appropriate. However, the SGP does not alter the basic fact that the EDP involves discretion. However, it creates presumptions about how certain of its elements will be exercised and increases the transparency of the procedure, in particular through requirements of reasoning and publication.[30] The SGP also re-allocates discretionary power, strengthening the role of Ecofin and weakening that of the Commission.

The Treaty makes the Commission the "gatekeeper" of the EDP. The Commission monitors the development of deficits and the stock of debt in the member states, *"with a view to identifying gross errors"*. Unless the Commission initiates the procedure by making a report, Ecofin has no power to decide that a member state has an excessive deficit. If the Commission does make a report, the Economic and Financial Committee (EFC) formulates an opinion on it. It is important to note that the EFC not only has its own defined role at various points in the excessive deficit and other procedures, but also subsequently prepares the work of Ecofin.[31] Once the EFC has given its opinion, the Commission then makes a judge-

---

[28] Art. 104 (11) (ex 104c(11)) EC.

[29] On the Monetary Committee see Andreas Kees, "The Monetary Committee as a promoter of European integration" in A. F. P. Bakker et al (eds), *Monetary Stability through International Co-operation: essays in honour of André Szász* (Dordrecht: Kluwer, 1994); A. F. P. Bakker, *The Liberalization of Capital Movements in Europe: the Monetary Committee and financial integration, 1958–1994* (Dordrecht: Kluwer, 1995). Like the Monetary Committee, the Economic and Financial Committee will be composed of officials from national central banks and finance ministries. (Proposal for a Council Decision on the detailed provisions concerning the composition of the EFC: COM/98/0110 final).

[30] See in particular Regulation 1467/97 Art. 4(2): Resolution, member states, points 2 and 6; the Commission, point 4; the Council, point 6. The SGP Resolution "invites" Ecofin always to state in writing the reasons which justify a decision not to act if at any stage of the excessive deficit or surveillance of budgetary positions procedures the Council did not act on a Commission recommendation, and to make public the votes of each member state in such a case.

[31] Art. 114(1) (ex 109c(1)) EC.

ment as to whether an excessive deficit exists, or may occur. If so, it must address an opinion to Ecofin.

The decision that a state has an excessive deficit is made by qualified majority of Ecofin, after an overall assessment and having considered any observations which the member state concerned may wish to make. The member state concerned has a vote, as do the non-participating states. (Other decisions in the EDP are governed by special voting rules).[32]

In making the decision that a member state has an excessive deficit, Ecofin acts on a recommendation from the Commission. A recommendation is an essential procedural step, but its substance is not binding on Ecofin. Ecofin could adopt a decision that there is an excessive deficit by qualified majority even against the Commission's recommendation. (In contrast, where the Council acts on a *proposal* from the Commission it can amend the proposal only by unanimity).[33] However, the Commission can block an excessive deficit decision by not making a recommendation. Article 115 (ex 109d) EC allows the Council or a member state to request the Commission to make a recommendation. The Commission must examine the request and "submit its conclusions to the Council without delay".

The SGP Resolution says that the Commission commits itself, following a request from the Council under Article 115 (ex 109d) EC, to make, "*as a rule*", a recommendation for a Council decision on whether an excessive deficit exists. The words "as a rule" appear to mean "normally, but not necessarily always". The intention, however, is clearly to reduce the gatekeeper role of the Commission and further concentrate the discretionary power to interpret and apply the deficit criterion in the hands of the EFC and Ecofin.

Once an excessive deficit decision has been made, it remains in force unless and until it is abrogated by Ecofin, again acting on a recommendation from the Commission. The member state concerned cannot vote and is excluded from the calculation of the qualified majority.

B. *the criteria and the reference values*

The Commission monitors budgetary discipline on the basis of two criteria. If a member state does not fulfil the requirements under either criterion, the Commission must initiate the EDP by preparing a report under Article 104(3) (ex 104c(3)) EC. The Commission may also prepare a report if it is of the opinion that there is a risk that an excessive deficit may

---

[32] The abrogation of an excessive deficit decision as well as recommendations under Art. 104(7) (ex 104c(7)) EC and decisions to make recommendations public under Art. 104(8) (ex 104c(8)) EC are made by a qualified majority of two thirds, excluding the votes of the states concerned. Non-participating states have a vote. On sanctions see *infra* section C, p.86.

[33] Art. 249 (1) (ex 189a(1)) EC.

occur, notwithstanding the fulfilment of the requirements under the criteria.

Each of the criteria incorporates a "reference value", specified in a Protocol on the EDP. The two reference values are three per cent for the ratio of the annual budget deficit (planned or actual) to GDP and sixty per cent for the ratio of government debt to GDP. In both cases "government" means general government; that is, central, regional and local government and social security funds. The debt and deficits of commercial operations, such as state-owned industries, are excluded.[34]

(i) the debt criterion

"Debt" for the purposes of the EDP means gross debt, consolidated within and between the different components of general government.[35] The reason for being concerned with the level of debt, rather than focusing exclusively on deficits, is that high levels of debt make the public finances more vulnerable to economic shocks, and their soundness more readily questioned by financial markets. From an economic perspective, however, there is no particular justification for a debt-to-GDP ratio of sixty per cent rather than a higher or lower figure. Sixty per cent appears to have been selected because it represented the EU average at the time when the Maastricht Treaty was being negotiated.

If the sixty per cent debt-to-GDP ratio is exceeded, the member state does not fulfil the requirements of the relevant criterion unless *"the ratio is sufficiently diminishing and approaching the reference value at a satisfactory pace"*. The terms "sufficiently" and "satisfactory" are not defined. "Approaching" could be understood to mean "coming near to" or "moving in the direction of". In practice, the latter interpretation prevailed: in May 1998 the excessive deficit decisions concerning Belgium and Italy were abrogated in order to allow them to be part of the "first wave" of the single currency, whilst their debt-to-GDP ratios were approximately double the reference value.[36] It would be premature, however, to conclude from this that the debt criterion is no longer of any significance and that all that matters is the deficit criterion. Two points in particular should be noted. First, the debt criterion provides the only legal basis for distinguishing between high and low debt states in the EDP. (Whether it is desirable or politically possible to make such a distinction is another question). Second,

---

[34] Protocol on the excessive deficit procedure, Art. 2. NB the exclusion of commercial operations means that the concept of general government deficit is narrower than the UK concept of the Public Sector Borrowing Requirement.

[35] Protocol on the excessive deficit procedure, Art. 2. "Gross" means that government-owned assets are not taken into account in the calculation. Consolidation means that debts owed by one part of general government to another are excluded (for example, debts owed by local government to central government).

[36] "Commission's recommendation concerning the third stage of economic and monetary union", 65 *European Economy* (1998).

it should not be assumed that changes in the debt-to-GDP ratio automatically correlate with levels of deficit. If real deficits are higher than recorded because of the accounting techniques used, the disparity may subsequently show up in the debt ratio as a "stock flow adjustment".

(ii) the deficit criterion

If the planned or actual deficit-to-GDP ratio exceeds three per cent, the member state does not fulfil the requirements of the relevant criterion unless one of two conditions is fulfilled:

> either the ratio has declined substantially and continuously and reached a level that comes close to the reference value; or alternatively, the excess over the reference value is only exceptional and temporary and the ratio remains close to the reference value.

According to the SGP Resolution, the Commission "commits itself" to prepare a report under Article 104 (ex 104c(3)) EC whenever the planned or actual deficit exceeds three per cent. Thus whereas the Treaty provides for an exercise of judgement by the Commission as to whether the criterion is fulfilled, the SGP envisages an automatic triggering if the reference value is exceeded. The effect is again to reduce the gatekeeper power of the Commission and concentrate the discretionary power to interpret and apply the deficit criterion in the hands of the EFC and Ecofin. However, the Commission's report must nonetheless include its judgement of whether the member state fulfils the requirements of the deficit criterion. According to the SGP Resolution, if the Commission's report considers that a deficit exceeding three per cent, is not excessive and this opinion differs from that of the EFC, the Commission commits itself to present in writing to the Council the reasons for its position.

investment expenditure

According to Article 104(3) (ex 104c(3)) EC, the Commission's report shall also take into account *"whether the government deficit exceeds government investment expenditure . . ."* The so-called "golden rule" (i.e. limit public borrowing to the amount necessary to finance investment expenditure[37]) is not a requirement as such, but is identified as a relevant factor to be taken into account alongside others. The Treaty, however, gives no indication of how it is to be taken into account. Presumably the fact that the amount of the deficit exceeds government investment expenditure could be weighed against other factors, which might suggest that the member state concerned fulfils the requirements of the deficit criterion despite having a deficit ratio which exceeds three per cent. On the other hand, if the deficit does not

---

[37] See also Art. 115(1) of the German Basic Law which states the principle that net borrowing by the Federal government shall not exceed the total of Federal investment expenditures.

exceed government investment expenditure, this could itself be taken as a reason to consider that the member state concerned fulfils the requirements of the deficit criterion despite having a deficit ratio which exceeds three per cent.

the economic cycle

Article 104(3) (ex 104c(3)) EC also refers expressly to *"the medium term economic and budgetary position of the member state"* as a relevant factor. The point here is that, as noted in section 2.1 above, the operation of the "automatic stabilisers" mean that the budget balance tends to deteriorate as the economic cycle moves downwards and improve towards the high point of the cycle. The significance of any given size of budget deficit therefore partly depends on the stage of the economic cycle at which it occurs. To show the underlying position, the Commission also produces figures for cyclically-adjusted budget deficits,[38] although the figures taken into account in the EDP are not cyclically-adjusted.

In practice, the question which is likely to arise in the EDP concerns deficits in an economic downturn: should the three per cent reference value be applied strictly in a recession? The corresponding question about the desirable budget balance at the *high* point of the economic cycle is, of course, unlikely to arise directly in the EDP. Underlying both questions is another: what should be the norm for the budget balance from which cyclical variations upwards and downwards deviate? According to the SGP Resolution, the member states: *"commit themselves to respect the medium-term budgetary objective of positions close to balance or in surplus . . .".* The recitals to Regulation 1467/97 make specific reference to this commitment. It would therefore be reasonable to expect that, within the EDP, deficits exceeding the reference value and which are inconsistent with the objective, will be considered "excessive". This, however, does not turn a political commitment into a legal obligation. A legal obligation arises only insofar as the deficit criterion is interpreted and applied though the EDP in a way that corresponds to the commitment.

As noted above, a member state meets the requirements of the deficit criterion despite a deficit that exceeds three per cent of GDP, provided that at least one of two conditions is satisfied. The first condition includes the requirement that the deficit ratio has "declined continuously". It is therefore irrelevant to a cyclical downturn, which tends to produce rising levels of deficit. The appropriate condition is therefore the second. This has two elements, both of which must be satisfied: (i) the ratio must remain *"close"* to the reference value and (ii) the excess over the reference value must be "exceptional and temporary". Neither "close" nor *"exceptional and temporary"* is defined by the Treaty. "Close" remains undefined, and this

---

[38] The methodology is explained in 60 *European Economy* (1995) 35–90.

remains the most significant discretionary element in the EDP. On the other hand, the SGP elaborates on the meaning of "exceptional and temporary" in Article 2 of Regulation 1467/97, which provides as follows:

1. The excess of a government deficit over the reference value shall be considered exceptional and temporary, in accordance with Article 104c (2) (a), second indent [now Article 104(2)(a), second indent], when resulting from an unusual event outside the control of the member state concerned and which has a major impact on the financial position of the general government, or when resulting from a severe economic downturn. In addition, the excess over the reference value shall be considered temporary if budgetary forecasts as provided by the Commission indicate that the deficit will fall below the reference value following the end of the unusual event or the severe economic downturn.
2. The Commission when preparing a report under Article 104c (3) [now Article 104(3)] shall, as a rule, consider an excess over the reference value resulting from asevere economic downturn to be exceptional only if there is an annual fall of real GDP of at least 2%.
3. The Council when deciding, according to Article 104c (6 [now Article 104(6)], whether an excessive deficit exists, shall in its overall assessment take into account any observations made by the member state showing that an annual fall of real GDP of less than 2% is nevertheless exceptional in the light of further supporting evidence, in particular on the abruptness of the downturn or on the accumulated loss of output relative to past trends.

These provisions would be easier to interpret if, in Article 2 (1), the words *"and temporary"* in the first sentence and "In addition", at the beginning of the second sentence had been omitted. It is not clear to the present writer whether this change would alter the intended meaning.[39] What is clear, however, is that the SGP here again concentrates discretionary power in the hands of the EFC and Ecofin. The Commission—but not Ecofin—is bound (albeit "as a rule", which here as elsewhere appears to mean, "normally, but not necessarily always") to consider that there is an excessive deficit unless there is an annual fall of real GDP of at least two per cent.[40] Furthermore, the factors which are particularly mentioned as ones that Ecofin can take into account (the abruptness of the downturn and accumulated loss of output relative to past trends), are based on counter-factual assumptions (what would have happened if)? Although it could be argued that the relevant statistical data should be supplied by the Commission (in application of Article 4 of the Protocol on the EDP), the

[39] The discussion that follows deals only with the Article as it relates to "severe economic downturns". However, it would be fascinating to speculate on what might be considered an "unusual event outside the control of the member state concerned". Presumably natural disasters are included, but what about a war or a collapse of the political system?

[40] It is, of course, much less restrictive to specify *real* GDP as opposed to *nominal* GDP. Even with low levels of inflation, a fall in nominal GDP is a rare event.

reference in Article 2(3) to "observations made by the member state" suggests that "further supporting evidence" may be supplied by the member state itself.

The SGP Resolution records that member states:

> commit themselves not to invoke the benefit of Article 2 (3) of the Council Regulation on speeding up and clarifying the excessive deficit procedure unless they are in severe recession; in evaluating whether the economic downturn is severe, the member states will, as a rule, take as a reference point an annual fall in real GDP of at least 0.75 %.

The last phrase contains a double qualification. First, the figure of a 0.75 per cent annual fall in real GDP is expressed to be a "reference point". Second, member states are to take the figure as a reference point "as a rule". It should also be remembered that the SGP Resolution contains political commitments, not legal obligations. From a legal perspective, the only provision of Regulation 1467/97 concerning the meaning of "exceptional and temporary" which imposes an additional obligation on Ecofin is the requirement, in certain circumstances, to take into account observations from the member state on a specific matter. There is no provision which, either expressly or by necessary implication, limits Ecofin in its power of "overall assessment".

C. sanctions

If it decides that an excessive deficit exists, Ecofin makes recommendations to the states concerned. The recommendations may subsequently be made public if there is no effective action in response.[41] The SGP Resolution "invites" the member states to make recommendations public on their own initiative. If a *participating* member state persists in failing to put the recommendations into practice, Ecofin may decide what deficit reduction is necessary and give notice to the member state to take measures within a specified time limit. It may also request the member state to submit reports in accordance with a specific timetable in order to examine its adjustment efforts.[42]

Article 104(11) (ex 104c(11)) EC and Articles 11-16 of Regulation 1467/97 provide for sanctions against a participating member state that fails to comply with an Ecofin decision taken in accordance with Article 104(9) (ex 104c(9)) EC. Decisions under Article 104 (9) and (11) (ex 104c(9) and (11)) EC are made by a qualified majority of two thirds of the participating member states, excluding the votes of the member state concerned. (Non-participating member states do not have a vote).[43]

---

[41] Art. (104(7) and (8) (ex 104c(7) and (8)) EC.

[42] Art. 104 (9) (ex 104c(9)) EC.

[43] Art. 104(13) (ex 104c(13)) EC; Art. 122(5) (ex 109k(5) EC. Non-participating member states do have a vote as regards the existence of an excessive deficit and the making of recommendations under Art. 104(7) (ex 104c(7)) EC.

Article 104(11) (ex 104c(11)) EC provides that Ecofin may decide to apply, or as the case may be, intensify one or more of the following measures:

- to require the member state concerned to publish additional information, to be specified by the Council, before issuing bonds and securities;
- to invite the European Investment Bank to reconsider its lending policy towards the member state concerned;
- to require the member state concerned to make a non-interest-bearing deposit of an appropriate size with the Community until the excessive deficit has, in the view of the Council, been corrected;
- to impose fines of an appropriate size.

Regulation 1467/97 specifies that whenever the Council decides to apply sanctions, a non-interest-bearing deposit shall, "as a rule", be required. The amount of the deposit is specified for cases when the excessive deficit is the result of non-compliance with the deficit criterion. It consists of a fixed component equal to 0.2 per cent of GDP, and a variable component equal to one tenth of the difference between the deficit as a percentage of GDP in the preceding year and the reference value of three per cent of GDP. The maximum amount of a single deposit is 0.5 per cent of GDP.

Each following year, until the excessive deficit decision is abrogated, the Council shall assess whether the participating member state concerned has taken effective action in response to the Article 104(9) (ex 104c(9)) EC notice. Unless it has, Regulation 1467/97 provides for the Council to decide, in accordance with Article 104(11) (ex 104c(11)) EC, to intensify the sanctions, but these do not have to take the form of an additional deposit. If an additional deposit is required, however, it shall be equal to one tenth of the difference between the deficit as a percentage of GDP in the preceding year and the reference value of three per cent of GDP, subject to the same maximum of 0.5 per cent of GDP per deposit.

After two years a deposit shall, *"as a rule"*, be converted into a fine, if the excessive deficit has, in the view of the Council, not been corrected.[44] According to Article 14 of Regulation 1467/97 the Council shall abrogate sanctions depending on the significance of the progress made by the participating member state concerned in correcting the excessive deficit. If Ecofin abrogates the excessive deficit decision, all outstanding sanctions are also abrogated. However, fines are not to be reimbursed.

It can be seen from the above that the SGP injects a considerable degree of automaticity into the EDP in relation to the type and amount of sanctions to be imposed. As regards the decision to impose sanctions at all, the first sentence of Article 6 of Regulation 1467/97 reads as follows:

Where the conditions to apply Article 104c(11) [now Article 104(11)] are met, the Council shall impose sanctions in accordance with Article 104c(11) [now Article 104(11)].

[44] Regulation 1469/97, Art. 13.

This could be understood to impose an obligation on the Council to impose sanctions. However, this interpretation would be inconsistent with the wording of Article 104(11) (ex 104c(11)) EC itself which provides that the Council *may* apply or intensify sanctions. It would also make redundant the provision of the SGP Resolution which *"invites"* the Council *"always"* to impose sanctions if a participating member state fails to take the necessary steps to bring an excessive deficit situation to an end as recommended by the Council. The purpose of the provision in question could therefore be to state more explicitly what the Treaty puts in the language of diplomacy ("apply . . . measures"); i.e. that Article 104(11) (ex 104c(11)) EC authorises Ecofin to impose sanctions on member states. The possibility of sanctions is what makes the EDP fundamentally different from the multilateral surveillance procedure.

5. Multilateral Surveillance

"Multilateral surveillance" was initiated by the Monetary Committee in 1987 and received a legal basis in a Council Decision of 1990.[45] Since the Maastricht Treaty came into force, multilateral surveillance has been based on Article 99 (ex 103) EC, which is also the basis for the adoption of "broad guidelines" of the economic policies of the member states and of the Community. Article 99(3) (ex 103(3)) EC provides that the Council shall:

> on the basis of reports submitted by the Commission, monitor economic developments in each of the Member States and in the Community as well as the consistency of economic policies with the broad guidelines and regularly carry out an overall assessment.

Article 99(4) (ex 103(4)) EC empowers the Council to make recommendations to a member state if its economic policies are not consistent with the broad guidelines, or if they risk jeopardising the proper functioning of EMU. The Council acts by qualified majority on a recommendation from the Commission. The Council may, acting by qualified majority on a proposal from the Commission, decide to make its recommendations public.[46]

---

[45] See 29th Report of the Monetary Committee, p. 18 and Council Decision 90/141/EEC of 12 March 1990 on the attainment of progressive convergence of economic policies and performance during stage one of economic and monetary union (OJ L078 24 March 1990, p. 23). Decision 90/141/EEC replaced a 1974 decision that had also provided for the Council to establish economic policy guidelines and for permanent consultation and monitoring in a co-ordinating group (Council Decision 74/120/EEC of 18 February 1974 on the attainment of a high degree of convergence of economic policies and performance 1974 OJ L63/16.

[46] This should be distinguished from the position under Art. 100 (ex 103a) where, acting on a proposal from the Commission, the Council is restricted by the need for unanimity when exercising its power to "decide upon the measures appropriate to the economic situation, in particular if severe difficulties arise in the supply of certain products".

As can be seen from the above, the Treaty envisages a central role for the broad guidelines in the multilateral surveillance procedure. The Luxembourg Resolution of the European Council considered that they should be developed into an effective instrument for ensuring sustained convergence of member states. It called for more concrete and country-specific guidelines giving more attention to improving competitiveness, labour-, product- and services-market efficiency, education and training, and to making taxation and social protection systems more employment-friendly.[47]

In practice, however, the detailed rules for multilateral surveillance, adopted in accordance with Article 99(5) (ex 103(5)) EC, are concerned with budgetary issues. Their effect is to make multilateral surveillance a procedure for re-inforcing and supplementing the EDP. The rules are contained in Regulation 1466/97,[48] and constitute one of the three elements of the SGP. They build on the experience of "convergence programmes".

A. Stability and Convergence Programmes

Convergence programmes derive from a suggestion made by the Monetary Committee to Ecofin in Spring 1991.[49] It was agreed that member states would draw up convergence programmes setting out multi-annual paths for inflation, debt and deficits and describing their policy measures for achieving them. Article 116 (ex 109e) EC subsequently provided a legal basis for these programmes to be submitted before the beginning of the second stage of EMU (i.e. 1 January 1994). Although there was no specific provision for updating or amendment of the convergence programmes, a procedure for this purpose was established and a code of conduct for convergence programmes was drawn up by the Monetary Committee and endorsed by Ecofin in February 1994. In practice, the monitoring and updating of convergence programmes became a key part of the preparations for the third stage of EMU. In particular, they played an important

---

[47] Resolution of the European Council on Economic Policy Co-ordination in Stage 3 of EMU and on Treaty Arts. 109 and 109b [now Articles 111 and 113 EC], 13 December 1997 points 4 and 6 and see point 44 of the Presidency conclusions.

The adoption of the broad economic guidelines involves a complex procedure which has four stages:

  (i) the Commission makes a recommendation;

  (ii) acting by qualified majority, Ecofin formulates a draft for the guidelines and reports its findings to the European Council;

  (iii) acting on the basis of the report from Ecofin, the European Council shall "discuss a conclusion";

  (iv) on the basis of this conclusion and acting by qualified majority, Ecofin adopts a recommendation setting out these broad guidelines.

[48] On the strengthening of the surveillance of budgetary positions and the surveillance and co-ordination of economic policies, OJ 1997 L209/1.

[49] Kees, *supra* n. 29, p.131.

role in the operation of the EDP during stage two of EMU. Ecofin's recommendations under Article 104(7) (ex 104c(7)) EC were largely based on the relevant member state's own targets and policies as set out in its convergence programme.

Regulation 1466/97 provides a legal basis for the substance of the convergence programme exercise to become a permanent feature of the third stage of EMU. Non-participating states continue to submit convergence programmes, whilst participating states submit "stability programmes". According to Regulation 1466/97, convergence and stability programmes are intended to prevent, at an early stage, the occurrence of excessive deficits and to promote the surveillance and co-ordination of economic policies. Both types of programmes are to be submitted before 1 March 1999 and updated annually thereafter. The programmes and updates must be made public.

In general, the provisions concerning the two types of programme are very similar and are identical as regards procedure. The legal obligations are therefore essentially the same for both participating and non-participating states. In what follows, however, reference is made only to stability programmes. Stability programmes must present the following information:

(a) the medium-term objective for the budgetary position of close to balance or in surplus and the adjustment path towards this objective for the general government surplus/deficit and the expected path of the general government debt ratio;
(b) the main assumptions about expected economic developments and important economic variables which are relevant to the realisation of the stability programme such as government investment expenditure, real gross domestic product (GDP) growth, employment and inflation;
(c) a description of budgetary and other economic policy measures being taken and/or proposed to achieve the objectives of the programme, and, in the case of the main budgetary measures, an assessment of their quantitative effects on the budget;
(d) an analysis of how changes in the main economic assumptions would affect the budgetary and debt position.

The information about paths for the general government surplus/deficit ratio and debt ratio and the main economic assumptions referred to in paragraphs (a) and (b) must be on an annual basis. They must cover, as well as the current and preceding year, at least the following three years.

The Commission and the EFC each make an assessment of the stability programme. Based on these assessments, Ecofin examines the following questions:

(a) whether the medium-term budget objective in the stability programme provides for a safety margin to ensure the avoidance of an excessive deficit;

(b) whether the economic assumptions on which the programme is based are realistic; and

(c) whether the measures being taken and/or proposed are sufficient to achieve the targeted adjustment path towards the medium-term budgetary objective; *and*

(d) whether the contents of the stability programme facilitate the closer co-ordination of economic policies and whether the economic policies of the member state concerned are consistent with the broad economic policy guidelines.[50]

Ecofin is to carry out this examination within two months of the submission of the programme. It then delivers an opinion on the programme, on a recommendation from the Commission and after consulting the EFC. If Ecofin considers that the objectives and contents of a programme should be strengthened, its opinion invites the member state concerned to adjust its programme. Updated stability programmes are to be examined by the EFC, on the basis of assessments made by the Commission. Examination by Ecofin only takes place "if necessary".

Implementation of the programmes is to be monitored by Ecofin as part of multilateral surveillance in accordance with Article 99(3) (ex 103(3)) EC. Monitoring is to be carried out on the basis of information provided by participating member states and of assessments by the Commission and the EFC,

> with a view to identifying actual or expected significant divergence of the budgetary position from the medium-term budgetary objective, or the adjust-ment path towards it, as set in the programme for the government surplus/deficit.

The monitoring process is intended to provide an early warning in order to prevent the occurrence of an excessive deficit. If multilateral surveillance identifies significant divergence of the budgetary position from the medium-term budgetary objective, or the adjustment path towards it, Article 99(4) (ex 103(4)) EC and Article 6 (2) of Regulation 1466/97 provide for Ecofin to address a recommendation to the member state concerned to take the necessary adjustment measures. If the divergence persists or gets worse, Article 6(3) of Regulation 1466/97 provides for Ecofin to make a recommendation to the member state concerned to take prompt corrective measures. Ecofin may also make the recommendation public.

Naturally, recommendations have no binding force as such.[51] However, the recommendations could nonetheless be effective for two reasons. First, the early warning procedure through multilateral surveillance both re-inforces and is re-inforced by the eventual possibility of an excessive deficit decision through the EDP. The "early warning" therefore relates to possible

---

[50] Art. 5(1)).   [51] Art. 249 (ex 189) EC.

sanctions. At the same time, the issuing of an early warning could make it more likely that an excessive deficit decision would actually be made by Ecofin if corrective action is not taken.

Second, the warning system could operate early enough to be taken into account in national budgetary procedures. Such procedures normally involve a variety of actors, some of whom (such as finance ministers) tend to favour budgetary consolidation (lower spending and deficits). Since stability programmes are to be public, it is natural for their annual updating also to become part of the national budgetary procedure. The overall effect of including a member state's stability programme as part of its budget planning and monitoring budgetary development according to the plans through multilateral surveillance, could be to strengthen the position of the finance minister in the national budgetary procedure.

6. Conclusion

As was perhaps to be expected, the SGP turns out to be a complex and in some ways ambiguous exercise. In section 2 above, we noted that the Pact reflects the tension between advocates of rules and advocates of discretion. The case for discretion is that, from an economic perspective, there is no right answer to the question "what is an excessive deficit?" The case for rules—put crudely—is that discretion could be misused, both by member states and by the Community institutions which participate in the EDP. In the debate between rules and discretion, the SGP clearly pushes the EDP further in the direction of rules without, however, eliminating discretion, either in the identification of an excessive deficit by Ecofin, or in the decision to impose sanctions.

However, the excessive deficit procedure is focused on the *maximum* size of deficit permitted. As we have seen, this question is bound up with another; "what should be the budget balance over the economic cycle?" The EDP cannot operate effectively without an answer to that question, because of the possibility that a deficit which exceeds the reference value may be permitted if the excess is "temporary and exceptional".

One way to proceed would be on a case-by-case basis, making a discretionary judgement every time the question arises. Instead, the SGP contains a political commitment to the principle of "a medium-term budgetary objective of positions close to balance or in surplus". It is impossible, however, to translate this commitment into a series of numbers that could constitute binding rules, to the effect that if GDP falls by x per cent, the deficit can be y per cent. This is impossible because the real economic relationships which could underlie such figures are not sufficiently stable, or at any rate our knowledge of them is too limited. Discretion in the application of this principle in the EDP is therefore unavoidable. It is hard to imagine, however, that debates about *application* of the principle could be prevented from also becoming debates about the meaning and/or the desirability of the principle. In other words, the procedures on which the Pact is based could become the setting for a debate about macro-economic policy, in which the advocates of expansionary policies (if there are any such advocates in Ecofin or the EFC) could expect to be heard alongside the advocates of budgetary consolidation.

5

EMU, *the European Central Bank, and Judicial Review*

PAUL CRAIG

THE emergence of the euro and the creation of the European Central Bank (ECB) clearly raise legal issues of major importance for the Community. In constitutional terms these developments prompt a whole series of more particular inquiries as to the impact of such developments on the economic constitution of the Community, the appropriate balance between central bank independence and democratic accountability, and the relationship between the ECB and the other major Community institutions. These issues have been discussed in the academic literature and will be touched on in the analysis which follows.[1] The principal focus of this paper is, however, rather different: it is to consider the role which may be played by the European Court (ECJ) within this area. The structure of the Treaty articles concerning Economic and Monetary Union (EMU) was laid down by the Maastricht Treaty and has not been altered markedly by the Treaty of Amsterdam. It is this framework which will, therefore, provide the legal basis on which a single currency is established, and within which the ECB and European System of Central Banks (ESCB) operate. It is clear, moreover, as will be seen, that some of the relevant Treaty articles draw upon more general provisions of the EC Treaty and that the interpretation of these Articles will be influenced by the Court's general jurisprudence. It seems timely then to consider the types of legal challenge which might arise concerning the operation of the single currency by the ECB and the ESCB, and the likely resolution of these conflicts. This is a topic of some importance in and of itself, given the role played by the Court in other areas of Community law. It will also enable us to come to some more concrete conclusions as to how far any democratic deficit of the ECB will be alleviated through judicial oversight.

---

[1] P. Brentford, "Constitutional Aspects of the Independence of the European Central Bank", (1998) 47 *ICLQ* 75; L. Gormley and J.de Haan, "The Democracy Deficit of the European Central Bank", (1996) 21 *ELRev.* 95.

1. Stage Three of EMU: The Legal Framework

It may be helpful at this juncture to set out briefly the legal framework which applies within stage three of EMU since this will facilitate the later discussion. The move to stage three has important consequences concerning institutional structure, regulatory power, monetary policy, economic policy and judicial control.

A. institutional structure

In institutional terms, immediately after the decision on the starting date for stage three has been taken, or immediately after 1 July 1998 (if, as it transpired, stage three had not by that stage commenced), the ECB is brought into being,[2] and the European Monetary Institute (EMI) goes into liquidation.[3] The ECB has legal personality.[4] It has an Executive Board and a Governing Council. The Executive Board is composed of a President, Vice-President and four other members, who must be recognised experts in monetary or banking matters. They serve for eight years and the posts are non-renewable.[5] The Governing Council consists of the Executive Board, plus the Governors of the national central banks.[6] The independence of the ECB is enshrined in Article 108 (ex Article 107) EC, which stipulates that the ECB shall not take any instruction from Community institutions, member states or any other body. This independence is reflected in the decision-making structure of the ECB: the President of the Council and a member of the Commission may participate in meetings of the ECB's Governing Council, but they do not have the right to vote.[7] The ECB is itself part of the ESCB, the other members being the national central banks.[8] The start of the third stage of EMU also sees the establishment of the Economic and Financial Committee, to be composed of no more than two members drawn from the member states, the Commission and the ECB. This Committee has a number of tasks, including:[9] delivering opinions to the Council or Commission; keeping under review the economic and financial situation of the member states and the Community; examining the situation regarding free movement of capital; and contributing to the preparation of Council work.

B. regulatory powers

Article 110 (ex 108a) EC contains the basic regulatory powers of the ECB. The ECB does not have a general power to make regulations. Article 110(1)

---

[2] Art. 123(1) (ex 109L(1)) EC.   [3] Art. 123(2) (ex 109L(2)) EC.
[4] Art. 107(2) (ex 106(2)) EC.   [5] Art. 112(2) (ex 109a(2)) EC.
[6] Art. 112(1) (ex 109a(1)) EC.   [7] Art. 113(1) (ex 109b(1)) EC.
[8] Art. 107(1) (ex 106(1)) EC.   [9] Art. 114(2) (ex 109c(2)) EC.

(ex 108a(1)) EC provides that it has this power to the extent necessary to implement the tasks defined in Article 3.1, first indent, Articles 19.1, 22 or 25.2 of the Statute of the ESCB, and in cases which shall be laid down in the acts of the Council referred to in Article 107(6) (ex 106(6)) EC. This Article therefore accords the power to make regulations either in the specific instances mentioned in the particular Articles of the ESCB Statute or pursuant to Article 107(6) EC.

The particular Articles of the ESCB Statute which are mentioned cover the following matters. Article 3.1 (first indent) accords the power to make regulations to "define and implement the monetary policy of the Community". While this provision is general in nature it is not all embracing, since it does not cover the conduct of foreign exchange operations, or the holding and managing of the official foreign reserves of the member states which are dealt with in the second and third indents of Article 3.1. Article 19.1 of the Statute gives the ECB power to make regulations relating to the holding by national credit institutions of minimum reserves with the ECB, and to impose sanctions in case of non-compliance. Article 22 of the Statute empowers the ECB to make regulations to ensure efficient and sound clearing and payment systems within the Community and other countries, while Article 25.2 enables the ECB to make such norms in relation to the prudential supervision of credit institutions within the Community, pursuant to a decision having been made by the Council under Article 105(6) of the EC Treaty.

Article 107(6) (ex 106(6)) EC, states that the Council, acting by qualified majority either on a proposal from the Commission and after consulting the European Parliament (EP) and the ECB, or on a recommendation from the ECB and after consulting the EP and the Commission, shall adopt the provisions referred to in Articles 4, 5.4, 19.2, 20, 28.1, 30.4 and 34.3 of the ESCB Statute. The combined effect of Articles 107(6) and 110 (ex 108a) EC would therefore seem to be as follows: the Council is under a duty imposed by Article 107(6) EC to adopt the provisions referred to in the particular Articles of the ESCB Statute set out above. Article 110 (ex 108a) EC is based on the premise that the Council may well, when making such provisions, choose to accord delegated power to the ECB to flesh out the details of the norms which the Council has enacted. This is the rationale for the power to make regulations given to the ECB by Article 110 (ex 108a) EC. Thus, to take an example, the Council has a duty to define the basis for the minimum and maximum reserves to be held by national credit institutions with the ECB, and the maximum permissible ratios between these reserves, as well as the appropriate sanctions in the case of non-compliance.[10] The Council may well decide to fulfil this duty in a way which would still leave room for further detailed regulation to be decided upon by the ECB, and

---

[10] Art. 19.2, ESCB Statute.

hence the latter would then be empowered by Article 110 (ex 108a) EC to make these further regulatory norms.

The ECB is given a general power to take decisions by Article 110(1) (ex 108a(1)) EC which are necessary for carrying out the tasks entrusted to the ESCB under the EC Treaty and the Statute of the ESCB. It is also empowered to make recommendations and deliver opinions.[11]

It is clear from Article 110(2) (ex 108a(2)) EC that the terms regulation, decision, recommendation and opinion have the same meaning as in Article 249 (ex 189) EC. Article 110(2) EC also stipulates that Articles 253–56 (ex 190–192) EC, concerning the duty to give reasons, publication, access to documents and the like, apply to regulations and decisions made under Article 110 EC. Article 110(2) EC further provides that the ECB, although under no obligation to publish recommendations, opinions and decisions, may decide to do so.[12] The ECB is entitled, subject to conditions adopted by the Council under the procedure laid down in Article 107(6) (ex 106(6)) EC, to impose fines or periodic penalty payments on undertakings for failure to comply with obligations contained in its regulations and decisions.[13]

It should not, however, be thought that the ECB can only regulate formally through regulations or decisions. It is clear from Article 12 of the ESCB Statute that it can also operate through less formal measures. This Article provides that the Governing Council of the ECB shall adopt guidelines and take the decisions necessary to ensure the performance of the tasks entrusted to the ESCB under the Treaty and under the Statute. Article 12 further stipulates that the Governing Council shall formulate the monetary policy of the Community including, as appropriate, decisions relating to intermediate monetary objectives, key interest rates and the supply of reserves in the ESCB, and shall establish the necessary guidelines for their implementation. The Executive Board of the ECB must then implement monetary policy in accordance with the guidelines and decisions laid down by the Governing Council.

C. consequences for monetary policy

The most important consequence in terms of monetary policy is of course the establishment of a single currency. At the start of the third stage the Council fixes the conversion rates at which the currencies of the member states without a derogation are irrevocably fixed.[14] The euro is then

---

[11] Art. 110(1) (ex 108a(1)) EC.

[12] It is surprising that Art. 110(2) (ex 108a(2)) EC does not mention the publication of ECB regulations, and neither are they covered by the provisions in Art. 254 (ex 191) EC on publication of regulations. Despite this strange omission, it can only be hoped that all ECB regulations will be published in the OJ.

[13] Art. 110(3) (ex 108a(3)) EC.

[14] This decision is made unanimously by those states which do not have a derogation, on a proposal from the Commission and after consulting the ECB; Art. 123(4) (ex 109l(4)) EC.

substituted for these currencies at this rate and becomes a currency in its own right. The Council is to take other measures necessary for the rapid introduction of the euro as the single currency of those member states.[15] The EC Treaty also contains important provisions concerning the objectives of Community monetary policy. These are set out in Article 105 (ex Article 105) EC. The primary objective of the ESCB is to maintain price stability. Without prejudice to this objective, the ESCB must support the general economic policies of the Community with a view to attaining the objectives set out in Article 2 (ex Article 2). The ESCB is to act in accordance with the principle of an open market economy with free competition, favouring the efficient allocation of resources and in compliance with the principles set out in Article 4. The basic tasks of the ESCB are:[16] to define and implement the Community's monetary policy; to conduct foreign exchange operations; to hold and manage the official foreign reserves of the member states; and to promote the smooth operation of the payment system. The ECB must be consulted on any Community act in its fields of competence, and subject to certain conditions, by national authorities regarding any draft legislative provision in its fields of competence.[17] It is the ECB which has the exclusive right to authorise the issue of banknotes within the EC.[18] The ESCB is to "contribute" to the smooth conduct of policies pursued by other competent authorities relating to the prudential supervision of credit institutions and the stability of the financial system.[19]

D. consequences for economic policy

The shift to stage three also has consequences for economic policy, in that more peremptory Treaty provisions now apply in this area. This is particularly noteworthy in relation to fiscal and budgetary matters. Member states will now have the obligation to avoid excessive government deficits, and not just to endeavour to avoid them.[20] The Council's powers to deal with states which do not adhere to its recommendations on excessive budgetary deficits are reinforced once the third stage of EMU has begun.[21]

E. judicial control

Article 35 of the Statute of the ESCB deals with judicial control and related matters. The general principle underlying this Article is that the ECB will

---

[15] *Ibid.*   [16] Art. 105(2) (ex 105(2)) EC.   [17] Art. 105(4) (ex 105(4)) EC.
[18] Art. 106 (ex 105a) EC. The ECB and the national banks can actually issue the banknotes.
[19] Art. 105(5) (ex 105(5)) EC.   [20] Art. 104(1) (ex 104c(1)) EC.
[21] Arts. 104(9) and (11) (ex 104c(9) and (11)) EC. However, Arts. 104(1), (9) and (11) do not apply to the UK as long as it remains outside the euro-zone; see Protocol on Certain Provisions Relating to the UK, Art.5.

be subject to the general rules on judicial review and the like laid down in the Treaty. Article 35.1 is the most important provision, and provides that the acts or omissions of the ECB shall be open to review or interpretation by the ECJ in the cases and under the conditions laid down in the Treaty. It also allows the ECB to institute proceedings in the cases and under the conditions provided for in the Treaty.[22] Article 35.3 makes it clear that in principle the ECB is subject to the liability rules contained in Article 288 (ex 215) EC, although the liability of national central banks is to be determined by their respective national laws.

Disputes between the ECB and its creditors, debtors or any other person are to be decided by the competent national courts, save where jurisdiction has been conferred on the ECJ.[23] The ECJ is expressly given jurisdiction in actions concerning the fulfilment by a national central bank of its obligations under the Statute.[24] The format of such actions is modelled on Article 226 (ex 169) EC. The ECJ also has jurisdiction to give judgment pursuant to an arbitration clause contained in a contract concluded by or on behalf of the ECB, whether that contract is governed by public or private law.[25]

2. Challenges to the ECB

It is clear from both Article 230(1) (ex 173(1)) EC, and Article 35 of the ESCB Statute, that the acts of the ECB, other than recommendations and opinions, are susceptible to judicial review in the normal manner. The general rules contained in Article 230 will, therefore, have to be satisfied. This requires an applicant to show that the challenged act is susceptible to review, that he or she has standing and that the ECB has infringed one of the grounds for review set out in Article 230(2). These issues will be considered in turn. Before doing so it might be helpful to identify some of the cases which might result in legal challenges.

A. challenges by applicants in the sphere of EMU

We are of course in the world of hypothesis, since it is only when the ECB has been fully operational for some time that we will truly know whether applicants will seek redress through the ECJ, and if so in what types of case. We can, none the less, hazard some guess as to the types of case which might lead to legal challenge.

[22] A decision by the ECB to institute proceedings before the ECJ is to be taken by the Governing Council; Art. 35.5 of the ESCB Statute.
[23] Art. 35.2 of the ESCB Statute.
[24] Art. 35.6. See also, Art.237(d) (ex 180(d)) EC.
[25] Art. 35.4. See also, Art.238 (ex 181) EC.

The obvious place to begin is by looking at the instances in which the ECB has explicit power to make regulations as set out in Article 110 (ex 108a) EC. The very breadth of the subject-matter dealt with in Article 3.1, first indent, which concerns the definition and implementation of the Community's monetary policy, necessarily means that many regulations will be made under this head. These may well range from the very broad, which are concerned with the general schema of price stability, to the very specific, which enshrine detailed rules limiting the conduct of national actors where it may be prejudicial to the Community's monetary objectives. It is perfectly possible that a non-privileged actor might feel inclined to challenge such a measure under Article 230 (ex 173) EC, more particularly one which is at the more specific end of this regulatory spectrum. This applies *a fortiori* to ECB regulations made under Article 19.1. This Article empowers the ECB to make regulations concerning the minimum reserves which credit institutions must hold with the ECB and national central banks in pursuance of monetary policy objectives. The possibility of challenge to such provisions is further enhanced by the fact that the ECB can levy interest and impose other sanctions in the case of non-compliance. It is equally possible to imagine challenges to ECB regulations in the field of prudential supervision of credit institutions. The Council may, under Article 105(6) EC, confer on the ECB specific tasks relating to this area. It is clear from Article 110 (ex 108a) EC that the ECB can choose to implement these tasks by the passage of regulations. Such regulations will, of course, vary considerably in terms of content and scope. It is, however, perfectly possible to imagine relatively specific norms being enacted which are not to the liking of those affected, who then decide to have recourse to judicial review under Article 230 (ex 173) EC.

Legal challenges may also be forthcoming in relation to regulations made by the ECB pursuant to acts adopted by the Council under Article 107(6) (ex 106(6)) EC. The rationale for this structure of power was explained above:[26] the Council will, in the specified areas, adopt the provisions needed to implement the objectives of the relevant Articles of the ESCB Statute, but it might well, when doing so, decide to leave further implementation to the ECB, which can itself then proceed to develop policy by way of regulation if it should choose to do so. An example will, hopefully, make this clear. The Council must adopt the general rules and conditions concerning the payment of penalties and fines, in accordance with the legislative procedure specified in Article 107(6). It is, however, open to the Council, having set out these general conditions, to leave further implementation to the ECB. The ECB may then choose to flesh out the interstices of the Council's conditions by its own regulations, as it is entitled to do under Article 110 (ex 108a) EC. It is perfectly possible that a

---

[26] See *supra*, p. 97.

non-privileged applicant may seek to challenge such ECB regulations, either on the ground that they depart from the conditions laid down by the Council, or on one of the other heads of review mentioned in Article 230(2) (ex 173(2)) EC.

The discussion thus far has concentrated on possible challenges to ECB regulations. The ECB also possesses, as we have seen, a general power to take decisions under Article 110 (ex 108a) EC. It is, moreover, clear, both in terms of principle and from the terms of the ESCB Statute, that such decisions may vary enormously in terms of their relative generality/specificity. At one end of the scale are the decisions referred to in Article 12 of the Statute, relating to the matters of general importance for the attainment of the Community's monetary policy. At the other end of the scale are decisions imposing penalties and fines for non-compliance with ECB norms. The ECB would also appear to have considerable latitude as to whether to develop policy in a particular area through regulation/rulemaking, or through decision/adjudication. It is therefore perfectly possible to imagine situations in which the ECB makes a decision which is formally addressed to one person or institution, which is felt to be of concern to others in a like position. The ECB might, for example, take a decision as to the minimum reserves which a credit institution has to hold with the ECB itself and national central banks which could have ramifications for other such bodies.

B. direct actions under Article 230 (ex 173) EC: acts which are amenable to review

In accordance with the general principles governing judicial review under Article 230 (ex 173) EC, the applicant will have to show that the challenged act is amenable to judicial review. This will not be a problem in relation to regulations. Nor, generally, will there be difficulties concerning the reviewability of decisions. The general jurisprudence of the ECJ dealing with the issue of whether an act does or does not have legal effects may, however, be of relevance in the context of the ECB. There are at least two types of case in which this problem may arise.

First, there may be instances where the ECB is considering the imposition of a fine or a penalty on an institution, and there may be steps which are preliminary to the issuance of the final decision which the affected party wishes to challenge. In cases of this nature the general jurisprudence of the ECJ flowing from the *IBM* case[27] will determine whether the measure is challengeable under Article 230 (ex 173) EC.

Secondly, interesting and important issues may well arise as to the reviewability of the guidelines to be adopted by the Governing Council of

---

[27] Case 60/81 *International Business Machines Corporation* v. *Commission* [1981] ECR 2639.

the ECB under Article 12 of the ESCB Statute. We have already seen that these guidelines are designed to deal with important matters relating to the implementation of the EC's monetary policy. It is extremely doubtful whether non-privileged applicants would be found to have standing to challenge measures of this nature. Such challenges may, however, be forthcoming from privileged applicants. The initial issue would then be whether the guideline was a reviewable act for the purposes of Article 230 (ex 173) EC.[28] It is clear from the *ERTA* case[29] that the ECJ will treat an act as open to review provided that it has binding force or produces legal effects, and that this is so even if the act in question is *sui generis*. It is then perfectly possible that guidelines made under Article 12 of the Statute will be open to review, although much will depend upon the content of any particular such measure.

C. direct actions under Article 230: standing

It is clear that challenges to the norms made by the ECB may be made either by privileged applicants, those mentioned in Article 230(2) (ex 173(2)) EC, or by non-privileged applicants, as dealt with by Article 230(4) (ex 173(4)) EC. There has, in general, been no difficulty concerning the former category (i.e. member states, the Commission and the Council), and therefore the discussion which follows will concentrate on the position of non-privileged applicants.[30]

It has never been easy for a non-privileged applicant to satisfy the standing criteria established by the ECJ, and continues to be difficult notwithstanding certain decisions which were thought to have liberalised the law in this area. The case law is complex, and the analysis which follows is therefore an outline of the main principles of the Court's jurisprudence. More detailed discussion can be found elsewhere.[31]

An individual is, according to Article 230 (ex 173) EC, only able to challenge the following types of measures: decisions which are addressed to that person; decisions which are addressed to another person, but which are of direct and individual concern to the applicant; and norms which are in the form of regulations, where the applicant contends that the "regulation" is in reality a decision which is of direct and individual concern to him or her. Cases which fall into the first of these categories have not proven to be

---

[28] See P. Craig and G. de Burca, *EU Law: Text, Cases and Materials* (Oxford, OUP, 1998, 2nd ed.), ch. 11; S. Weatherill and P. Beaumont, *EU Law*, (London, Penguin, 1999, 3rd ed.), ch.8.

[29] Case 22/70 *Commission* v. *Council* [1971] ECR 263.

[30] The position of quasi-privileged applicants, namely the European Parliament, the Court of Auditors and the ECB, is that they have standing "for the purpose of protecting their prerogatives" (Art 230 (3) ex 173(3) EC).

[31] See Craig and de Burca *supra* n. 28, Ch. 11; Weatherill and Beaumont *supra* n. 28, Ch. 8.

problematic. Attention will therefore be focused on the other two types of case.

The seminal decision governing challenges to decisions which are addressed to another person is still the *Plaumann* case.[32] In 1961 the German Government requested the Commission to authorise it to suspend the collection of duties on clementines imported from third countries. The Commission refused the request, and addressed its answer to the German Government. The applicant in the case was an importer of clementines, who sought to contest the legality of the Commission's decision. The ECJ adopted the following test to determine whether the applicant was individually concerned by the decision addressed to the German Government:

> Persons other than those to whom a decision is addressed may only claim to be individually concerned if that decision affects them by reason of certain attributes which are peculiar to them or by reason of circumstances in which they are differentiated from all other persons and by virtue of these factors distinguishes them individually just as in the case of the person addressed. In the present case the applicant is affected by the disputed Decision as an importer of clementines, that is to say, by reason of a commercial activity which may at any time be practised by any person and is not therefore such as to distinguish the applicant in relation to the contested Decision as in the case of the addressee.
>
> For these reasons the present action for annulment must be declared inadmissible.

It is the application of the test to the facts of this and other cases which has rendered it such a difficult hurdle for applicants to surmount. The applicant failed because it practised a commercial activity which could be carried on by any person at any time. This is open to criticism both pragmatically and conceptually. In pragmatic terms the application of the test can be criticised as being economically unrealistic. If there are, for example, only a very limited number of firms pursuing a certain trade this is not fortuitous, nor is the number of those firms likely to rise overnight. The presently existing range of such firms is established by the ordinary principles of supply and demand: if there are two or three firms in the industry this is because they can satisfy the current market demand. The Court's reasoning is also open to criticism in conceptual terms, since it renders it literally impossible for an applicant *ever* to succeed, except in a very limited category of retrospective cases. The applicant failed because the activity of clementine-importing could be carried out by anyone at any time. On this reasoning the applicant would fail even if there were only one such importer at the time the challenged decision was made, since it would always be open to the Court to contend that others could enter the industry. No applicant could ever succeed since it could *always* be argued

---

[32] Case 25/62 *Plaumann & Co.* v. *Commission* [1963] ECR 95, [1964] CMLR 29.

that others might engage in the trade at some juncture. To regard any category as open merely because others might notionally undertake the trade in issue means, of course, that any decision which has any future impact will be unchallengeable because the category will be regarded as open.

The other type of case which has been problematic is where an individual asserts that, although the challenged measure was in the form of a regulation, it was in reality a decision which was of direct and individual concern to him or her. Until recently the ECJ applied the abstract terminology test, as exemplified by the *Calpak* case.[33] The ECJ acknowledged that the objective of allowing challenges of this nature was to:

> prevent the Community institutions from being in a position, merely by choosing the form of a regulation, to exclude an application by an individual against a decision which concerns him directly and individually.[34]

The ECJ then denied the applicant's standing on the ground that the contested measure applied to objectively determined situations and produced legal effects with regard to categories of persons described in a generalised and abstract manner. The nature of the measure as a regulation was not, moreover, called in question by the mere fact that it was possible to determine the number or even identity of the producers to be granted the aid which is limited thereby.[35]

The problem with the abstract terminology test is that, rather than looking behind form to substance, it comes perilously close to looking behind form to form. A regulation will be accepted as a true regulation if, as stated in *Calpak*, it applies to "objectively determined situations and produces legal effects with regard to categories of persons described in a generalized and abstract manner". However, it is always possible to draft norms in this manner, and thus to immunise them from attack, more especially as the Court makes it clear that knowledge of the number or identity of those affected will not prevent the norm from being regarded as a true regulation.

The abstract terminology test was normally the sole criterion employed by the ECJ: if a regulation was a "true" regulation as judged by this test,

---

[33] Cases 789 and 790/79 *Calpak SpA and Società Emiliana Lavorazione Frutta SpA* v. *Commission* [1980] ECR 1949, [1981] 1 CMLR 26. See also Cases 103–109/78 *Beauport* v. *Council and Commission* [1979] ECR 17, [1979] 3 CMLR 1; Case 162/78 *Wagner* v. *Commission* [1979] ECR 3467; Case 45/81 *Alexander Moksel Import-Export GmbH & Co Handels KG* v. *Commission* [1982] ECR 1129; Cases 97, 99, 193, 215/86 *Asteris AE and Greece* v. *Commission* [1988] ECR 2181, [1988] 3 CMLR 493; Case 160/88R *Fédération Européenne de la Santé Animale* v. *Council* [1988] ECR 4121; Case C–298/89 *Gibraltar* v. *Council* [1993] ECR I–3605, [1994] 3 CMLR 425; Case C–308/89 *Codorniu SA* v. *Council* [1994] ECR I–1853.

[34] Cases 789 and 790/79, *supra* n. 33, para. 7.

[35] *Ibid.*, para. 9.

then the Court would stop the inquiry at that point, and conclude that the applicant did not have standing. There has, however, been some shift in the Court's position, in the sense that it is now willing to accept that a regulation might well be a "true" regulation as judged by the abstract terminology test, *but* to admit that none the less it might well be of individual concern to certain applicants. This approach was initially employed in the context of anti-dumping,[36] but has now been used outside this area, as exemplified by the *Codorniu* case.[37] The applicant challenged a regulation which stipulated that the term *cremant* should be reserved for sparkling wines of a particular quality coming from France or Luxembourg. The applicant made sparkling wine in Spain and held a trade mark which contained the word *cremant*. However, other Spanish producers also used this term. The Council argued vigorously that the measure was a regulation within the *Calpak* test, and that it could not be challenged irrespective of whether it was possible to identify the number or identity of those affected by it. The ECJ repeated the abstract terminology test, but then held that although the contested measure was "legislative" as judged by this test, that did not prevent it from being of individual concern to certain traders. The test for individual concern was that laid down in *Plaumann*, and this was held to be satisfied because the contested measure would have prevented the applicant from using its trade mark.

It would be rash, however, to assume that this development has revolutionalised Article 230(4) (ex 173(4)) EC so far as private applicants are concerned. An applicant will still have to show individual concern, *and* the criterion for this is the *Plaumann* test. We have already seen the difficulties with satisfying this test. If, therefore, the change in the Court's approach to regulations is to be meaningful it will have to be accompanied by a more liberal interpretation of the *Plaumann* test. If this does not occur then individuals will be no better off than they were before: they will, in principle, be able to challenge real regulations, but they will find it impossible to satisfy the requirement of individual concern. It is, therefore, crucially important to determine the meaning given to individual concern in this more recent jurisprudence. It may come as no surprise that differing interpretations can be detected in the case law. Three approaches can be distinguished.

The first may be termed the "infringement of rights or breach of duty" approach. The former is exemplified by *Codorniu* itself. The applicant was held to be individually concerned because it possessed a trade mark right which would have been overridden by the contested regulation. An example of the latter is to be found in *Antillean Rice*.[38] The applicants

---

[36] Case C–358/89 *Extramet Industrie SA v. Council* [1991] ECR I–2501, [1993] 2 CMLR 619.

[37] Case C–309/89 *Codorniu SA v. Council* [1994] ECR I–1853, [1995] 2 CMLR 561.

[38] Cases T–480 and 483/93 *Antillean Rice Mills NV v. Commission* [1995] ECR II–2305.

challenged a decision fixing a minimum import price for certain goods. The Court of First Instance (CFI) held that the contested measure was in reality of a legislative nature.[39] It held that the applicants were nonetheless individually concerned because the relevant article on which the contested decision was based meant that the Commission was under a duty to take account of the negative effects of such a decision introducing safeguard measures on the position of those such as the applicants.[40]

The second may be termed the "degree of factual injury" approach. On this view the existence of individual concern will be determined by a largely factual inquiry into the significance for the applicant of the contested regulation. This approach is exemplified by *Extramet*[41] where the ECJ allowed the applicant to challenge an anti-dumping regulation on the ground that it was individually concerned. The Court reached this conclusion because the applicant was the largest importer of the product on which the dumping duty was imposed, the end user of the product, its business activities depended to a very large extent on the imports, and because it would be very difficult for it to obtain alternative sources of supply of the relevant product.

The third approach which is apparent in the case law may be termed "pure *Plaumann*". It is important to understand that this approach appears to be the "default position": it will be applied unless the applicant can bring itself within one of the other two. Applicants will be denied standing by applying the *Plaumann* test *in the same manner* as in *Plaumann* itself. The fact that the applicant operates a trade which could, *in the sense considered above*, be engaged in by any other person, will serve to deny individual concern. The existence of particular factual injury to the applicant will not be relevant, unless the case can be brought within the narrow exception for completed past events. There are a number of cases which have adopted this approach. In *Buralux*[42] the applicants were linked companies which sought to challenge a regulation concerning the shipment of waste within the EC. The ECJ held that the mere fact that it was possible to determine the number or even identity of those affected did not mean that the regulation was of individual concern to them, so long as the measure was abstractly formulated.[43] Individual concern was to be determined by the *Plaumann* test.[44] The applicants failed to satisfy this test since they were affected only as "economic operators in the business of waste transfer between Member States, in the same way as any other operator in that business".[45] The applicants' contention[46] that the CFI had erred by paying insufficient attention to the

---

[39] *Ibid.,* para. 65.   [40] *Ibid.,* paras. 70, 76.

[41] Case C–358/89, *supra* n. 36, para. 17; Case T–164/94 *Ferchimex SA* v. *Council* [1995] ECR II–2681.

[42] Case C–209/94P *Buralux SA* v. *Council* [1996] ECR I–615.

[43] *Ibid.,* para. 24.   [44] *Ibid.,* para. 25.   [45] *Ibid.,* para. 28.   [46] *Ibid.,* para. 14.

factual circumstances of the applicant's position was rejected by the ECJ. The ECJ held that the fact that the applicants were the only companies engaged in shipment of waste between France and Germany was not relevant, since the regulation applied to all waste shipments in the EC.[47] This same approach has been applied in a number of other cases concerned with challenges to regulations.[48] It is also evident in more recent challenges to decisions as exemplified by the *Greenpeace* case.[49] The CFI specifically rejected the applicants' argument that it should adopt a more liberal approach and accord standing based solely on the fact that loss or detriment would be suffered from the harmful environmental effects of the Commission's alleged unlawful conduct. The CFI held that the *Plaumann* test was applicable irrespective of the nature, economic or otherwise, of the applicant's interest which was affected, and it refused to apply a sufficiency of interest test to Article 230(4) (ex 173(4)) EC.[50] The CFI concluded that the applicants did not have any attribute which distinguished them sufficiently from all other persons for the purpose of the *Plaumann* test. The CFI also rejected the claim that the applicant associations, such as Greenpeace, should be afforded standing in their own right: an association formed to protect the collective interests of a category of persons could not, normally, have *locus standi* where the individual members of the association were unable to demonstrate individual concern as judged by the *Plaumann* test.

It is clear that the central issue in the post-*Codorniu/Extramet* case law is the meaning to be accorded to individual concern. It is of course true, in one sense, that the interpretation of this term will be dependent on the facts of the particular case. This should not, however, serve to conceal the fact that the *test itself* is being given different meanings in various cases. It is important to emphasise the real differences which exist between them. The second approach, which is based on a showing of some factual injury to the applicant which marks it out, is very different from the third, the pure *Plaumann* approach, which excludes such factual considerations and denies standing if the category of applicants is open in the sense exemplified by *Plaumann* itself and many subsequent cases. Under this latter

---

[47] *Ibid.*, para. 29.

[48] Case T–472/93 *Campo Ebro Industrial SA* v. *Council* [1996] 1 CMLR 1038; Case T–489/93 *Unifruit Hellas EPE* v. *Commission* [1996] 1 CMLR 267; Case T–116/94R *Cassa Nazionale di Previdenza a favore degli Avvocati e Procuratori* v. *Council* [1996] 2 CMLR 79; Case T–122/96 *Federolio* v. *Commission* [1997] All ER (EC) 929.

[49] Case T–585/93 *Stichting Greenpeace Council (Greenpeace International)* v. *Commission* [1995] ECR II–2205. The decision of the CFI has been upheld on appeal in Case C–321/95P *Stichting Greenpeace Council (Greenpeace International)* v. *Commission* [1998] ECR I–1651. See also, Case T–117/94 *Associazione Agricoltori della Provincia di Rovigo* v. *Commission* [1995] ECR II–455; Case T–60/96 *Merck & Co Inc* v. *Commission* [1997] All ER (EC) 785.

[50] *Ibid.*, para. 51.

approach it will not suffice for a trader to show particular harm, unless the case comes within the narrow exception for completed past events. Nor will the fact that all present traders might be seriously affected by a regulation suffice for them to be accorded standing. While this attitude persists many cases are doomed to failure.[51]

It will, in the light of the case law considered above, be difficult, to say the very least, for non-privileged applicants to surmount the standing hurdle to challenge acts of the ECB. The types of regulation or decision made by the ECB which might generate legal challenges were considered above. While little difficulty will be encountered by an applicant who seeks to contest a decision addressed to itself involving, for example, the imposition of a penalty, non-privileged applicants are likely to fare much less well when seeking to challenge regulations or decisions addressed to a third party. If the ECJ and CFI continue to classify these cases within category three set out above, and apply what was termed the "pure *Plaumann*" approach, then such applicants will not be accorded standing and the doors to review under Article 230 (ex 173)) EC will remain firmly closed.

D. indirect actions under Article 234 (ex 177) EC.

The difficulty of securing standing under Article 230 (ex 173) EC may well convince those who seek to contest norms made by the ECB to use Article 234 (ex Article 177) EC as an alternative route by which to get the substance of the case before the ECJ. This has certainly been the option tried by many applicants who wished to challenge Community norms in other substantive areas, and found that the Article 230 route was not open to them.

It is clear in principle that the option of using Article 234 (ex 177) EC is available: Article 234(1)(b) provides that the ECJ can give preliminary rulings concerning, *inter alia*, the validity and interpretation of acts of the ECB. The initial difficulty for an applicant who seeks to use this route in order to contest an act of the ECB will be how to frame the cause of action. In order for a matter to be referred by a national court to the ECJ under Article 234 there has to be an action of some kind between two parties which has been started at national level.

In areas where applicants have used this indirect mode of challenge it has been common for the other party to be, for example, a national intervention agency which is applying the Community regulation which the private party wishes to have reviewed. This regulation may, for example, require the forfeiture of a deposit which has been given by a trader. The trader

[51] The approach of the Community courts towards standing in particular areas such as competition, state aids and anti-dumping continues to be more liberal, certainly when compared to the third approach set out above. Space precludes a detailed examination of this case law. See the books cited, *supra* n. 28, for a discussion of this case law.

believes that this forfeiture, and the regulation on which it is based, are contrary to Community law. If the security is forfeited, the trader may then institute judicial review proceedings in the national courts, claiming that the regulation is invalid. It will then be for the national court to decide whether to refer the matter to the ECJ under Article 234(1)(b).[52]

It is not immediately apparent who the other party would be in the context of a challenge to a norm made by the ECB. There is, as yet, no ready analogy with national intervention agencies which operate in the agricultural sphere. It is, however, possible that measures taken under Article 12.1, paragraph 3, will provide the answer in this respect. This provision states that the ECB may, to the extent to which it deems it possible and appropriate, have recourse to the national central banks to carry out operations which form part of the tasks of the ESCB. It is therefore open to the ECB to enlist the support of the national central banks in the implementation of Community monetary policy. The ECB may decide that this is the most efficient mechanism for the effective application of some, at least, of the regulatory norms which it will make. If this should prove to be so then the action in the national court which seeks to challenge the ECB norm could be initiated against the national central bank. If the ECB does not develop Article 12.1 along these lines, then an applicant will have to find some other relevant party against whom to bring the claim. Where the ECB's decision or regulation imposes an obligation on the state, then the state itself could be the appropriate defendant or respondent before the national courts.[53]

Any attempt to use Article 234 (ex 177) EC to challenge a norm enacted by the ECB will, of course, have to comply with the general rules which govern such actions. Thus, an applicant will, as decided in the *TWD* case,[54] not be allowed to use Article 234 (ex 177) EC if a direct action under Article 230 (ex 173) EC would have been available. It seems, therefore, that a challenge under Article 234 (ex 177) EC will not be possible if the matter could have been raised by a person who had standing under Article 230 (ex 173) EC, and who knew of the matter within the time limits for a direct action. Where it is unclear whether the applicant would have had standing for an Article 230 (ex 173) EC action, the ECJ is likely to be more willing to admit the indirect action. Thus in the *Accrington Beef*

---

[52] In other instances the matter may arise somewhat differently. Thus, if a regulation contains a demand for a levy which the trader believes to be in breach of Community law, then the trader's strategy might be to resist payment, be sued by the national agency, and then raise the alleged invalidity of the regulation on which the demand is based by way of defence. Once again, it would then be for the national court to decide whether to refer the matter to the ECJ.

[53] See by way of analogy, Case 216/82 *Universität Hamburg* v. *Hauptzollamt Hamburg-Kehrwieder* [1983] ECR 2771.

[54] Case C–188/92 *TWD Textilwerke Deggendorf GmbH* v. *Germany* [1994] ECR I–833. See also, Case C–178/95 *Wiljo NV* v. *Belgium* [1997] ECR I–585, [1997] 1 CMLR 627.

case[55] the ECJ distinguished *TWD* and held that the failure to challenge a regulation under Article 230 (ex 173) EC was no bar to an Article 234 (ex 177) EC action, since it was not obvious that the Article 230 (ex 173) EC action would have been admissible. The ECJ is also likely to be more receptive to actions under Article 234 (ex 177) EC where the applicant would not have known of the relevant measure in time to challenge it under Article 230 (ex 173 EC).

It must not, however, be forgotten that while Article 234 enables an applicant to circumvent the very narrow standing criteria under Article 230, the progress of the action is still dependent on the willingness of the national court to refer the matter to the ECJ.

E. the substance of the challenge

The discussion thus far has been concerned with the ways in which an applicant might seek to get a case before the ECJ or CFI in order to contest the legality or validity of an ECB norm. For an applicant—privileged or otherwise—to succeed it will obviously be necessary to show that the ECB has been guilty of one of the types of error listed in Article 230(2) (ex 173(2)) EC: lack of competence; infringement of an essential procedural requirement; infringement of the Treaty or of any rule of law relating to its application; or misuse of powers. General analysis of these heads of review can be found elsewhere.[56]

A bare reading of these does not, however, convey their import. What it fails to reveal is the fact that the ECJ and CFI have considerable judicial discretion as to the intensity with which they will apply these grounds of challenge.[57] It is clear that the Community courts apply the principles of judicial review less intensively where the subject-matter involves complex economic determinations, more especially when these are combined with the necessity for the primary decision-maker to balance conflicting policy considerations in order to arrive at a decision. There are many judicial decisions which attest to this in, for example, the agricultural sphere[58] and in relation to state aids.[59]

---

[55] Case C–241/95 *R. v. Intervention Board for Agricultural Produce, ex p. Accrington Beef Co. Ltd.* [1997] 1 CMLR 675.

[56] See the books cited, *supra* n. 28.

[57] Craig and de Burca, *supra* n. 28., pp. 501–05.

[58] See, for example, Cases 197–200, 243, 245, 247/80 *Ludwigshafener Walzmühle Erling KG v. Council* [1981] ECR 3211; Case 8/82 *KG in der Firma Hans-Otto Wagner GmbH Agrarhandel v. Bundesanstalt für Landwirtschaftliche Marktordnung* [1983] ECR 371; Case 283/83 *Firma A. Racke v. Hauptzollamt Mainz* [1984] ECR 3791; Case 5/73 *Balkan-Import-Export GmbH v. Hauptzollamt BerlinPackhof* [1973] ECR 1091, 1112; Case C–331/88 *R. v. Minister of Agriculture, Fisheries and Food and the Secretary of State for Health, ex. p. FEDESA* [1990] ECR I–4023, 4061; Case C–8/89 *Vincenzo Zardi v. Consorzio Agrario Provinciale di Ferrara* [1990] ECR I–2515, 2532–3.

[59] See, for example, Case C–56/93 *Belgium v. Commission* [1996] ECR I–723; Cases

It will, therefore, not be easy for an applicant to convince the ECJ or CFI that the ECB has erred in, for example, setting the reserves which credit institutions should hold with the ECB, or in devising the rules for the prudential supervision of credit institutions. If the applicant can show some procedural error in the making of such norms, such as a failure to give reasons, or a failure to publish, then the chances of success in the review action will be enhanced. If, however, the applicant relies on a substantive ground of challenge the Community courts will almost certainly require that a manifest error be proven before they will intervene. It will not be easy for an applicant to convince the Court that this is so, more especially when the ECB has to take decisions or make regulations under severe time constraints in order to respond to market pressures.

3. Challenges by or on Behalf of the ECB

The discussion thus far has focused on the ways in which the ECB might be made legally accountable for its actions before the Community courts and the difficulties which applicants will face in this respect. It should not, however, be thought that the ECB will necessarily always be the "defendant" in any such legal action. It is possible for the ECB itself to have recourse to the courts. This is made clear by Article 230(3) (ex 173(3)) EC which provides that the ECJ shall have jurisdiction in actions brought by the ECB for the purpose of protecting its prerogatives. The position of the ECB is therefore treated by way of analogy with that of the European Parliament (EP). We can envisage a number of different types of case in which the ECB might itself seek to bring proceedings before the ECJ pursuant to Article 230(3) (ex 173(3)) EC. Inter-institutional disputes of this nature have been a common feature of the Community, whether between the Council and Commission, the EP and Commission or the EP and the Council. Resort to the ECJ should, not, therefore, be regarded as merely a hypothetical possibility.

The first, and most obvious, instance in which the ECB would wish to do so would be where the other Community institutions failed to consult the ECB as required by various Articles of the EC Treaty, most notably Articles 105(4), 105(6) 106(2) and 107(6).[60] It is clear, from the Court's jurisprudence in relation to the EP, that a failure to consult, or a failure to wait for the EP's opinion, will render the relevant Community act void.[61]

T–244 and 486/93 *TWD Textilwerke Deggendorf GmbH* v. *Commission* [1995] ECR II–2265, [1996] 1 CMLR 332, upheld on appeal, Case C–355/95P *TWD* v. *Commission* [1997] ECR I–2549.

[60] Ex Arts. 105(4), 105(6), 105a(2) and 106(6) EC.

[61] Case 138/79 *Roquette Frères* v. *Council* [1980] ECR 3333; Case C–65/93 *European Parliament* v. *Council (Re Generalised Tariff Preferences)* [1995] ECR I–643, [1996] 1 CMLR 4; Case C–156/93 *European Parliament* v. *Commission (Re Genetically Modified Micro-Organisms in Organic Products)* [1995] 3 CMLR 707.

A further consultation may be required if the measure has been subject to significant changes after the initial consultation has taken place and before its adoption by the Council.[62] The possibility of such a challenge is enhanced by the very generality of Article 105(4) which provides that the ECB shall be consulted "on any proposed Community act in its field of competence". The breadth of the ECB's sphere of competence, and the difficulties of drawing the line between monetary policy and broader aspects of economic policy, to be considered below, means that there may well be genuine differences of opinion between the Community institutions as to whether Article 105(4) "bites" or not in any particular instance.

Secondly, the ECB might also avail itself of judicial review to protect the participation rights which it is afforded by the Treaty in contexts other than the passage of Community acts. For example, Article 113(2) (ex 109b(2)) EC states that the President of the ECB shall be invited to participate in Council meetings when the Council is deliberating on matters relating to the objectives and tasks of the ESCB. The participation rights secured to the ECB by this Article would surely also be regarded as falling within the prerogatives of the ECB which the ECJ would be willing to protect via judicial review if necessary.

The third type of case where the ECB might consider legal action is if it believes that its autonomy, as enshrined in Article 108 (ex 107) EC and related Articles, has been infringed. There is no doubt that the ECB's autonomy would be regarded as within its prerogatives, and hence that it would be protected via judicial review under Article 230(3) (ex 173(3)) EC. Article 108 (ex 107) EC states that neither the ECB, national central banks or their decision-making bodies, shall seek or take instructions from Community institutions or bodies, from any government or a member state or from any other body. The Community institutions and the member states undertake to respect this principle and shall not seek to influence the members of the decision-making bodies of the ECB or of the national central banks in the performance of their tasks. It is readily apparent that Article 108 (ex 107) EC is central to the entire schema of monetary union, and is the principled cornerstone of the ECB's autonomy. It provides the foundation for other, more specific, Treaty provisions which are designed to safeguard the ECB's independence. Articles 112 and 113 (ex 109a and

---

[62] Case C–388/92 *European Parliament* v. *Council* [1994] ECR I–2067; Case C–417/93 *European Parliament* v. *Council (Re Continuation of the TACIS Programme)* [1995] ECR I–1185, [1995] 2 CMLR 829; Case C–21/94 *European Parliament* v. *Council (Re Road Taxes)* [1996] 1 CMLR 94. Where the changes are either technical or in accordance with Parliament's wishes reconsultation may not be necessary: Case 41/69 *ACF Chemiefarma* v. *Commission* [1970] ECR 661; Case 817/79 *Buyl* v. *Commission* [1982] ECR 245; Case C–331/88 *R.* v. *Minister of Agriculture, Fisheries and Food and Secretary of State for Health, ex p FEDESA* [1990] ECR I–4023.

109b) EC are themselves of central importance to the overall institutional autonomy of the ECB. Article 112 (ex 109a) EC stipulates that the members of the Executive Board of the ECB shall be appointed from those who have professional expertise in monetary or banking matters, and that they should hold office for a fixed term of eight years. Article 113 (ex 109b) EC reinforces this point by making it clear that although the President of the Council and a member of the Commission may participate in the meetings of the ECB's Governing Council, they do not have a vote.

It is possible to imagine a number of situations where the ECB might choose to have recourse to the ECJ on this ground. The deal struck over the Presidency of the ECB furnishes an example. This deal was almost certainly illegal when viewed against the Treaty provisions. Article 112(2)(b) (ex 109a(2)(b)) EC is mandatory: the term of office of the President shall be eight years. It would make a nonsense of the entire scheme of the Treaty if it could be circumvented by a "gentlemen's agreement", the import of which was that the initial Dutch incumbent of the post would be appointed for eight years, but resign after four, and that the successor would be a particular French banker. Such an agreement should be held to be illegal, or of no effect, both because it undermines Article 112(2)(b) (ex 109a(2)(b)) EC, and because it would constitute an undue fetter on the discretionary power to choose a new ECB President after the initial eight years had elapsed. There is no doubt that this issue would be held to come within the prerogatives of the ECB itself. Four years is a long time in banking as well as in politics. The fact that the President of the ECB seemed to accept the deal does not mean that he could not have a change of heart within the next four years.

The fourth type of case in which a legal action might be brought by the ECB, or on its behalf, overlaps with the third, but should be treated separately for reasons which will become apparent. It is clear that Community monetary policy is based on collaboration between the ECB and national central banks. This is reflected in the composition of the ECB's Governing Council, which is made up of the Executive Board plus the Governors of the national central banks;[63] in the requirement that member states ensure that their national central banks have the requisite independence to take part in monetary union;[64] and in the fact that Article 108 (ex 107) EC concerned with autonomy is framed in terms of national central banks as well as the ECB.[65] The ECB itself clearly has an interest in ensuring that the autonomy of national central banks is preserved. This raises interesting questions as to possible legal redress should a member state seek to influence its own national bank. Let it be assumed for the sake of argument that the national bank bows to such pressure, and, for example, gives special credit facilities to a public authority in breach of

---

[63] Art. 112(1) (ex 109a(1)) EC.   [64] Art. 109 (ex 108) EC.   [65] Art. 108 (ex 107) EC.

Article 101 (ex 104) EC. There would be no possibility of the ECB using Article 230 (ex 173) EC, since the contested action would be that of an individual member state, rather than a Community institution. The Commission might bring an Article 226 (ex 169) EC action against the member state. For its part, the ECB could bring the national central bank before the ECJ for its alleged failure to "fulfil an obligation under" the ESCB Statute.[66]

Other provisions in the ESCB Statute also touch on this issue in an interesting way. Article 14.2 provides that a Governor of a national central bank may be relieved of office only if he no longer fulfils the conditions required for the performance of his duties or if he has been guilty of serious misconduct. Such a decision can be referred to the ECJ by the Governor concerned or by the Governing Council of the ECB on the grounds of infringement of the Treaty or of any rule of law relating to its application, subject to a two months time limit.

The final instance which could give rise to legal action is in some ways the most interesting. It concerns the boundaries between monetary policy and economic policy. The Treaty Articles make it clear that while the ECB has considerable power and autonomy over the former, the Commission and the Council have the primary say over the latter. Economics as a discipline does not, however, respect formal Treaty boundaries. The line between monetary policy and economic policy may not always be pristinely clear, and in any event the two obviously interact, a point recognised forcefully in the Luxembourg European Council meeting in December 1997. There might well therefore be cases brought by the ECB which raise issues on the borderline between economic and monetary policy.

4. Conclusion

We shall have to wait and see how far the ECJ is used to resolve disputes brought by privileged applicants or individuals against the ECB, and how far the ECB itself seeks to make use of the ECJ in the types of situation mentioned above. There is but little doubt that, particularly in the latter category, the ECB will initially attempt to resolve any disputes through political rather than legal means. The history of the Community is, however, replete with examples of resort to the courts in order to resolve inter-institutional disputes, and it would be surprising if such disputes were to be entirely absent from this area.

[66] Art. 35.6 ESCB Statute and Art. 237(d) (ex 180(d)) EC.

PART THREE

European Governance

6

The Constitutional Law of the Euro?
Disciplining European Governance

MICHELLE EVERSON

1. Introduction

MONEY, as systems theory would often have it,[1] is imbued with a complexity all of its own and is thus no business of the law. The many connections between an abstract currency form on the one hand, and real economic wealth, political/economic power and social pre-occupations on the other, are too dense and too intricate to be easily assessed by or slotted into the simplifying—i.e., discipline-internal—normative frameworks with which lawyers are wont to work.[2] Equally, however, as several centuries of legal experience have also impressed upon us, "real" law in all its pretension to be a positive instrument of social justice, would seem to be an exclusive matter for individual nations, or more specifically, the constitutional nation state.[3] Only that form of law which is eternally and irrevocably wedded to and guided by constitution-ally-delimited democratic processes, can claim for itself a legitimate role in determining the exact contours of an acceptable and accepted distribution of monetary wealth within society.

Seen in this sober light, the Maastricht Treaty's explicit efforts to deploy "de-nationalised" European law to create an Economic and Monetary Union (EMU) would seem, from the lawyer's point of view at least, to be

---

[1] D. Baecker, *Information und Risiko in der Marktwirtschaft* (Frankfurt a.M, Suhrkamp, 1998), pp. 96 *et seq*; N. Luhmann, *Die Gesellschaft der Gesellschaft* (Frankfurt a.M, Suhrkamp, 1998) Vol I, pp. 348 *et seq,* with references to earlier works.

[2] In Luhmann's tradition of thought, the problem is not merely one of law's inability to connect with external (non-legal) systems of organisation; rather, the fatal mismatch between law and money derives from money's currency as a broker of "real power" or reflection of the world as it "is" and the law's contrasting pre-occupation with prescriptive power or the world as it "should" be.

[3] Thus, stateless nations such as Scotland, Catalonia and Quebec do not possess their own currency.

exceptionally ill-advised. First, it leads the law into a monetary morass of technical provisions and political considerations; and so demands formal legal adjudication upon matters which wise lawyers might prefer to leave to be governed by a tandem of elected politicians and expert communities. But secondly, it also makes absolute the decree *nisei* which has seen European law slowly parted from its supposedly socio-politically neutral, functionalist/technocratic roots; the quasi-constitutional enshrinement of a European monetary policy founded upon price-stability seemingly requiring it to take positive action which cannot but have an immediate impact upon the financial status of individual Europeans and thus adjust nationally-determined notions of wealth distribution and social balance.

Given its novel involvement in a monetary field which it might prefer to shun, and the noted lack of constitutionalised political direction which would furnish European law with a conventional legitimacy to alter national notions of social balance,[4] it is thus unsurprising that law in Europe has—to date at least—made able use of loopholes in the EU Treaty and Community institutional structure in its efforts to place the responsibility for EMU firmly back upon the shoulders of those politicians and experts who first set it in motion. Both national and European law have resisted the temptation legally to enforce a rigidly monetarist vision of European Union: with the *Bundesverfassungsgericht* citing the "flexibility" of the convergence criteria under Article 121 (ex 109(j)) EC as the reason why the *Bundesregierung* and not itself bears responsibility for German entry into EMU;[5] and European law being equally content to include[6] within the regulation of economic convergence the European Council Resolution on the Stability and Growth Pact (SGP)—or a law so "soft" as to be no law at all[7]—along with regulations that leave significant political discretion to the Ministers in the Council.

In short, or so it would seem, law in Europe appears first, to have taken to heart the view of those European integration theorists who argue that

---

[4] J.H.H. Weiler, "Does Europe Need a Constitution?", (1995) 1(3) *European Law Journal* 259; more precisely, the claim that whilst the European treaties, with their corollary doctrines of direct effect and supremacy, have taken on a *de facto* status as a "European Constitution", the underlying lack of an effective form of "European Constitutionalism"— or direct and irrevocable relationship between European law and conventional constitutional values such as democratic sovereignty—nonetheless determines that the European Constitution entails no broader legitimacy to direct or govern issues traditionally consigned to democratically-legitimated law.

[5] Decision 2.4.1998, 2 *BvR* 1877/97 and 2 *BvR* 50/98.

[6] Although the other instruments which make up the Stability and Growth Pact are in the "hard law" form of regulations; See Reg. 1466/97 and Reg. 1467/97. See further Ch. 4 *supra*.

[7] Resolution of the European Council on the Stability and Growth Pact, Annex I of Presidency Conclusions, Amsterdam European Council, 16–17 June 1997, in *European Documents*, No. 2043, 21 June, pp. 2–3. For the concept of "soft" law, cf, Francis Snyder, *New Directions in Community Law* (London, Weidenfeld & Nicolson, 1990).

stateless and thus putatively "non-majoritarian" European law should avoid all potentially redistributive issues and concern itself with "micro" rather than "macro-economic" policy implementation.[8] And would seem second, to have conceded the "deliberative" point that much of current European integration is about and should thus be guided by sensitive and flexible political "governance," rather than a formalised law with an inexorable and inevitable logic of its own.[9] In its EU Treaty guise as a rigid normative legal framework, EMU is uncompromising and unforgiving. As it is instead evolving, through political and technical compromise, it is developing a potential to ease the political and social conflicts which might otherwise blow monetary union off course.

The monetary shyness of national and European legal systems notwithstanding, this chapter nonetheless attempts to argue that law should not fully withdraw from the management of EMU. The reasons for and the proposed nature of legal supervision of EMU are, however, complex. Certainly, any effort to take a more direct role in the legal operationalisation of EU Treaty criteria would be misconceived: monetary/economic discretion is indeed the better part of legal valour. Nonetheless, if viewed as an on-going attempt to "socialise" European economic relationships— or impose a common and politically/normatively determined social balance upon a mutual European economic area—the various indistinct political/technical debates and more concrete institutions which make up EMU would appear urgently to be in need both of guiding and discourse-constitutive normative/constitutional principles, and of more prosaic legal mechanisms of institutional control.

Supposed Treaty-law rigidity notwithstanding, the normative and institutional contours of EMU have yet to be settled: the exact degree of monetary convergence and national economic stability remaining a matter for flexible technical and political decision-making.[10] Such matters apart, however, EMU—and with it the euro—will nevertheless ultimately stand or fall by virtue of its "credibility"; that is, on the one hand, the institu-

---

[8] See for example, Giandomenico Majone who, at his theoretically purest, stresses that issues of governance having redistributive effects are the exclusive concern of majoritarian democracy and should never be delegated to non-political or purely legal processes; G. Majone, "Regulating Europe: Problems and Perspectives", (1989) *Jahrbuch zur Staats und Verwaltungswissenschaften* 3.

[9] See for example, C. Joerges and J. Neyer, "From Intergovernmental Bargaining to Deliberative Political Processes: The Constitutionalisation of Comitology", (1997) 3(3) *European Law Journal* 273–99; more precisely, the claim that the expansion of the EC's competence into areas of social, rather than purely economic, regulation has correctly determined that politically-neutral technocratic governance has been superseded by an explicitly political form of governance which is structured and disciplined by its continuing "deliberative" respect for technocratic and economically-rationalising Treaty aims—or by its willingness to subject "politics" to the proportionality imposing yardsticks of technical and economic advice.

[10] See Chs. 1 and 5 *supra* and Ch.8 *infra*.

tional credibility of the bodies (European Central Bank and European System of Central Banks (ECB and ESCB)) administering European monetary policy;[11] and on the other, the stabilising credibility of—or degree of wider political support for—the outcomes of the fluid technical/political debates which underpin European economic and social policy.[12] Thus, while law has no part to play in material European governance and must leave politicians and experts sufficient room to determine the substantive contours of EMU, it can attempt to discipline such governance, or find and apply both credibility-securing structural yardsticks and "higher" legal principles. On the one institutional hand, it must guarantee "non-majoritarian" or independent yet accountable monetary policy. And on the other—possibly more important—political/technical hand, it must also endeavour to ensure that the necessarily fluid discourses which will determine European economic policy are both civil and deliberative— showing sufficient regard both for set Community goals and for specific and possibly unforeseen national sensibilities and problems. The future of EMU (and European Union) undeniably lies in the hand of elastic technical/political governance rather than rigid law; yet, if EMU (and European Union) is to succeed, European (monetary and economic) governance must entail far more than "chance" political/technical outcomes— being instead normatively disciplined by European law.

2. Evolving "Socialisation" of the Free European Market and Common Economic Area

It is common to view the process of economic and monetary integration within Europe in one of two distinct ways. On the one hand, it is regarded by some as a narrow "technical" project, which removes the "distorting" factor of currency fluctuations from internal market exchanges and is thus consolidating of the micro-economic gains of European economic integration.[13] On the other, it is also widely considered to be an explicitly "political" programme: a further step upon the road to the establishment of a European polity.

Importantly, however, the notion of "EMU as a political programme" is likewise marked by a sharp dichotomy between two views on the exact nature of EMU and the form of European polity to which it will give rise. First—a stereotypically French view—EMU is deemed to be a mere precursor to and catalyst for fully-fledged political European Union: a

---

[11] Arts. 105–111 (ex 105–109) EC.

[12] Arts. 98–104 (ex 102a–104c) EC and the Stability and Growth Pact.

[13] C. Goodhart, "The Political Economy of Money" in P. Kenen (ed.), *Understanding Interdependence: The Macroeconomics of the Open* (Princeton, Princeton University Press, 1995).

simple monetary spur to the creation of a European federal state with wide-ranging and potentially interventionist powers of economic and social management. Secondly—in a contrasting and "ordo-liberally flavoured" German analysis—EMU is argued to represent the final crystallisation of "codified," or technocratically rather than politically-determined monetary policy,[14] and thus to be a sound basis for the evolution, not of interventionist, but of "restrained" and economically-rationalising European "governance".[15] Equally, in this latter view, EMU need not logically culminate in federal statehood. Rather, with monetary policy safe in the insulating hands of "experts", complementary programmes of (national) economic stability and the establishment of a (Europe-wide) social balance, may either be entrusted to centralised European political bodies or, alternatively, be shared—by means of strictly-structured legal institutions and agreements—amongst the various national, supranational and even regional layers of Europe's "multi-level" governance structures.[16]

A. the disputed EMU telos[17]

The varying modes of assessing EMU and the European polity which it should give rise to, however, have their historical roots in the very varied

[14] Cf, for a recent and comprehensive analysis of "ordo-liberal" thought, E.J. Mestmäcker, "On the Legitimacy of European Law", (1994) *Rabels Zeitschrift für ausländisches und internationales Privatrecht*, 615–635. In brief summary, the ordo-liberal tradition has long sought to cast European integration in a politically-neutral light, arguing that European economic management is not a matter of the creation of substantive policies of economic intervention. Rather, member states have joined together to rationalise various limited areas of economic oversight: the defining characteristic of such an enterprise being the creation of (European) legal structures which protect liberalised market exchange from direct political interference. Of course the policy objective of "liberalised market exchange" is in itself a political choice.

[15] Alternatively, monetary policy may and should be distinct from overall economic and social policies: the politically-neutral management of money nonetheless, and in turn, shaping both economic and redistributive programmes, imposing a tight budgetary discipline and so preventing large-scale and competition distorting interventionism. In this sense, "governance" as opposed to "government" is likewise a crucial distinction: monetary, economic and social management no longer being a mere matter of the implementation of transient political programmes, but instead being "pre-conditioned" by fixed normative goals such as price stability.

[16] Note, that ordo-liberals themselves reject any notion that the European Union is upon the path to full (federal) statehood (E. J. Mestmäcker, *Rise im Europäischen Social Contract* (Hans Martin Schleyer, Stiftung, 1997)—a view not always shared by the German political establishment. Nonetheless both groups have historically concurred in the views that monetary policy should be distinct from economic and social policy and be pursued through very different institutional structures. From this it follows that such distinct institutional structures may be found either at the same level of governance, or alternatively be shared between national, supranational and regional bodies.

[17] The history of the disputed *telos* is not examined in full: readers wishing for more

political and technocratic views which were to emerge and dominate in each stage of the long and complex process of political and technical negotiation which marked intensifying European economic and monetary integration.

Thus, with the European Community in its integrationist infancy, an unbounded micro-economic optimism prevailed, the Commission's "Initiative 1964" clearly stating that:

> [T]he aim of the Community is not merely to expand trade between the Member States; it implies merging the six markets in a single internal market and the establishment of an economic union. It therefore appears indispensable to adapt the monetary policy of the Six to the degree of integration attained in other fields.[18]

Nonetheless, money's intricate connections with political and economic power, as well as broader social considerations, inevitably determined that the simple and narrow technical link made between the efficient functioning of the internal market and monetary co-ordination, was soon to be placed into question. While the Commission began to harness technocratic and expert skills to the integrationist goal and, more particularly, established a "guiding" committee of Governors of the national central banks,[19] the member states nevertheless sought to retain their guiding position. The process of economic and monetary union was accordingly also to be marked by intense and conflicting political negotiations.

In particular, the "Barre Plan", presented by the Commission to the Council in 1968,[20] explicitly called for closer co-ordination of short-term national economic policies and a convergence in longer-term national economic policy orientations. It therefore clearly exposed the inevitable linkage between monetary integration and overall national economic and social management. Equally, the Commission's recommendation was to mark the beginnings of a distinct and discourse-defining rift between those politicians who assumed that monetary union would lead simply and

---

detail should refer to Francis Snyder's invaluable analysis, *EMU Revisited: Are we Making a Constitution? What Constitution are we Making?*, Working Paper of the Department of Law No. 98/6 (EUI: Florence); also the shorter version with the same title in P. Craig and G. de Burca (eds.), *The Evolution of EU Law* (Oxford, Oxford University Press, 1999).

[18] Although political considerations may have played a part in the 1960 implementation of the First Capital Directive (under Article 67 EEC), the French Government feeling there be a need to protect European currencies from the "vagaries of the US dollar", L. Tsoulakis, "Economic and Monetary Union: The Primacy of High Politics" in H. Wallace and W. Wallace (eds.), *Policy-making in the European Union* (Oxford, Oxford University Press, 1996, 2nd ed.); cf, also F. Snyder, *supra* n. 17.

[19] Cf, F. Snyder, *supra* n. 17.

[20] "Commission Memorandum to the Council on the Co-ordination of Economic Policies and Monetary Co-operation within the Community," (*Second General Report on the Activities of the Community 1968*: February 1969).

inevitably to total political integration,[21] and those who more cautiously weighed up the question of the establishment, at European level, of a meaningful relationship between money, economic policy, social balance and politics. This latter group were thus quickly to call for an initial convergence of national economic policies,[22] and similarly expressed a preference for the immediate establishment of centralised institutions of European economic and social co-ordination.

The constant and conflicting interplay between the Commission's narrow micro-economic integrationist goal, the largely anti-inflationary views of ever more powerful technocrats and epistemic communities, and the member states' wider desires either for monetary union to become political union, or for a more careful approach to the creation of (politicised) relations between Europe's economic, social and monetary policies, was to characterise increasing European monetary integration throughout the 1970s and 1980s. Council Decisions and Resolutions on economic stability, the Snake, the European Unit of Account, the European Monetary System, the European Currency Unit and further Capital Directives, were all marked in their preparation and composition by the diverse nature of the political/technical actors involved in their negotiation, and the sometimes indistinct—even competing—views reflected in their provisions.[23] Certainly, views in favour of initial and economically stabilising convergence, or the "coronation theory", appeared to be gaining the upper hand.[24] However, measures such as the Third Capital Directive which almost completely alienated national authority over capital movements, together with the Exchange Rate Mechanism which—in its effects at least—diluted national control over exchange rates,[25] likewise appear to have lent some credence to the notion that monetary union might precede economic convergence.

In short, monetary and economic integration was to see both an increasing dichotomy between the technical and political direction of

---

[21] Cf, G.G. Rosentahl, *The Men Behind the Decisions* (Lexington Books, 1975), in particular France, "There is no such thing as monetary Europe. . . Europe is either political and has a currency or it does not exist and has no currency", (Michel Debré, French Minister of Defence).

[22] So that the imposition of strict monetary discipline would be supported by financial/economic discipline in the member states; and would likewise not have too detrimental an impact on the social and economic status of "weaker" nations.

[23] See J. Usher in Ch. 1 *supra* and in *The Law of Money and Financial Services in the European Community* (Oxford, Clarendon Press, 1994).

[24] See the measures taken in the 1970s like the 1974 Convergence Decision and Stability Directive when it was expected that monetary union would be achieved by 1980. This was not realised and by the mid 1980s the Treaty amendment provided for by the Single European Act, Art. 102a of the then EEC Treaty, called upon member states to co-operate in matters of economic and monetary convergence but stopped short of prescribing the goal of full monetary union.

[25] C. Goodhart, *supra* n. 13.

European policy-making, and a large degree of conflict amongst various groups as to what EMU should be dedicated to, how it should be slotted into supranational/national/regional structures, and thus how it would determine the future shape of the European polity. That a final quasi-coherent design for EMU was achieved at all, is probably due only to an unusual convergence of views between national politicians and technical experts which allowed Jacques Delors to draw up a comprehensive report on the preferred stages for EMU,[26] which in its turn provided the final impetus for the EC Treaty's normative commitment to monetary union and co-ordinated economic policy created by the Maastricht Treaty. With the late 1980s witnessing the withdrawal of most European states from interventionist economic policies,[27] and seeking expert advice upon how to deal with increasingly volatile international capital markets and intensifying international economic interpenetration, the time was at last ripe for coalition with anti-inflationary economic experts and a move to EMU.

B. EMU and the Maastricht Treaty: uncertain goals and structures

Drawn up by the heads of the national central banks and various economic experts appointed by the member states, the Delors Report, presented in 1989, was consequently unsurprisingly cohesive and price-stability flavoured in orientation. It entailed a clear vision both of the aims of European monetary and economic integration, and of the particular European polity which would ensue. Following an initial period of convergence, an independent central bank would have exclusive control of European monetary policy. Firmly agreed upon European legal frameworks and procedures would constitute and control anti-inflationary national economic policy. Meanwhile a common fiscal policy and increased aid under structural and regional funds would mirror national social instruments, such as the German *Finanzausgleichgesetz*,[28] so allowing for redistribution between richer and poorer regions and countries. Equally, the latter instrument would likewise constitute the common political establishment—through co-ordination of national budgetary policies—of a Europe-wide social balance. An ordo-liberally flavoured construct in a non-state setting, the Delors Report first codified monetary and economic policy—leaving monetary policy in the exclusive hands of experts and price-stability oriented economic policy to be largely determined by Brussels technocrats.[29] And secondly, provided for a limited and flexible

---

[26] A position agreed at the 1988 Hanover meeting of the European Council; cf, for full details F. Snyder, *supra* n. 17.

[27] G. Majone, "The European Community Between Social Policy and Regulation", (1992) 30 *Journal of Common Market Studies* 3(1), 153.

[28] Which governs transfers of fiscal income between richer and poorer *Länder*.

[29] By virtue of their drafting prerogative.

degree of political union in the matter of redistribution and social stability.

Significant as it was in furnishing the impetus for the Maastricht Treaty's normative commitment to monetary union—and, in particular, for the normativisation of the "coronation" theory of stages of economic convergence—the Delors plan nonetheless still fell victim to national sensibilities prior to Maastricht, and public disquiet in the wake of the Maastricht Treaty. Concerns largely focused on worries about the dexterity and legitimacy of a technocratic approach to European monetary and economic integration. As a consequence, while price-stability remained the key goal, the more nuanced approach to the division of competence in fiscal policy and the Maastricht and Amsterdam Treaties' creation of more indistinct economic and social management arrangements—in particular the more flexible structures of the Stability and Growth and Employment Pacts agreed at Amsterdam[30]—were nonetheless to leave room for doubt as to the exact aims of EMU and the governmental levels at which monetary, economic and social policy will be pursued.

With regard first to EMU's guiding normative goal of price stability, the limited harmonisation of Community fiscal policy and the lack of a clear link between employment/social policy and economic governance in Europe, would seem, on the one hand, to hint at an uncompromisingly monetarist vision of European growth and social balance. In the light of the apparent imposition of strict budgetary discipline upon the member states by both the Maastricht Treaty and individual convergence pacts and stability programmes, and with an equal eye to the supposedly treaty-secured independence of the ECB, social balance would now appear to be a sole matter for market-led re-adjustments. Labour mobility, and not exchange rate policy or public borrowing, is seemingly the most appropriate means to secure growth and compensate for economic shocks. On the other hand, however, such putative and seemingly unforgiving monetarism, would also appear to be vulnerable to national attempts at potentially interventionist modification, with disruptive mechanisms including: first, the wide margin of discretion in the Maastricht Treaty's convergence criteria; secondly, the similar flexibility in the individual national convergence and stability programmes negotiated with the Commission; thirdly, increasing attempts to politicise the work of the "independent" central bankers (in particular, French attempts to water-down independence through a reduction of the ECB President's term from eight to four years); and fourthly, the introduction of a potentially economically-interventionist incubus—the Economic and Financial Committee (EFC)[31]—into the building if not the offices of the ECB. As ever, differing political and technical opinions have marked the final creation of EMU, leaving their contrasting imprints upon the laws and agree-

---

[30] *Agence Europe No. 6993*, Thursday, 12 June 1997, pp. 6–7.
[31] See Art. 114(2) (ex 109c(2)) EC.

ments which will guide it. The fight for the normative contours of EMU, it would seem, is thus not over but only just beginning.

Equally, however, as a mirror to the normative uncertainty about EMU goals, the levels of its governance remain largely indistinct. While monetary policy would appear, by virtue of the Maastricht Treaty's constitutionalisation of the independence of the ECB, to be a clear-cut supranational matter, more recent national "claw-back" mechanisms, or attempts to influence the appointment of the ECB President, have the potential to undermine this status. Similarly, economic policy—though structured by the EC Treaty and convergence/stability programmes—might primarily appear to be a matter for the member states, but may likewise take on a more inter-governmental—if not fully supranational—hue, by virtue of multi-lateral surveillance programmes[32] and emerging institutions such as the EFC. Similarly, those few socially-corrective (redistributive) policies which do exist, are clearly in an extreme state of multi-level flux: an issue for the supranational structural funds,[33] a matter for the inter-governmental co-ordination of employment policies, and a theme to be tackled by a quasi-supranational Social Chapter which seems steadily but surely to be attempting to constitute its own "European" polity through the incorporation of emerging transnational "social partners" within legislative negotiations.[34]

In short, in the matter of governmental levels at least, the most remarkable feature of the post-EMU European Union (EU) would not seem to be its apparently revolutionary step of fully disassociating monetary, economic and social policy from one another; but rather its inability to determine to which supranational, inter-governmental, governmental or even social level each newly liberated policy should be allotted.

C. evolving socialisation

Caught between technical knowledge and political considerations, potentially interventionist and restrained ordo-liberal (if not monetarist) notions of economic management, and located between states, supranational organisations, inter-governmental agreements and private actors—European monetary and economic union is uncertain both as to its normative characteristics and the governmental structures, or polity, within which it is embedded.

As such, it is perhaps wise initially to characterise EMU as a further example of the indeterminate but evolving "socialisation"[35] of the free

---

[32] Introduced by the Madrid Summit in December 1995.

[33] See Ch.7 *infra* by J. Scott and S. Vousden.

[34] A new polity prompted by the Amsterdam Treaty which has integrated the Social Protocol into the Treaty and brought all fifteen member states back on board, see Title XI (Arts. 136–150).

[35] For greater detail on the notion of socialisation, cf, M. Everson, "Constitutionalising

European market and emerging European economic space. The historic integration project being the creation of a free market, which was secured by primary European law from the predatory attentions of interventionist member state governments, European integration has likewise witnessed the establishment of an autonomous sphere of economic interchange: an economic area which is no longer subject to the "command" management of national polities. As such, the integration project has embodied a fundamental challenge to modes of social organisation; deploying European law to disconnect the traditional (hierarchical) linkages once maintained between society, politics and the market-place. Equally, however, more recent, substantive market re-regulation, and, indeed, grand economic designs such as the EMU, in their turn, represent a contested attempt to re-establish relations between all three political, social and economic areas within Europe. Doubts clearly remain as to the ultimate goal of European integration: will Europe become a state or will it remain a limited, technocratic enterprise? Equal uncertainty reigns with regard to the legitimate character of a European polity: are member states still the constituent units of the EU, or is governance now more a matter for the technocratic concerns of the Commission and its attendant experts, or indeed, of emerging and Europe-wide private interests? Consequently, the exact form which renewed linkages will take is still unclear. Instead, "socialisation", or the re-introduction of the market-place into its broader social and political context, is an evolving and disputed process: a result of the daily decisions and compromises reached within the integration project.

Seen in this light, whatsoever monetarist, ordo-liberal, interventionist, statist, intergovernmental or supranational form comes to dominate EMU, the process of European monetary and economic union is undeniably an attempt to impose some form of order upon what is a state of (international economic) nature—seeking to create one European approach to issues of wealth redistribution and the establishment of "social balance." National economic, monetary and social policies were once disjointed and determined simply by the vagaries of economic exchanges within a free European market, or—viewed from the standpoint of national economic policy—an international exchange rate system which has become increasingly vulnerable to currency speculation. With the arrival of EMU, however, a potential now exists for the establishment of some form of order or common European balance between market and society.

The flexible provisions of the EC Treaty and emerging forms of co-operative national, intergovernmental and supranational decision-making, thus provide nascent and highly permeable governance structures within which a disputed European polity might meet to mediate and decide upon

European Administrative Law: Legal Oversight of a Stateless Market" in C. Joerges and E. Vos (eds.), *EU Committees: Social Regulation, Law and Politics* (Oxford, Hart, 1999).

conflicting views of the social balance to be struck within Europe. EMU, like European integration itself, is an evolving and contested project. Neither its goals are clear, nor is it certain whether its normative contours will be determined by traditional national politics and politicians or by more neutral technical expertise and experts. Nonetheless, for all its indeterminacy, it clearly does represent the institutional beginnings of the effort to "socialise" once unmanageable capital flows and create and sensitively govern an emerging European economic area.

3. Law's Caution

Since their inception, the European Communities and Union have clearly been creatures of the law: sustained by a legal dynamic which has seen European law eagerly deploy treaty provisions with a potential for subjectivisation as individual rights (most notably, the Four Freedoms),[36] in an intense and economically-rationalising legal campaign against unduly restrictive member state market regulation. Such a subjectivisation of treaty principles has, on the one hand, clearly served the Community goal of the establishment of the internal market. On the other hand, however, it has cut deep into the autonomy of national economic and social policy-making: on many occasions, simply sweeping aside social stability mechanisms founded in interventionist economic regulation.[37]

European law has traditionally been willing to engage in the hands-on rationalisation of market regulation/economic management within Europe; and has repeatedly been prepared—even in the face of censure by national constitutional courts[38]—to risk any claim which it may have to be a body of law dealing solely with technical rather than redistributive issues, and thus not to require any form of traditional and politically-constituted legitimation. Given these traits, the overwhelming silence with which European legal circles have greeted a treaty-enshrined and price-stability oriented European monetary and economic policy—and, more specifically,

---

[36] Arts. 39, 43, 49 and 52 (ex 48, 52, 59 and 63) EC Treaty; though a de-personalised Art. 28 (ex 30) EC has also had its part to play in this rationalising process, cf, M. Poires Mauduro, *We the Court* (Oxford, Hart, 1998).

[37] In other words, much of restrictive national economic regulation served aims other than simple market regulation; pursuing instead, through mechanisms such as support for the competitive position of declining industries, social goals such as full employment; cf, C. Joerges, "Product Safety in the European Community: Market Integration, Social Regulation and Legal Structures" (1992) *Journal of Behavioural and Social Sciences* 38, 132–148.

[38] Cf, the *Brunner* judgment of the *Bundesverfassungsgericht*, [1994] 1 CMLR 57; more particularly, its criticism of the extensive ECJ interpretation of Art. 28 (ex 30) EC, and consequent tendency to set aside national economic arrangements established through the national democratic process.

the possible treaty infringements that may already have taken place[39]—is striking indeed.

Certainly, such apparent caution cannot be traced to any more specific historical unwillingness to help to shape *supra-national* economic governance: the combination of Article 81(1) and (3) (ex 85 (1) and (3)) EC on competition policy, often having been used both to strike down national economic regimes and to refashion them on the European level.[40] Instead, uncharacteristic legal caution may be argued to derive from the specific difficulties associated with the management of money, and the deep social and political ramifications of explicit macro-economic policy-making.

A. technical complexity and social intricacy

Perhaps the most eagerly awaited of all responses to the final decision to move into the third stage of EMU, the *Bundesverfassungsgerichts's* judgment of 2 April 1998 [41] on the compatibility of EMU with German democratic processes and, more particularly, the legality of the Community's (lax) application of Maastricht's convergence criteria nature, sheds much explanatory light upon legal caution in monetary matters. In a certain sense the judgment was a foregone conclusion—the earlier *Brunner* judgment[42] having both confirmed EMU's compatibility with the democratic requirement's of the German Constitution and, as an analogous consequence, recognised the European Court of Justice's(ECJ) (constitutionally transferred) competence to review Treaty-based convergence criteria.[43] The *Bundesverfassungsgericht's* summary dismissal of both pleadings is nevertheless—in the specific terms in which it was delivered—of vital interest: representing the response to EMU of the national court most cognisant of the ordo-liberal model of monetary and economic union upon which it is loosely based.

In this regard, possibly the most interesting facet of the judgment was not simply the German Justices' recognition of the fact that highly technical and politically sensitive anti-inflationary economic policy-making lies somewhere "between technical knowledge and political constructivism", and consequent refusal to engage in any assessment of what must always be a discretionary—political/technical—process of adjudication:

> Die Kriterien für die Beurteilung der rechtlichen und wirtschaftlichen Konvergenz hat der EGV in klaren Tatbestände als rechtsverbindliche Entscheidungsgrundlage geregelt. Allerdings bestehen, wie das Gericht schon

[39] Largely in the matter of convergence criteria; though the attempted reduction in the term of the ECB president may also constitute an infringement. See J. Usher in Ch. 1 *supra* and P. Beaumont and N. Walker in Ch. 8 *infra*.

[40] C. Joerges, *supra* n. 37.

[41] *Supra* n 5, commonly known as "the Four Professors" judgment.

[42] *Supra*, n. 38.   [43] *Ibid*.

im Maastricht-Urteil gesagt hat, insoweit Einschätzungs-, Bewertungs- und Prognoseräume. Die Prüfung und Bewertung der vom Europäischen Währungsinstitut und der Kommission vorgelegten Daten verlangen empirische Feststellungen, Einschätzungen und Bewertungen, die sich nur annährend auf Erfarhrungswissen stützen können. In diesem Bereich *zwischen ökonomischer Erkenntnis und politischer Gestaltung* weist das GG die Entscheidungsverantwortlichkeiten Regierung und Parlament zu.[44]

But rather, the pronouncement that, while the German Constitution[45] and EC Treaty[46] may be founded upon the notion of price-stability, and indeed the subjective property right[47] can be read as imposing an obligation upon the German Government to maintain price-stability, such a constitutional notion cannot be transformed into a general and enforceable subjective right. Instead, its implementation must remain within the discretion of the political process:

> Sie sind von den politischen Organen zu verantworten, die für eine *Gesamtbeurteilung allgemeiner Entwicklungen* zuständig sind und ihre Entscheidungen entwickulngsbegleitend überprüfen und korrigieren können.[48]

An "overall [political] judgment of general developments," furnishes the key to the embeddedness of ordo-liberal principles within a constitution which is similarly dedicated to the maintenance of a just social balance.[49]

---

[44] Point II.1.2aa), emphasis added. In the Court's approved translation: "[T]he criteria for this convergence are regulated by the Treaty in clear sets of facts as legally binding bases for decision (Art. 109j(1) taken together with Art. 104c [now Art. 121(1) taken together with Art. 104] and the Protocol on the convergence criteria pursuant to Art. 109j [now Art. 121] ECT and the Protocol on the excessive deficit procedure). This legal criterion admittedly opens room for assessment, evaluation and forecast (*BVerfGE* 89, 155, 203): the verification and examination of the figures presented by the EMI and the Commission call for empirical findings, assessments and evaluations that can be based only approximately on empirical knowledge. Assessing the developments takes analyses and predictions using practical reason that allow only probability judgements but do not convey certainty. The overall assessment of a high degree of lasting convergence and the associated forecast for a durable stability community call for decisions from the responsible bodies in which factual findings, empirical values and deliberate creativity are mixed in fluid transitions".

[45] Art. 23, para. 3 GG.

[46] Art. 105 EC.

[47] Art. 14(1) GG.

[48] Point II.1.2e), emphasis added. In the Court's approved translation: "[T]hey are to be justified by the political bodies competent for an overall assessment of general developments and able to check and correct their decisions in the light of developments".

[49] Generally the German Constitution recognises the higher legal principle of a just social balance within society through its preamble's designation of the German State as a *Sozialstaat*. Such a principle is confirmed in much constitutional jurisprudence: most spectacularly in the *Finanzausgleich* judgment (*BVerfG 86 148, at 168*) which responded to the Federal Government's attempt to discipline the economic policy of various *Länder* (Bremen, Hamburg, Saarbrücken) through a reduction in fiscal transfers to them, by reminding the *Bund* that the principle of just social balance precluded any federal attempts to bankrupt individual states.

The necessarily competing and conflicting constitutional values of currency/price stability and social justice/equality lays the basis for an eternal and mediating political dance between considerations of economic stability and social balance. While law places the notions of price-stability, anti-inflationary economic policy and equal living conditions in the constituted political world, it can neither materially judge nor create equilibrium between these conflicting concepts. Such a process of balance is instead to be left to the political process.

B. political governance and law: from materialisation to proceduralism

This final observation perhaps provides the key to uncharacteristic European legal silence. To subjectivise a European commitment to price-stability, or strictly review EC Treaty convergence provisions upon formal application by individual Europeans, would be to materialise an incomplete and contested—arguably even monetarist—European economic policy. This would not only present a danger of false judicial assessment of constantly developing and complex technical data. It would also leave—and more importantly so—very little room for the political establishment of an equilibrium between social policy and an emerging European/national economic and monetary policy. European law would thus, by implication, be the source of a new (neither constitutionally nor democratically legitimated) European social balance; one seemingly based solely upon the normatively-bereft ground of labour mobility.

Clearly, European law must hold back from a material, or substantive, pursuit of the monetary and economic principles established in the EC Treaty. However, as the following section will argue—and the *Bundesverfassungsgericht* has itself in the past highlighted[50]—law might still have a role to play in the safeguarding of the credibility of the euro and EMU, protecting Europe's deep and dual normative commitment to the maintenance of a successful currency and acceptable social conditions through "proceduralisation"; and thereby adopting the role of oversight over the policy-making of supranational, national, and inter-governmental institutions and more diffuse (private/technical) interests.

4. Supervising Governance?

As noted, the as yet ill-formed and multi-level institutions through which a normatively disputed EMU is developing, may be regarded as the framework within which an evolving "socialisation" of the internal market and

---

[50] *Finanzausgleich* judgment, *supra* n. 49, and *infra* n 66.

common European economic area is taking place. Both technical/economic experts and politicians may accordingly be argued now to bear a dual duty of mediating between conflicting views upon EMU and the social balance to be struck within Europe, and ensuring the on-going credibility of the euro in the intervening period. This latter point is, however, crucial. Certainly, given EMU's troubled history, it cannot be hoped that a disputed monetary/economic integration *telos* can quickly be brought to a non-contested conclusion. However, the EC Treaty undoubtedly makes a firm "quasi-constitutional" commitment to the creation of a credible European currency:[51] a commitment which, with its final concretisation, has now inevitably become the cornerstone of the entire project of European Union. If the euro and EMU fail, so too does EU. Maintaining their credibility is quite simply an imperative.

Seen in this light, the function of European law is therefore surely to aid politicians and technocrats in their dual task: on the one hand, ensuring the institutional credibility of the euro; and on the other, regulating the process of debate on EMU's contested structures and normative goals. These two elements, however, are irrevocably intertwined. From the convergence theory standpoint, the credibility of the euro is now fully dependent upon general acceptance for the outcomes of the on-going process of political/technical interchange at the supranational or inter-governmental level: any isolated national deviation from stability-oriented economics, placing European anti-inflationary monetary policy into possibly fatal doubt.[52] Equally, however, the civility and sensitivity of the political/technical debate which characterises EMU, will likewise be far easier to establish and maintain in the shadow of a strong rather than a weak currency.[53]

A. ECB: monetary policy, independence and accountability

Prior to French attempts to hijack the ECB presidency, the foundation of EMU's long-term credibility was generally considered to be the treaty-guaranteed independence of the ECB.[54] Having exclusive control over

[51] Alternatively, and in the German vernacular, the commitment to the maintenance of a credible currency entails a further step in the elaboration of Europe's Economic Constitution (*Wirtschaftsverfassung*), or on-going attempt to concretise and make norma-tive (through higher European law) the exact shape of the common economic area upon which the European Union is founded.

[52] A national defection perhaps being caused by the national public's unwillingness to submit itself to economic and social policy disciplining regimes established by an intergov-ernmental or supranational; interchange which is perceived to be insensitive to national social needs, or even unjust.

[53] Some support for this argument may be evident from the reaction to the weakening euro in the first seven weeks of its existence in 1999.

[54] Arts. 108 and 112 (Ex 107 and 109a) EC.

money supply and interest rates, and a substantial degree of influence over member state borrowing, the ECB would ensure long-term anti-inflationary monetary policy, and thus the stability of the euro. In short, or so it would seem, the European partners had agreed on a *Bundesbank* model for European monetary policy.

However, as has become increasingly apparent, there is much public disquiet about the legitimacy of a technocratic approach to monetary policy, and recent events have seen the ECB's independence threatened as various member states have sought to influence its workings. Clearly, such manoeuvring derives from concerns that too independent an ECB might be insensitive to individual national difficulties and impose too rigid an anti-inflationary policy.[55] Such difficulties might broadly—and surprisingly perhaps—be argued to stem from the fact that whilst the ECB is often claimed to be a *Bundesbank* clone, it nonetheless differs crucially from it.[56] Thus, the *Bundesbank* was not —prior to the Maastricht Treaty at least— an institution whose independence was constitutionally guaranteed. Rather, its sheltered institutional status derived from secondary constitutional jurisprudence,[57] which itself—in a Habermasian twist—was based upon a demonstrable and general political and social consensus that the historically-conditioned German spectre of inflation was best exorcised by a pluralist—*i.e.*, regime-limiting—approach to the institutional control of monetary policy. In short, Germany wanted anti-inflationary monetary policy to succeed and so was prepared to accept the quasi-independence of the *Bundesbank*. Meanwhile, the danger that the Central Bank might be too insensitive to political and social needs was combated through its cultural, if not institutional, embeddedness in German political society: with officers of the Bank, as public figures, subject to wide-ranging political and public scrutiny, if not control. Common interest and the largely invisible, but nonetheless binding norms of social and cultural interaction would ensure reasonably close co-operation between the Central Bank and political power. In the European setting, however, both common interest and dense social interaction are absent, suggesting that a quasi-constitutionally independent Central Bank might appear to pose a danger of insensitive sledgehammer monetary governance.

Accepting fears that a culturally and politically disembodied ECB might

[55] See A. Scott in Ch. 2 *supra*.

[56] For details of the *Bundesbank's* culturally, rather than constitutionally, secured independence, cf. C. Joerges' comments on P. van Themaat, "Some propositions on the Legal Aspect of the Planned Economic and Monetary Union in its Political, Economic and Social Context before and after the Ratification of the Treaty of Maastricht" in F. Snyder (ed.), *Constitutional Dimensions of European Economic Integration* (London, Kluwer, 1996).

[57] Based upon Article 14 GG; a complex dogmatic dance determining that subjective property rights also entail an obligation of the German State to the maintenance of price stability.

not show due regard to the social and political complexities of the management of European money, it might nonetheless be argued that modern institutional design indicates that European law can play a part in compensating for a long history of consensual and cultural interaction between technocrats and society/politics. The goal of law is thus to achieve both "independence" and "accountability", and to determine that while no-one controls the policy-makers, the policy-makers are under control. Equally, the founding statutes of non-majoritarian institutions provide the tableau upon which the legal instruments of control might be painted.[58]

Prior to examining such measures—and as a sociological conditioning factor—it should also be noted that the ECB will itself be eager to maintain links with political governance. If "coronation" theorists are correct in their assumptions, much of monetary policy's success is itself dependent upon the price-stabilising orientation of national economic policies. The ECB will accordingly in any case seek contact with political processes—and will, in all likelihood, and in return for general stability, be content for the Council or national governments to arrange short-term aid to or flexibility for those nations in need.[59] Such sensitive and conditional co-operation can be assured and reinforced by the various institutional/ legal mechanisms incorporated within the Bank's founding statute.

First, wide-ranging review of the ECB by European parliamentary committees can both ensure that the Bank's technical decisions be subject to scrutiny from beyond its institutional structures, and can bring the ECB's underlying policies and principles to the notice of a wider European public.[60] Secondly, annual review of the Bank's budget by the European Parliament and the Court of Auditors will provide a means to control the ECB's yearly policy-agenda. And thirdly, measures such as institutionalised meetings between national economic representatives and the Bank, wide-ranging publication duties, and the appointment of a President acceptable to all, rather than a few, national governments, will all raise general acceptance for the Bank, maintaining its links with national political systems and the wider European public.

In a complex modern polity, political oversight does not necessarily rely upon political presence within institutional structures.[61] The ECB's independence is the foundation of the euro's credibility and must be

---

[58] Both the concept of independence and accountability and the legal/institutional mechanisms of accountable/independent non-majoritarian governance are taken from Giandomenico Majone's work; cf, for a concise explanation of accountable non-majoritarian institutions, G. Majone, "Independence vs Accountability", Working Paper in Social and Political Sciences No. 94/3 (Florence, European University Institute, 1994).

[59] For a less optimistic view about the likelihood of fiscal transfers see A. Scott Ch. 2 *supra* and P. Beaumont and N. Walker Ch. 8 *infra*.

[60] See Art. 113 (ex 109b) EC.

[61] Although some political presence is there, see Art. 113 (ex 109b) EC discussed in ch. 8 *infra* by P. Beaumont and N. Walker.

jealously guarded. Political accountability and cultural embeddedness can be achieved by means other than direct political control.

B. EMU *and the higher principles of deliberation*

Far more complex a question than that of ECB independence, however, is the issue of the legal structuring of the sharply-polarised political and technical debates which will continue to characterise EMU in the matter of national economic stability and social policy. As noted, European law is faced by two particular problems in this regard. First, the exact structures and governmental instances within which such discourses will be undertaken have yet to be settled. Economic policy may remain a matter largely for individual national states, controlled by the GSP.[62] Alternatively, it may take on intergovernmental and even supranational characteristics by virtue of multi-lateral surveillance and increasing cohesiveness within the EFC. In other words, the exact division of competences remains unclear. Equally, however, such debates and discourses will revolve around legally unbalanceable goods. There are no neutral criteria for balancing social justice against anti-inflationary measures. No objective assessment can be made which will establish a natural equilibrium between degrees of price stability and redistributive demands.[63] As a consequence, law—if it wishes to maintain its neutrality—cannot settle disputes through material "legal policy".

Yet, there is already potential for ECJ intervention into EMU. Could a member state ask the ECJ to review a financial penalty imposed under Article 104 (ex 104c) EC?[64] Will the ECB be drawn to seek judicial aid to discipline errant states? Whatsoever the cause, European law may find itself in the never-never regions between technical knowledge and political constructivism; or, on the uncertain ground of an overall judgment of general developments.

Here it would thus seem necessary to begin to address the question of the proceduralisation of European law and the establishment of higher legal principles for the guiding of EMU-determining discourse. Law cannot materially decide exactly which visions of social balance, economic policy or monetary stability should properly guide EMU; but it may be able to establish the legitimacy of and general public support for the fluid political/technical debates which will determine EMU, ensuring that the political and technical groupings who engage in such discourses and take decisions having an effect upon European and national social balances, do so in a civic and deliberative manner. Principles must thus be found to

[62] See I. Harden Ch.4 *supra* for detailed analysis.

[63] Though price stability and redistribution of wealth are not necessarily incompatible, the deflationary pressure associated with price stability may stagnate economic growth, which in turn may make redistribution of wealth more difficult.

[64] See P. Craig Ch.5 *supra* for further treatment of the ECJ's role.

ensure that the outcomes of such debates are not merely a reflection of strategic behaviour and that discussion is marked by a due regard for the views and concerns of all who are affected by EMU.

The higher legal principles which might act as yardsticks for the quality both of civility and of deliberation are at hand; being readily derivable from existing European treaties and the constitutional/cultural traditions of the member states. Price stability and a credible currency are clear and quasi-constitutional European goals. They are plainly stated within the EU Treaty, and those who have chosen to take part within EMU should accordingly display a degree of "vertical solidarity" with such European aims. Equally, however, the principle of social solidarity is firmly enshrined in all of the member states constitutions/political cultures and has likewise become a part of a European legal tradition: the EC Treaty's Social Chapter (invigorated by the Treaty of Amsterdam) signalling the Union's commitment to the establishment of a measure of social justice within Europe. Similarly, a duty of co-operation is one of the Union's most cherished constitutional principles.[65] As a consequence, the Community goal of regulatory growth and development needs to be pursued with a measure of "horizontal solidarity" for social needs and particular economic problems in the member states; with all national governments, and institutions of European governance, such as the central bank co-operating amongst themselves to find the most appropriate solutions to individual national problems.[66]

As a concluding note, however, the very real difficulties of establishing the formal legal mechanisms which might give voice to such higher principles can be briefly highlighted. On the one hand, the application of such principles may appear to be a simple matter: the ECJ simply calling upon the principle of vertical solidarity to justify the imposition of financial sanctions upon a member state which had chosen to flaunt price stabilising convergence criteria. On the other, however, much of EMU's long-term

---

[65] Art. 10 (ex 5) EC.

[66] The notions of "horizontal" and "vertical solidarity" are taken from the *Bundesverfassungsgercht's Finanzausgleich* judgment, *supra* n. 49 In brief, the Court, faced by a serious clash between the economic policies/ideologies of the *Bund* and several *Länder*, ruled that a principle of vertical solidarity determined that individual states might not pursue economic policies which would be fatal to the policies of federal government. By the same measure, however, a principle of horizontal solidarity, also prescribed that federal government must take note of the specific economic conditions and difficulties of individual states; and might thus not formulate its own policies so as to make the financial position of those states untenable. As such, the judgment is a noteworthy example of "proceduralised constitutionalism", the Constitutional Court avoiding a material role in the settlement of a complex fiscal transfer dispute, but nonetheless playing an active role in structuring discussion between the *Bund* and the *Länder* in an attempt, first, to make debate "deliberative", or receptive to the needs of all concerned, and secondly, to provide "civility-imposing" guidelines (social justice and equal respect for the outcomes of federal/state political processes) to lessen the danger of discussion being simply dominated by strategic interests.

credibility will rest upon the ability of national and European technocrats and politicians convincingly to balance the possibly competing values of just social balance and rational economic development, and here very real legal difficulties may arise. How then can European law formally guarantee that technical/political discourse will give rise to equitable solutions which pay due regard both to (national or European) social crises (horizontal solidarity) and to Europe's continuing commitment to rational economic development (vertical solidarity)? Certainly, some form of rule of reasons requirement,[67] might be used to ensure that the actors within any decision-making process have at least heard all technical or political views concerned; such discursive plurality, theoretically at least,[68] forcing any national or European policy-maker fully to ground their preferred options in the face of possibly competing views. However, given the necessarily fluid and dispersed nature of the supra-national, national and intergovernmental debates which will shape EMU, this may be a very difficult, if not impossible task for the law to achieve. Nonetheless, given the vital need to maintain the credibility of EMU (and thus of the Union) the law and legal science must, at the very least, begin to investigate such issues.

5. Conclusion: Constitutionalising EMU and European Law

As an overall conclusion, it should finally be noted that the process of European political and monetary integration adds to the general and growing perception that European law needs to urgently re-assess its own normative foundations. With the arrival of EMU, the legitimising claim that a European law devoid of constitutionalised political legitimation might nonetheless—through the subjectivisation of European Treaty provisions—insinuate itself deep into national legal orders on the basis of its purely functionalist and technocratic orientation, has now been fully exposed for the fallacy which it is and has always been.[69] Normativised EMU provisions represent a deep and highly visible incursion into the social balance struck by the constitutions and political processes of the member states; and a materialised/subjectivised legal approach to EMU would thus be completely devoid of political or constitutional legitimacy.

However, European law does have a vital role to play in the regulation of the fluid and flexible governance which is determining the normative contours and institutional structures of an evolving European social balance. Law can add much needed legitimacy to this process, ensuring that the on-going socialisation of the single market and European

---

[67] Derived from Art. 253 (ex 190) EC.

[68] C. Joerges and J. Neyer, "From Intergovernmental Bargaining to Deliberative Political Processes: The Constitutionalisation of Comitology", *supra* n. 9.

[69] *Supra*, n. 37.

economic area is informed by publicly articulated and deliberated normative principles, and is not simply the result of undeclared or untested
strategic self-interest.

Here, however, where once European lawyers scanned the Treaties for
material norms amenable to subjectivisation, they must now survey
European law for provisions and principles upon which they might build in
an effort to create a proceduralised framework for European governance.
In other words, the effort legally to oversee EMU may contribute to the
constitutionalisation of European law; such a constitutionalisation,
however, must be founded in procedural rather than substantive notions of
justice.

7

Economic and Social Cohesion and the Euro

JOANNE SCOTT and STEPHEN VOUSDEN

1. Introduction

IN 1996 the Commission presented its first *Cohesion Report*.[1] This text represents the first "comprehensive examination" of national and Community policies to promote economic and social cohesion in the European Union (EU).[2] The concept of economic and social cohesion, though introduced into the EC Treaty in 1987 when the Single European Act came into force, is not defined.[3] The Cohesion Report proposes a broad and multi-faceted conception of cohesion. This is presented by the Commission as encompassing both a geographic (spatial) and a social dimension. The former is understood in terms of a reduction in disparities between member states, and between regions, in the EU. While the Commission acknowledges the limitations of a quantitative assessment in evaluating geographic cohesion, two primary indicators are employed in assessing recent trends: per capita Gross Domestic Product (GDP) and (un)employment. The social dimension of cohesion is, the Commission recognises, more difficult to define. Again, two primary indicators are deployed, relating to income and employment.[4] In terms of income, the Commission attaches particular importance to measuring inequalities between households by reference to levels of household expenditure. It does so with a view to assessing levels of poverty. Poverty is conceived as a relative rather than an absolute concept.[5] When it comes to social cohesion

---

[1] COM(96) 542 final.   [2] *Ibid.*, p. 13.

[3] See Art. 2 and Arts. 158–162 (ex 130a–130e) EC. Art. 158 (ex 130a) EC provides that the Community shall "in particular" aim at reducing disparities between the levels of development of the various regions and the backwardness of the least-favoured regions. It is thus apparent, on the basis of the text of the Treaty, that cohesion encompasses a regional dimension.

[4] *Supra* n. 1, p. 38.

[5] The Commission observes in this respect that "[t]he degree to which society suffers from poverty is generally assessed in terms of the poverty line, which is a relative rather than an absolute concept, usually defined as the proportion of households with income of 50% or

and employment, the Commission focuses not only upon overall levels of unemployment but upon the issue of access to employment for specific social groups, such as women, young people, older workers and the long-term unemployed.

The second chapter of the Commission's Cohesion Report makes for depressing reading. This analyses the scale of the "cohesion gap" in the EU and the extent to which this has expanded or contracted over the past two decades. It paints a complex picture of mixed fortunes, but a picture which is indicative of the pronounced and enduring nature of economic and social disparities between and within the member states. In terms of cohesion between member states, the gap between richest and poorest has increased quite dramatically over the last twenty years, with average income in the two poorest member states (Greece and Portugal) some forty per cent below that in the four richest (Belgium, Denmark, Luxembourg and Austria). This, of course, may be partly attributed to the relatively rapid enlargement of the Community during this period. More reassuringly, the per capita income of the four "cohesion" member states has increased from sixty-six per cent to seventy-four per cent of the average of the Union as a whole.[6] At the regional level, the report highlights the largely unchanging scale of disparities in income, with average incomes in the ten richest regions being (in 1993) 3.3 times higher than those in the ten poorest. "Excluding the new German Lander, the regions making up the two groups [have] remained remarkably similar over the 10 year period".[7] The Report notes further that average disparity in income per head in the EU is twice that of comparable regions in the US. In terms of social cohesion, the statistics presented demonstrate an increase in rates of poverty (assessed with reference to household expenditure) in most member states during the 1980s, albeit that in three of the four cohesion states the proportion of households below the poverty line declined. Comparable data is not available for the 1990s, but figures on household income (rather than expenditure) for 1993 reveal both growing inequalities between households and a higher incidence of poverty.[8]

The findings of the Cohesion Report are most hard-hitting when it comes to assessing employment trends, most notably at the regional level. It is in these terms that regional disparities are "particularly acute and show little

less of the average for the country as a whole". *Ibid.* p. 45. It is interesting to note that whereas regions are defined as "lagging" or "backwards" on the basis of their average GDP relative to the Community average, poverty is assessed according to national rather than Community norms in terms of expenditure levels.

[6] The four cohesion states are Spain, Portugal, Ireland and Greece. This figure conceals substantial differences in terms of economic performance between these states and, in particular, the remarkable success of the Irish economy where, in 1995, average income exceeded 90% of the Community average; and the poor performance of Greece where average income increased from 62% to 65% of the Community average.

[7] *Supra* n. 1, p. 21.   [8] *Ibid.*, p. 45.

sign of narrowing".[9] Whereas for the regions least affected by unemployment in the mid-1980s, there has been little change in average unemployment, for those most seriously affected there has been a significant increase over time.[10] Average unemployment in the ten most seriously affected regions is nearly seven times as high as that in the ten least affected. Youth unemployment (under the age of twenty-five) is a particular problem, averaging twenty-one per cent across the Union as a whole. In Spain youth unemployment equals forty per cent, and in Italy thirty-five per cent of the registered unemployed. In certain regions of Italy, notably Campania, nearly two-thirds of young people are unemployed. The Union is also characterised by high and persistent long-term unemployment, with nearly half of those out of work and seeking work unemployed for at least one year (compared to twelve per cent in the US). This is a particular problem for women, older workers and for those with low skills and few qualifications.

It would be possible to go on. Statistics abound in the Cohesion Report and speak, albeit obliquely, of the scale of the EU's cohesion challenge. It is against this backdrop that this paper should be read. It should also be read in the light of the contribution of Andrew Scott to this volume.[11] One of the central propositions put forward in his paper is that if things are bad now in terms of cohesion, they are likely to get worse with the introduction of economic and monetary union (EMU). While the thesis that EMU will tend (at least in the short and medium-term) to exacerbate incohesion in the Union is not one which is universally accepted, it is a conclusion which has been endorsed by a number of high level reports prepared for the institutions of the EU.[12] Many of the arguments supporting this thesis are elaborated and explored by Andrew Scott. These relate not merely to the direct fiscal implications of convergence at national and regional level, and the constraints on expenditure which these imply, but also to the reduction of member state autonomy in the area of monetary policy. In the absence of control over either exchange rates or interest rates, the capacity of states to adjust to changing economic circumstances, especially asymmetric

---

[9] *Ibid.*, p. 25.

[10] For the ten worst-affected regions this amounts to a 7% increase. For the twenty-five worst affected this amounts to a 5% increase.

[11] See Ch. 2 *supra*.

[12] See especially the MacDougall Report, *Report of the Study Group on the Role of Public Finance in European Integration: Volumes I and II.* (Commission, 1977); the Delors Report, *Report on Economic and Monetary Union in the European Community* (Commission, 1989); Beggs and Maye, *A New Strategy for Social and Economic Cohesion After 1992* (European Parliament, 1991). For a more sanguine view see Emerson et al, *One Market, One Money: An Evaluation of the Potential Benefits and Costs of Forming an Economic and Monetary Union* (Oxford, OUP, 1992) and Molle, Sleijpen and Vanheukelen, "The Impact of an Economic and Monetary Union on Social and Economic Cohesion: Analysis and Ensuing Policy Implications" in K. Gretschmann (ed.), *Economic and Monetary Union: Implications for National Policy-Makers* (Martinus Nijhoff, 1993).

economic shocks, is attenuated. It is notable in this respect that it is the Union's least favoured regions which tend to diverge most dramatically from the Community norm in terms of economic profile. In the context of a single macro-economic policy articulated at Community level, it is these regions which may be most vulnerable to such shocks and whose adjustment problems may be anticipated to be most severe.[13] It is indicative of such fears that seventy economists in the Netherlands recently signed a declaration to the effect that they believe that in a period of deep recession the Maastricht criteria will send the EMU into a fatal spiral of budget cuts and unemployment.[14] One of the important characteristics behind this prophecy is that the economists believe that the European Central Bank (ECB), as required by the Treaty, will privilege price stability over employment and social welfare. Nonetheless, it must be stressed, these arguments are complex and contested. They represent the domain of the professional economist, and economists, like lawyers, rarely agree. What, however, is clear is that the EU was characterised by significant economic and social incohesion as it approached the third stage of monetary union, and there is a grave risk that incohesion will be exacerbated in view of the manner in which EMU is to be constructed in Europe. Thus far, success in achieving (nominal) convergence has not been matched by success in achieving cohesion (real convergence).

The purpose of this chapter is to examine the nature of the Community's cohesion policies in the context of EMU. It will focus upon the Community's financial instruments for cohesion, especially the structural and cohesion funds. Reform of these funds will occur shortly after the start of the third stage of EMU, and the Commission's current reform proposals will form one focus for analysis in this chapter. Before turning to these proposals, however, the next section will look briefly at the functioning of the Community's financial instruments for cohesion, highlighting the principal characteristics of both the structural and cohesion funds.

---

[13] Beggs and Maye *ibid.*, note in this respect that "The question, therefore, is whether regions currently less favoured within a Member State will be more or less disadvantaged by joining an EC-wide EMU . . . If the region's characteristics are more similar to the Community norm than is its Member State then it may gain. If it is even less like it then the forces of divergence will be enhanced. On the whole, regions which are most dissimilar also tend to be the least favoured. As a result, the adverse effects of EMU are likely to be greatest for the less favoured regions in the less favoured Member States".

[14] G. Reuten, K. Vendrik, and R. Went, *De prijs van de euro – de gevaren van de Europese monetaire unie* [The price of the Euro – the risks of European Monetary Union] (Van Gennep, 1998).

2. Community Financial Instruments for Cohesion

From modest beginnings the Community's financial instruments for cohesion have come to assume enormous quantitative significance in terms of the proportion of the overall Community budget which they absorb. Outdone only by spending on agricultural intervention, these instruments today represent more than one-third of total Community expenditure. The rapid rise in spending in this area, particularly over the past decade, reflects the ambitious nature of the broader integration agenda over this period. The financial resources dedicated to structural funding doubled pursuant to the reforms of 1988, and again pursuant to those of 1993.[15] In terms of timing, significant reform of structural funding has followed closely in the wake of major Treaty revision, especially in the context of the Single European Act and the Maastricht Treaty. This has led many to conceive such funding as essentially "compensatory" in nature; compensating member states for the (risk of) uneven spatial effects associated with these grand inter-governmental bargains.[16] Thus these financial instruments are presented as having evolved functionally on the basis of a political logic, and as of critical importance in constructing a consensus around initiatives such as the single market programme and EMU. As David Allen observes, "[a]s we continue to trace the evolution of the structural funds . . . broad Community deals involving both enlargement and EMU are always significant explanatory factors".[17]

Community funding in the name of economic and social cohesion can be divided into two broad categories; the structural funds (ERDF, ESF and Guidance Section of the EAGGF) and the more recently established cohesion fund.[18] Funding in these two categories is governed by different principles and premises. A number of these differences betray the EMU-

[15] The 1988 reforms resulted in the adoption of five new regulations providing a common legislative framework for the functioning of the three structural funds; the European Regional Development Fund (ERDF), the European Social Fund (ESF) and the Guidance Section of the European Guidance and Guarantee Fund (EAGGF). These regulations, though still in force, were amended comprehensively in 1993. See Council Regulations 2081/93 (framework regulation), 2082/93 (coordination regulation) and 2083–85/93 (individual regulations pertaining to each of the three funds) in OJ 1993 L193.

[16] See P. MacAleavey, *The Political Logic of the European Community Structural Funds Budget: Lobbying Efforts by Declining Regions* (EUI Working Paper, RSC, No. 94/2), M. Pollack, "Regional Actors in an Intergovernmental Play: The Making and Implementation of EU Structural Policy" in Mazey and Rhodes (eds.), *The State of the European Union: Volume III* (Lynne Riener, 1995).

[17] "Cohesion and Structural Adjustment" in Wallace and Wallace (eds.), *Policy-Making in the European Union* (Oxford, OUP, 1996, 3rd ed.), pp.212–13.

[18] On the Cohesion Fund see Council Regulation 1164/94 OJ 1994 L30/1. This was preceded by a Cohesion Financial Instrument adopted pending the entry into force of the Maastricht Treaty.

origins of the cohesion fund, specific competence for the establishment of which was conferred by the Maastricht Treaty.[19] A brief comparison of these two distinct categories of funding will serve to exemplify the primary characteristics of the Community's financial instruments for cohesion, as these have operated during the current programming period (1994–99).

The cohesion fund may be distinguished from the structural funds most obviously in terms of the relative scale of funding. The former is less than ten per cent of the size of the latter. Moreover, under each category, such funding as there is, is allocated according to different premises. The cohesion fund represents an instrument of cohesion between member states, eligibility for funding being determined at national level. There are, at present, four cohesion states (Greece, Portugal, Spain and Ireland) selected on the basis that there per capita GNP is (or was at the relevant time) less than ninety per cent of the average for the Union as a whole. By way of contrast, in so far as the structural funds seek to promote spatial cohesion, they do so at a regional rather than a national level. Five objectives were articulated in the context of the 1988 reform of structural funding, three of which are regional in nature; objective 1 (promoting the development and structural adjustment of regions whose development is lagging behind), objective 2 (converting the regions, frontier regions or parts of regions seriously affected by industrial decline), and objective 5(b) (facilitating the development and structural adjustment of rural areas). A sixth objective was added further to the enlargement of the Union in 1995. This is concerned with promoting the development and structural adjustment of sparsely populated (Nordic) regions.

In addition, three objectives of a "horizontal" nature were established, funding on the basis of which currently accrues throughout the entire territory of the Union. In their pursuit of these horizontal objectives, concerned broadly with combating unemployment and the occupational integration of young people, and with agricultural and forestry assistance, the structural funds may be conceived as instruments of social rather than geographic cohesion. It is significant—and this is a point to which we will return later in the chapter—that nearly seventy per cent of total structural funding accrues under objective 1 to the Community's so-called "lagging" regions; regions which (in principle) have a per capita GDP which is less than seventy-five per cent of the Community average.[20] An additional

[19] Art. 161 (ex 130d) EC. The cohesion financial instrument was established pursuant to Art. 308 (ex 235) EC. This reflected in particular the concerns of the Spanish government surrounding the spatial impact of EMU, and the insistence of this government that such a fund be established as a quid pro quo for signing up to EMU.

[20] We say "in principle" here because a list of objective 1 regions is included in an annex to the structural funds "framework regulation". This is adopted unanimously pursuant to Art. 161 (ex 130d) EC, on the basis of a Commission proposal, with the assent of the European Parliament, and following consultation of the Economic and Social Committee and the Committee of the Regions. This quantitative criteria has consequently been subject

eleven per cent of funding accrues under objective 2, with objectives 3 and 4 absorbing around the same amount.

There is one further difference separating eligibility criteria in respect of cohesion and structural funding. The cohesion fund, unlike the structural funds, is underwritten by the operation of a conditionality principle. It is a condition of such funding that member states have in place a programme leading to the fulfilment of the conditions of economic convergence referred to in Article 104 (ex 104c) EC. Thus this fund operates as an instrument of convergence as well as national cohesion. Conditionality, in this sense, represents an on-going feature of the fund. Where the Council determines that an excessive deficit exists in any one of the cohesion states, and where that decision is not abrogated within one year or any other period specified, no new projects (or in the case of multi-stage projects, no new stages) shall receive assistance from the fund. Suspension of funding will cease where the Council abrogates its decision on the existence of an excessive government deficit. Exceptionally, in the case of projects directly affecting more than one member state, the Council may, acting by a qualified majority on a Commission recommendation, decide to defer suspension.[21]

Also explicable in terms of this link between convergence and the budgetary discipline which this implies, and EMU, is the watering down in the context of the cohesion fund of the principle of additionality; a source of such acrimony between the Community and certain member states (especially the UK under the Tory government) for so many years. This requires that member states shall not deploy structural funding to replace comparable national funding, but that Community funding be additional to it. To this end, member states are required to maintain their level of public structural or comparable expenditure at the level at least of that made available during the previous programming period (1988-1993). This requirement was softened somewhat even in the context of structural funding in 1993, whereby member states were permitted to take account of macro-economic circumstances, as well as a number of more specific economic considerations, such as privatisations, the unusually high level of public structural expenditure undertaken in the previous period, and business cycles in the national economy.[22] In view of the link between

---

to political pressures and has not always been strictly applied. The Highlands and Islands in Scotland is a case in point.

[21] *Supra* n. 18, Art. 6. According to the Commission's current reform proposals conditionality will continue to apply to those cohesion states participating in the euro. On the basis of these proposals funding would be suspended pursuant to a Commission recommendation pursuant to Art. 6(3)of Council Regulation 1466/97 (OJ 1997 L209/1), or pursuant to Art. 3(2) of Council Regulation 1467/97 (OJ 1997 L209/6) (the Stability and Growth Pact). See I. Harden, Ch. 4 *supra*, for a full analysis of the Stability and Growth Pact.

[22] *Supra* n. 15 (coordination regulation), Art. 9.

macro-economic stability and the cohesion fund, and its role in mitigating the fiscal constraints implied by convergence, it is entirely logical that the concept of additionality, though relevant, does not bind the cohesion states in so far as cohesion funding is concerned. While the preamble to the cohesion fund regulation observes that member states have undertaken not to decrease investment efforts in those limited fields to which the fund applies (transport infrastructure and environmental protection), and while the Commission's annual report on the activities of this fund is to include information on this matter, no formal mechanisms of verification are laid down. This link between convergence and cohesion funding is further reflected in the higher rate of part-financing which this fund, compared to the structural funds, may provide.[23]

Finally, before moving on to consider the Commission's reform proposals, one last distinction in terms of the operation of the cohesion and structural funds may be noted. Whereas the former operates on the basis of an individual project-based approach, each project requiring specific Commission approval, the latter have evolved gradually in the direction of a programme-based approach. Under the structural funds the bulk of expenditure accrues on the basis of "operational programmes". Such programmes represent the third stage of the development planning process, following the preparation of regional plans by member states and the establishment of Community Support Frameworks.[24] The latter are adopted by the Commission (in accordance with the comitology procedures laid down) pursuant to the plans submitted, acting on the basis of "partnership".[25] Operational programmes too are approved by the Commission, but are defined in broad, thematic terms, leaving substantial discretion in terms of implementation to the member state concerned. Such programmes are multi-annual in nature and have been likened to "incomplete contracts" between the Commission and the member states:

> . . . the European Commission exchanges the guarantee of multi-annual structural funding for the commitment by national authorities to allocate the

---

[23] In the case of the cohesion fund the ceiling (in terms of total Community assistance from all aid sources) is 90% of total expenditure. In the context of structural funds the ceiling is often less than, and rarely exceeds, 75% of total cost. See *supra* n. 15 (framework regulation), Art. 13.

[24] Since 1993 it has been possible to compress two stages of the development planning process into one. Member states may, at the time of submitting their plans, include applications for operational programmes and the relevant information required in support of such applications. In this event the Commission will adopt a Single Programming Document rather than a Community Support Framework. This represents Commission approval of these applications in respect of the operational programmes concerned. On the development planning process generally, see *supra* n. 15 (framework and coordination regulations, esp. Arts. 8–11 of the former and Arts. 5–16 of the latter).

[25] For a discussion of this concept of partnership see section 4 *infra*.

resources within a framework, into the design of which the Commission has made some input.[26]

While member states enjoy, within the framework of structural funding, enormous substantive discretion in terms of the choice of projects to be financed, Community legislation establishes a regulatory framework which imposes not only certain procedural obligations in terms of implementation, but also minimum guarantees for the effectiveness of expenditure on the basis of scrutiny of national arrangements for management and financial control.[27] We will return later in this chapter to examine implementation arrangements for structural funding in more detail, and to consider the constitutional implications of these arrangements in evaluating the legitimacy of Community fiscal intervention in an age of subsidiarity. Before doing so, however, it is necessary to turn to the Commission's current proposals for the reform of the Community's financial instruments for cohesion. In so doing, a number of critical issues, central to the operation of these funds in the specific context of EMU, will also be explored.

3. The Commission's Reform Proposals: Community Cohesion Policy for the New Millennium

The emphasis in the Commission's reform proposals[28] is on the quality, rather than the quantity, of funding during the next programming period. The overall budgetary ceiling in terms of cohesion support is to be maintained at the level of 0.46 per cent of the Union's GDP. While, in view of anticipated growth rates, this would imply an overall increase in the funding available (275 billion euro for 2000-2006 compared to 200 billion for 1993-1999[29]) a large tranche of this additional funding (45 billion euro at 1997 prices) would accrue by way of pre-accession financial assistance to

---

[26] P. MacAleavey, *Policy Implementation as Incomplete Contracting: The European Regional Development Fund* (EUI PhD thesis, 1995), p. 163.

[27] See for example, Council Regulation 2064/97 OJ 1997 L290/1, establishing detailed arrangements for financial control of operations co-financed by the Structural Funds.

[28] These are available on the DG XVI web site. The full texts of the proposed regulations governing structural and cohesion funding, and the establishment of the new instrument for structural policies for pre-accession (ISPA) are accompanied by explanatory memoranda. Negotiations are on-going and, as we write, (October 1998) at an early stage. Moreover, as things stand, there is clearly pressure for changes to be introduced, especially as regards the functioning of the ESF.

[29] At 1997 prices. This is equivalent to 286.4 billion euro compared to 208 billion euro at 1999 prices.

the states of Central and Eastern Europe (CEEs).[30] Budgetary rigour is a fact of political life for the Community as well as for its member states.

In terms of quality, the Commission returns to a familiar theme: that of the need to further concentrate resources. As in the past, concentration of assistance is conceived in terms which are both geographic and functional. In terms of functional concentration, the Commission proposes a reduction in the number of priority objectives pursued, two of which would be regional and one social in nature.[31] The new objective 1 would essentially consolidate existing objectives 1 and 6, whereas the new objective 2 would encompass all areas (industrial and rural) undergoing economic and social conversion, thus combining existing objectives 2 and 5(b). A third horizontal objective would focus upon the development of human resources, supporting the adaptation and modernisation of policies and systems relating to education, training and employment. Each of these three objectives would be conceived as mutually exclusive and hence objective 1 and 2 regions would not be eligible for support under objective 3. This stands in contrast to current arrangements where, as noted above, objectives 3 and 4 are "horizontal" in nature, accruing throughout the territory of the Union, not excluding those areas eligible for regional assistance.

Particularly significant in terms of geographic concentration is the Commission's proposal to reduce the percentage of the Union's population covered by structural funding, from the present level of fifty-one per cent to between thirty-five and forty per cent. Crucial to the success of this endeavour is the task of selecting regions eligible for assistance under objectives 1 and 2. As far as objective 1 regions are concerned, the Commission proposes to maintain the existing criterion for selection (per capita GDP of less than seventy-five per cent of the Union average) but to ensure its strict application.[32] To this end, if the Commission's proposals are accepted in this respect, the Commission would come to enjoy complete authority to draw up the list of objective 1 regions, thus reducing

[30] Pre-accession financial assistance will involve, alongside Phare and pre-accession agricultural assistance, the establishment of a new instrument for structural policies for pre-accession. This will be subject to an indicative allocation between the ten CEEs and will function according to broadly the same principles as the cohesion fund. Not only will assistance be concentrated in the spheres of environment and transport infrastructure, and operate on a project basis, but it will be underwritten by the application of conditionality. The relevant conditionality rules are laid down in the Accession Partnership Regulation. See Council Regulation 622/98 (OJ 1998 L85/1) on assistance to the applicant states in the framework of pre-accession strategy, and in particular on the establishment of accession partnerships.

[31] It also proposes a reduction in the number of Community initiative programmes receiving assistance, from thirteen to three.

[32] Except for those sparsely populated regions currently eligible for assistance under objective 6, which would in the future come to enjoy objective 1 status, and the "most remote regions" of the Union (French Overseas Departments, the Azores, the Canary Islands and Madeira) which would continue to enjoy objective 1 support.

the influence of the member states in the selection process. In the case of objective 2 regions, the criteria for selection are broad (and getting broader) and less than precise in their definition. Here the Commission proposes that no more than eighteen per cent (compared to twenty five per cent during the current programming period) of the Union population should be eligible for such assistance.[33] The Commission is to fix a population ceiling in respect of each member state. At the insistence of the UK, the Commission appears to have accepted that no more than one-third of any member state's objective 2 regions should forfeit this status pursuant to the current reforms. Given the expanded substantive scope of the new objective 2, the degree of concentration proposed by the Commission presents a significant challenge. The procedure for the selection of eligible regions under objective 2 has long been contested. In 1988 it was for the Commission to establish an initial list, acting in accordance with an advisory committee procedure. By 1993 it was for the member states to propose a list to the Commission and for the Commission, in close consultation with the state concerned, to adopt the list, again acting on the basis of the advisory committee procedure. Hence during this period a degree of authority passed from the Commission to the member states, representing "a retreat to a more national style of policy-making".[34] Today, the Commission proposals sanction the continuing capacity of the member states to draw up the initial list, but insists that the final decision be adopted by the Commission acting in "close concertation" with the state concerned, but not apparently within the framework of an advisory committee constituted by national representatives.

In terms of geographic concentration and the selection of eligible regions it should be observed that the Commission has its eye firmly on political reality. On the basis of its current proposals, a number of regions in as many as eight member states would be deprived of their objective 1 status. It is thus not surprising to find the Commission seeking to soften the blow. It does so by proposing that financial assistance be withdrawn gradually from such regions, on the basis of lengthy transitional arrangements. In general terms, funding would continue to accrue to existing objective 1 regions on a transitional basis for six years, and for four years in the case of objective 2.[35]

It is also significant, from the perspective of financial concentration, that

---

[33] This is in addition to the 2% of the population covered by objective 1 transitional aid, and which meet the eligibility criteria for objective 2.

[34] Hooghe and Keating, "The Politics of European Union Regional Policy" (1994) 1 *Journal of European Public Policy* 367, p. 419.

[35] See Art. 6 of the Commission's proposed regulation on the reform of the structural funds for the details of the transitional arrangements it proposes, *supra* n. 28. For certain regions transitional support will continue to accrue throughout the entire programming period.

the Commission proposes to continue to allocate roughly two-thirds of structural funding to the Community's "lagging" (objective 1) regions. This reflects a privileging of the geographic dimension of cohesion, and also the essentially "structural" nature of the Community's regional policy, this being concerned principally to tackle the causes of incohesion rather than to mitigate the social effects. Thus, the bulk of funding under objective 1 is dedicated to improving basic infrastructure, especially communications, and to investment in productive activities. "Lagging" is defined in economic terms (per capita GDP), and development, in the context of objective 1, is also conceived in such terms. This is further reflected in the nature of the priorities which the Commission identifies in its explanatory memorandum accompanying its current reform proposals. Here, emphasis is placed upon infrastructure, the development of human resources, support for the productive sector, as well as upon the environment and equal opportunities between men and women.

This emphasis upon the economic and geographic aspects of cohesion and upon structural funding as a tool to assist the "lagging" regions to "catch-up" in economic terms with their more money-rich neighbours, is readily understandable in view of the often repeated criticism that Community funding constitutes a regional policy in name only; in reality representing no more than an excessively sophisticated, and wasteful, mechanism of redistribution between member states and regions.[36] Yet while such emphasis (rhetorical and financial) upon the structural basis for cohesion is explicable in political terms, it does highlight the qualitative shortcomings of the Community policy response to the cohesion challenge, in a context of EMU. There appears to be something of a mis-match between the nature of the cohesion problem generated by EMU, and the nature of the Community response. This is not to say that the Community response, as represented by the structural funds is inappropriate, merely that it is excessively uni-dimensional in view of the multi-faceted impact of EMU upon cohesion. Two points, in particular, may be made in support of this argument.

First, the functioning of the structural funds is characterised by a high degree of rigidity. From the perspective of EMU, and the uncertain impact of EMU upon cohesion, the funds are insufficiently flexible in their operation. Such is the operation of the funds that they do not serve to promote budgetary transfers to alleviate the adjustment problems associated with unforeseen, temporary, economic shocks.[37] This stems principally from the

---

[36] See for example, B. de Witte, "The Reform of the European Regional Development Fund" (1996) 23 *CMLRev.* 419.

[37] Ironically many economists argue that it is in response to precisely this kind of temporary shock that centralised budgetary transfers can be justified. See, for example, P. de Grauwe, *The Economics of Monetary Integration* (Oxford, OUP, 1997, 3rd ed.), pp. 208–09. See also A. Scott, Ch. 2 *supra*.

multi-annual programming approach which has underpinned these funds since 1988. Funding is allocated, on a national basis, at the start of what is now to be a seven year programming period.[38] Hence while, as will be seen below, there is a degree of flexibility in terms of how the money is spent, no more or less money will be made available during this period according to the nature of the economic cycle in the various member states, or the impact of asymmetric economic shocks. Whereas within member states, the tax and benefit systems in place adjust automatically to relative economic fortunes, in the Community the policy response is set out in advance, notwithstanding the unknown and essentially unknowable cohesion impact of EMU.

Second, as noted above, Community cohesion funding (encompassing both the structural and cohesion funds) may be conceived as social policy only at its margins. It is principally preoccupied, as is apparent from the focus of expenditure, with facilitating structural adjustment. It enjoys only a marginal capacity to address directly social inequalities, and poverty, in the EU. This is not to deny that Community cohesion policies encompass a social dimension. They do. It is rather to emphasise the relative insignificance of this dimension within the Community cohesion regime as a whole. It is, however, significant in this respect to have regard to the Commission's current reform proposals, especially as these concern the new, expanded, objective 2. As seen, this is to be devoted to economic and social restructuring and to bring together measures for non-objective 1 regions suffering from structural problems. These are areas undergoing economic change (in industry or services), declining rural areas, crisis-hit areas dependent on the fishing industry or urban areas in difficulty. The criteria for the selection of such regions are laid down in some detail in the Commission's proposed regulation. These range from the relatively precise (for example, average levels of unemployment or population density) to the usefully vague (this is especially the case in relation to urban areas where criteria such as a high level of poverty, including precarious housing conditions and a high crime rate or a low level of education are included). In so far as the nature of the definition of incohesion may be anticipated to inform the policy response, this new, broader, definition for objective 2, may imply a broader conception of regional development and, in particular, suggest a greater focus upon the social as opposed to the economic, and the qualitative as opposed to the quantitative. This implies an

---

[38] According to the Commission's current proposals a 10% slice of total funding is to be withheld at the start of the programming period, to be allocated mid-term. However, this reserve is to be allocated, not on the basis of changing economic fortunes, but on the basis of a mid-term performance review. The criteria to be applied will be laid down in advance in the regulation. See Art. 43 of the Commission proposed regulation for the reform of the structural funds, *supra* n. 28. Compliance with the principle of additionality will be one crucial aspect of this performance review.

increasing emphasis upon tackling problems of social exclusion and those associated with deprived and degraded urban environments. This is a trend which is already apparent in the cohesion rhetoric of the Commission. The DGXVI Commissioner (Monika Wulf-Mathies) observes in this respect that:

> As we approach the end of the twentieth century, our towns and cities are becoming the focus of a host of pressing social, economic and environmental problems. Social exclusion threatens the very basis of our society, founded as it is on a partial redistribution of wealth generated by the economy. Environmental degradation in many cities has undermined the quality of life for those living there, who total some 280 million people, or 80% of the population of the Union. This means that today's cities must bear a large part of the burden of reconciling economic competitiveness with social cohesion and sustainable development.[39]

Highly pertinent to this discussion of the social dimension of cohesion, and the nature of Community policy in this respect, are the successive "poverty programmes" instituted at Community level. It is to these programmes that the next section will briefly turn. This discussion serves further to highlight the high level of political sensitivity and disagreement associated with Community financial intervention in the social sphere.

4. The Community Poverty Programmes

The Community has established fields of direct expenditure to support specific initiatives to tackle poverty and social exclusion, but these have been of a somewhat sporadic and modest nature and they have been funded from the ESF. The development of the Community's "poverty programmes" reflects a continual mismatch between prevailing economic realities, the quality of intervention under the ESF and the shifting power of the member states. These factors have been endemic since the inception of the ESF and have contributed to the relative failure of ESF intervention to achieve economic and social change. Whilst the ESF was established to increase employment and worker mobility, the onset of the oil crisis and the re-emergence of structural unemployment, presented a challenge to which it was unable to respond. In the Commission's view, one explanation for this failure was that the Community institutions were powerless over the member states, which enjoyed almost complete *de facto* autonomy over the manner in which the fund was to be spent. Consequently, over time, the Commission sought more control in the management of the fund and

---

[39] See preface to *Europe's cities: Community measures in urban areas* on http://www.inforegio.org/wbdoc/docgener/presenta/cities/1_index/indx_en.htm. and also COM(97) 197 final, *Towards an Urban Agenda in the EU.*

established specific support initiatives to represent the Community interest.[40] Therefore, as the second phase of the ESF commenced, the first European plan to combat poverty was introduced, in the form of a pilot programme, on the basis of Article 308 (ex 235) EC.[41]

The "Poverty 1" programme was launched to undertake scientific studies on the nature of poverty and to create thirty pilot projects to search for new ways to tackle poverty. Although this initiative ended in 1980 without any immediate follow-up, four years later a second plan, the imaginatively named "Poverty 2", was spawned.[42] Poverty 2 tripled the number of projects funded and also formalised a network for mutual information and co-operation. As this drew to a close in 1988, statistical information established that while the macro-economic situation in the Community as a whole had improved, growing numbers of people were living in either traditional poverty or under "new" forms of poverty resulting from changing family and employment structures.[43] The Commission's concerns were of sufficient gravity to justify the renegotiation and the further renewal of this Community initiative. It was against this socio-economic background that "Poverty 3" was established in 1989, with a view to integrating, both economically and socially, less privileged groups into society.

The noble theme of the third poverty programme echoed around the Community institutions but was accompanied by negligible funds. The scale of the imbalance between, on the one hand, the rhetorical concerns about old and new poverty and exclusion and, on the other, the budgetary baseline for financial support is striking. Back in 1974, "Poverty 1" had started on a budget of 20 million ECU. Some twenty years later, and despite the overall expansion in ESF funding, the poverty budget was fixed at a miserly 55 million ECU. Luyten and Lammertyn note, in this respect, that this sum is for a multi-annual (four year) project and, more strikingly, that the entire amount devoted to the poverty programme represents one half of the annual amount spent by the Community on food aid to the poor.[44]

Nonetheless, the strength of "Poverty 3" lay in the ability of the Community to generate its own ideas. It began to be able to develop a view on social exclusion that was not completely dependent upon national traditions. Thus, despite being muffled by the limited budget, the Council managed to produce, within the framework of this programme, a clear

---

[40] In this context "more control" should not be equated with complete centralisation of responsibility. See section 5 *infra*.

[41] Council Decision 75/478/EEC OJ 1975 L199/34.

[42] Council Decision 85/8/EEC OJ 1985 L2/24.

[43] Commission, *Poverty, A New Programme Proposed by the Commission*, (1989) Social Europe 2/89, pp. 66–69.

[44] D. Luyten, and F. Lammertyn, *De welzijnszorg in de Vlaamse Gemeenschap: voorzieningen en overheidsbeleid* [*Public welfare care in the Flemish Community: the provision of services and government policy*] monografie 2, Het (kans-) armoedebeleid, (1990, Sociologisch Onderzoeksinstituut, KUL), pp. 30–31.

policy message that shattered the old, uni-dimensional, definition of poverty conceived as a matter of people having inadequate resources. Instead, the Community stressed that it was "structural changes, such as the increased difficulty in gaining access to the labour market" that caused the process of social exclusion.[45] A reflection of this new multi-faceted definition of social exclusion can be found in the kinds of initiatives that were funded by "Poverty 3". Apart from the thirty-nine actions that attempted to integrate citizens through the labour market, twelve innova-tive actions, relating to quality of life, such as housing projects, were also launched. Together the actions were distinctly multi-dimensional in their approach to combating social exclusion and, just as importantly, they involved the collaboration of all the most important actors in the projects and the participation of the group to be integrated.

Once again, as the mandate for "Poverty 3" was due to expire, the Commission commenced negotiations to establish a fourth programme. This, however, came at a time when the dominant mood across the Community was one of achieving the criteria for EMU. Indeed, such was the fervour of the member states as they set about converging towards these goals, that concern was expressed by the Economic and Social Committee about the fact that EMU had been pressing the member states to reduce their budget deficits and that this had created a new constraint on public spending which was affecting the funding of social protection schemes.[46] However the ability of the Community to respond effectively to this shifting economic context and climate was limited. Policy in the area of social exclusion was influenced by the doctrine of subsidiarity. The Commission's own report on the implementation of the third poverty programme stressed the quality of intervention and confirmed the success of the programme's multi-faceted approach, the partnerships and the participation. The conclusion was that "Poverty 4" should seek to build upon the principles established in the third programme, but seek also to emphasise further national-level model actions, as well as transnational networks of projects and multi-objective integrated strategies. However, the report reflected an underlying sense of disappointment at the effect of "added Community value", another expression of the subsidiarity principle. Hence, while the projects might gain recognition for their "ability to prompt debate . . . in the fight against social exclusion, which exceeds by far their immediate impact" on a national level, the programme "has not always been enough, at least at this stage, to trigger the knock-on effect hoped for"—despite the explicit dove-tailing of the projects with

---

[45] Council Resolution on Combating Social Exclusion, OJ 1989 C277/1.

[46] Opinion on Social Exclusion OJ 1993 C352/48. For a discussion of the dramatic series of fiscal reforms taken in Italy with a view to meeting the EMU criteria see, F. Reviglio, *Come Siamo Entrati in Europa (e perche potremmo uscirne)* [*How we entered into Europe (and why we could leave it)*] (Utet Libreria, 1998).

specific national programmes for combating poverty in some member states such as Ireland, Spain and Portugal.[47]

The re-negotiation of the poverty programme unleashed an unprecedented degree of acrimony, not from the states criticised in the Commission's report, but rather on the part of the richer states. This fierce resistance was most forcefully articulated by the UK and Germany and, notwithstanding the extensive and protracted diplomacy designed to appease their antagonism, the other members of the Council were unable to convince these member states to lift their block on the proposal. The UK Government adopted a stance that was consistent with its broader approach to Community social policy initiatives, by viewing the proposed poverty programme as implying a further extension of Community intervention in this sphere. The German Government claimed that to renew and extend the programme, on the basis of Article 308 (ex 235) EC, would be contrary to the principle of subsidiarity, reflecting also the sensitivity associated with recourse to this legal basis since the decision of the German Constitutional Court in the famous *Brunner* case.[48] Ironically perhaps, the German Government argued that a more appropriate legal basis could be found in the Treaty chapter specifically concerned with the establishment and functioning of the ESF.[49] Implementation decisions here are to be adopted by way of the co-operation procedure, and hence on the basis of qualified majority voting in Council. What is significant about the German opposition to the fourth programme is its concern to restrict the quality of Community intervention to the labour market and to exclude "quality of life" projects relating, for example, to education, housing and participation in society.

By late June 1995, the dispute surrounding the fourth poverty programme had not been resolved and the Council had still not approved the programme. However, because the general budget of 1995 had been approved by the European Parliament, from which the programme would be funded, the Commission decided to use its own initiative and to allocate 6 million ECU to fund eighty-six projects combating social exclusion. The projects included assistance for lone-parent families, women afflicted by poverty, the long-term unemployed, families in extreme poverty, as well as for the improvement of urban amenities and access to urban services. However, predictably, the Commission's intervention was viewed as an

[47] COM(93) 435 final, *Report on the Implementation of the Community Programme for Social and Economic Integration of the Least Privileged Groups (1989–1994)*, p. 65.

[48] Debates of the European Parliament, No. 4–452/209, 27 October 1994. *Brunner* v. *European Union Treaty* [1994] 1 CMLR 57.

[49] Arts. 146–148 (ex 123–125) EC. This position suggests that the German Government's opposition was as much tied up with the broader, constitutional, question of expanding Community competences under Art. 308 (ex 235) EC, as with specific concerns as regards the nature of Community intervention to combat poverty.

attempt to circumvent the stalemate in Council and it met with an action for judicial review brought by the UK, and supported by Germany, Denmark and the Council.[50] It was claimed that the Commission did not have the power to commit the spending of this part of the budget to these projects because the Commission did not possess a decision authorising the expenditure. The Commission relied on the only exception to this principle: that no such decision was required where the spending was "non-significant", and that the 6 million ECU for pilot projects constituted such "non-significant" expenditure. The Commission's arguments were regarded with obvious scepticism by the European Court:

> . . . the purpose of the projects to be funded was not to prepare future Community action or launch pilot projects. Rather, it is clear from the activities envisaged, the aims pursued and the persons benefited that they were intended to continue the initiatives of the Poverty 3 programme, at a time when it was obvious that the Council was not going to adopt the Poverty 4 proposal, which sought to continue and extend Community action to combat social exclusion.[51]

As a result of this judgment, the Commission decided in June 1998 to freeze temporarily, any course of Community action for which there was no legal basis. The freeze included measures in favour of the family and children, measures combating racism, health and well-being, and a number of projects concerned with the disabled and the elderly.

Since the "Poverty 4" debacle, but before the Court's judgment, there have been important further twists to the institutional dialogue that is developing the social dimension of Community policy. In particular, both the Commission and the Council have recently conveyed their standpoints, the former in a Communication,[52] and the latter in the issuing of Employment Guidelines.[53] Although these instruments are not binding legal acts, they are examples of "soft law" and are, as such, useful in tracing attempts in the Community to generate new law in a politico-economic context which is not conducive to the enactment of formal measures.[54]

The Commission's Communication begins by making a political gesture. As if to wipe the legislative slate clean of the institutional combat surrounding the renegotiation of the poverty programmes, the

---

[50] Case C-106/96 *United Kingdom* v. *Commission* [1998] ECR I–2729.

[51] *Ibid.*, para. 34.

[52] COM(97) 102 final, *Modernising and Improving Social Protection in the European Union*.

[53] Council Resolution on the 1998 Employment Guidelines, OJ 1998 C 30/1.

[54] According to Winter, Communications and Guidelines are equivalent to types of acts that have no binding effect, such as recommendations and opinions. See G. Winter, "Reforming the Sources and Categories of EC Legal Acts" in G. Winter (ed.), *Sources and Categories of European Union Law: A Comparative and Reform Perspective* (1996, Nomos), p. 15.

Communication announces that social exclusion is a "new phenomenon", and it proceeds to produce a matching novel definition in policy terms that begins with long-term unemployment.[55] This offers the Commission two advantages: the first is that exclusion becomes quantifiable as half of Europe's jobless are long-term unemployed.[56] The second is that this definition of exclusion addresses the old UK complaint that there is "no generally accepted definition of social exclusion let alone reliable evidence about the most effective way to tackle its causes".[57] This focus upon the labour market reflects not merely a shift in discourse towards an avowed Community belief in the labour market's ability to combat social exclusion, but also the relatively greater solidity of the Community's claim to competence in this area. It can be seen, therefore, that the apparent institutional amnesia which the Communication betrays can be viewed as an attempt by the Commission to spring partially from the political leg-iron of subsidiarity that has shackled its social exclusion initiatives since the end of the third poverty programme.

The drafting of the Commission Communication also demonstrates the immense influence of monetarist ideas in the creation of the euro. The Commission merely sketches part of the problem faced by member states and warns of the need to reform national social protection systems so as to respond to current economic conditions; "internal" conditions that require a consolidation of public finances in order to avoid heavy debt services crowding out future expenditure. In choosing to stress the need to keep debt under control, the Commission coyly obscures half the economic story, given that debt control has piggybacked on cuts in public expenditure, in part driven by the goal of achieving nominal economic convergence within the framework of the Maastricht Treaty.

The 1998 Council Guidelines focus on four themes: i.) improving employability by focusing on youth and long-term unemployment; ii.) developing entrepreneurship by exploiting the opportunities for job creation in the social economy linked to needs not yet established by the market; iii.) encouraging adaptability, by asking the social partners to negotiate flexible working patterns such as part-time work and; iv.) strengthening policies for equal treatment, in order to reduce the gap in unemployment rates for men and women. These Council Employment Guidelines are annual and member states can use ESF monies to support their mainstream labour market policies subject, of course, to the additionality principle. The 1999 Guidelines on Employment, proposed by the Commission, do not substantially modify these underlying principles, but they do remind member states that the Commission has tabled policies to reform the structural funds, including the ESF, (see section 4 above), which

---

[55] *Supra* n. 52, p. 9.
[56] EUROSTAT, "Labour Force Survey: Principle Results of 1996" No. 8/97.
[57] Quoted by P. Spicker, "Exclusion" (1997) 35 *JCMS* 133, p. 134.

make an explicit link between the developing European employment strategy and the proposed new objective 3.[58]

It is thus apparent that following more than two decades of Community experimentation in tackling poverty, including symptoms as well as causes, budgetary constraints, legislative paralysis, and subsidiarity, currently operate to lead the Community back in the direction of labour market, rather than non-labour market measures, for social and economic cohesion. Even in the sphere of social cohesion, the "structural" is again, even in terms of rhetoric, being privileged at the expense of measures designed to mitigate the consequences and hardship associated with social exclusion. The mis-match, noted above, between the fiscal implications of nominal convergence at national level and the Community level fiscal response, is thus further exemplified by recent experiences in respect of Community anti-poverty initiatives. Nonetheless, as is clear from the political context of negotiations for the renewal of the Community poverty programme, Community level initiatives for economic and, particularly, social cohesion raise important issues concerning the proper distribution of authority between different levels of governance. It is to this theme that the next section of the paper will turn.

5. Fiscal Federalism and Subsidiarity

It is not difficult to see that with EMU, and with the fiscal and monetary constraints this imposes upon member states, comes an increase in pressure for an enhanced fiscal capacity at Community level; principally in the name of economic and social cohesion. Consequently, that very same Treaty (Maastricht) which extended the scope of application of the concept of subsidiarity not only removes considerable powers from the hands of the member states, in favour of an autonomous central bank, but also generates pressure for an expanded Community budget and a move towards what has been termed "fiscal federalism". While the language of fiscal federalism is commonly deployed in the name of greater regional autonomy within states (notably in Italy), in the context of the EU this is often presented as militating in the direction of a strengthening of the Community's budgetary position. Such arguments are not new. Indeed, in 1977 the MacDougall report concluded that a "small public sector" federal budget equal to five to seven per cent of Community GDP might be "capable of sustaining an economic and monetary union".[59] For it to do so, however, this report emphasised that:

> . . . the transfers and expenditure under the budget equalisation mechanism for "social and welfare services" and "economic services" would have to be not

[58] 14 October 1998.
[59] MacDougall, *supra* n. 12 (volume 1), p. 70.

only strongly redistributive, but also capable of a sensitive and large-scale response to short-term changes in the economic fortunes of regions and states. Simulations made by the [MacDougall] Group . . . suggest that the budget of the small public sector federation could attain the standards of redistributive power seen elsewhere in fully integrated economies (e.g. equalising up to 40% of per capita regional differentials), but the technical design of the budgetary instruments to do this would have to be strongly and deliberately biased in favour of these objectives.[60]

The functional logic of this approach is in a sense unassailable. Efficiency in achieving spatial and social equality between social groups, regions and states demands, where the starting point is one of profound inequality, the fiscal empowerment of a higher political authority which can mediate distributive relations fairly between them. Subsidiarity, in so far as it is predicated upon conceptions of comparative efficiency, conse-quently militates forcefully in favour of, rather than against, a Community level response to the cohesion challenge. As soon as the objective to be achieved is understood in terms of cohesion between regions in different member states, and between member states as a whole, as well as in terms of cohesion between social groups across the various member states, it is clear that in the absence of a supranational response implying redistribu-tion between member states, such an objective is incapable of realisation.[61] One may seek to challenge the legitimacy or rationale of the Community's cohesion objective but, that objective having been laid down, "fiscal feder-alism" emerges as a necessary policy response; and one which, formally, is in keeping with the efficiency inspired conception of subsidiarity laid down in Article 5 (ex 3b) EC.

Subsidiarity is, however, not the only principle which constrains the Community in the exercise of its legislative competence under the Treaty. Also significant is the principle of proportionality which concerns the nature and intensity of the Community's legislative response. This requires, *inter alia*, that:

Regarding the nature and the extent of Community action, Community measures should leave as much scope for national decision as possible, consis-tent with securing the aim of the measure and observing the requirements of the Treaty. While respecting Community law, care should be taken to respect well established national arrangements and the organisation and working of Member States legal systems . . .[62]

---

[60] *Ibid.*

[61] This is, to an extent, more problematic in relation to social cohesion given, as noted above, that poverty is defined in relative terms, by reference to the national rather than Community norm.

[62] Protocol on the Application of the Principles of Subsidiarity and Proportionality, annexed to the Treaty establishing the EC (as inserted by the Treaty of Amsterdam) OJ 1997 C340/106.

Community structural funding may be conceived as a case study in the application of the proportionality principle. It constructs a model of "fiscal federalism"—albeit a very modest one in quantitative terms—which is not predicated upon a simple choice between different levels of governance, but upon a sharing of responsibility across these different levels. It implies a form of governance which is both multi-level and multi-actor. It does so through recourse to the novel – in operation if not in name—concept of "partnership". While decisions about the size of the overall financial envelope, and its distribution between member states, continue to be adopted at Community level, within the framework of inter-governmental decision-making, decisions relating to the allocation of funding vis-à-vis specific programmes and projects are adopted within the framework of "partnership". While this implies a role for Community level institutions—specifically the Commission—this role is not an exclusive one. The Commission is to act in close consultation with the member state concerned and the competent authorities and bodies including, within the framework of each state's national rules and current practices, the economic and social partners designated by the member state at national, regional, local or other level.[63] In its current proposals the Commission is committed to consolidating and strengthening the application of the partnership principle and to promote a broader and deeper conception of this principle. Breadth, in terms of partnership, is concerned with access to the partnership and with the range of actors included within it. In particular, the Commission insists that

> [t]he participation of regional and local authorities, environmental authorities, and economic and social partners, including non-governmental organisations, must be guaranteed by Member States.

"Depth" in this context, refers to the need to involve the partners throughout the various stages of the development planning process, including the preparation of the development plans and detailed programming and evaluation. Still, however, the definition of partnership included in the proposed reform regulation is imbued with considerable (excessive) flexibility. This provides (Article 8(1)) that:

> Community action shall contribute to corresponding national operations. They shall be drawn up in close consultations, hereinafter referred to as the "partnership", between the Commission and the Member States, together with:
> - the regional and local authorities and other competent authorities;
> - the economic and social partners;
> - the other competent bodies.
>
> Each Member State shall within its own institutional, legal and financial system, choose and designate the most representative partners at national,

---

[63] Art. 4(1), framework regulation, *supra* n. 15.

regional, local or other level referred to in the first indent through as wide an association as possible including where appropriate the bodies active in the field of environment and in the promotion of equal opportunities between men and women.

It is readily apparent that recourse to terms such as "within its [the member state concerned] own institutional, legal and financial system" and "where appropriate" will operate to undermine the coercive potential of this concept. Member states will continue to operate, to some extent, as "gate-keepers" to the partnership; a role which, in the UK at least, has resulted in the dominance of central government and the *de facto* exclusion of the social partners.[64]

There are certainly shortcomings in the operation of partnership. These have been well documented in the UK.[65] But, these notwithstanding, the concept is important, and exciting, in considering the constitutional implications of "fiscal federalism" in Europe. While this demands, in the name of economic and social cohesion, a more pronounced redistributive effort at Community level, it does not necessitate, even according to current models, the transfer to the Community institutions of sovereign authority in the relevant spheres of development and social welfare. What is remarkable about partnership as a constitutional model for fiscal federalism, is the manner in which it succeeds (conceptually at least) in transcending the Community/member state, as well as the public/private, divide in terms of the allocation of authority. It constructs a polity which is simultaneously big and small; big enough to be efficient in the context of the politics of redistribution, and yet small enough to be inclusive and participatory, and responsive to national, as well as sub-national needs.

It is significant in this respect that the Commission, in its current reform proposals, seeks to ensure a "re-focusing [of] the Commission's responsibilities"[66] in respect of structural funding. In particular, the political responsibility of the Commission is to be more clearly defined and its essentially strategic role clarified. Implementation of structural funding is to be further decentralised, with the partners within the member states assuming greater responsibility. In keeping with the proportionality principle, scope for national (and sub-national) decision is to be enhanced. The current reform proposals are thus characterised by a move towards devolution in decision-making and a reduction in the substantive prescriptiveness of Community

---

[64] On experience in the United Kingdom in this respect see Roberts and Hart, *Regional Strategy and Partnership in European Programmes: Experience in Four UK Regions* (Rowntree Foundation, 1996); R.A.W. Rhodes, *Understanding Governance: Policy Networks, Governments, Reflexivity and Accountability* (Open UP, 1997), I. Bache, *The Politics of EC Regional Policy* (Sheffield University Press, 1999) and J. Scott, "Law, Legitimacy and EC Governance: Prospects for 'Partnership'" (1998) 36 *JCMS* 175.

[65] *Ibid.*

[66] Explanatory Memorandum accompanying the proposed reform of the structural funds, *supra* n. 28, p. 10.

level intervention as regards the manner in which Community funds are to be spent. At the same time, however, it is notable that the Community is seeking to exert greater control over member states' procedures for the implementation of structural funding. The Community's commitment to proportionality is in this respect qualified, in so far as this principle also implies respect for well established national arrangements. The price to be paid for increasing substantive flexibility in implementation, is a higher degree of control over the administrative mechanisms and procedures for implementation. Regardless of national administrative and constitutional predilections and practices, sub-national government is to be associated with the implementation task as, crucially, are the social and economic partners. There is an irony here. Proportionality, like subsidiarity, represents one strand of the Community response to its "crisis of legitimacy". Yet procedural norms laid down at Community level, even where (and sometimes especially where) these disrupt established national arrangements, may serve to foster legitimacy by enhancing the responsiveness of implementation practices and by increasing their participatory basis. It may well be the case that:

> historical experience of the American New Deal and European welfare states shows that the expansion of redistributive social policies has been one of the main causes of political and administrative centralisation in this century.[67]

But, as the concept of partnership illustrates, re-distribution may take shape within a framework of "shared governance" which is as much predicated upon a devolution of political authority, as it is upon its centralisation.

6. Conclusion

This chapter has explored the nature of the Community's financial instruments for economic and social cohesion. It has done so in the light of the Commission's current reform proposals and in the light of the cohesion challenge presented by EMU. It has sought to illustrate both the extent of the "cohesion gap" in the EU and the shortcomings (quantitative and qualitative) of the Community's policy response. What is clear is that monetary union in Europe is not to be accompanied by fiscal transfers between member states on a scale which is comparable to those which customarily take place in established federations.[68] To the limited extent that transfers do take place, these seek principally to address the structural, rather than the social, dimension of cohesion. Community policy in this respect continues to be predicated upon a privileging of economic

---

[67] G. Majone, "Europe's 'Democracy Deficit': The Question of Standards" (1998) 4 *ELJ* 5, p. 14.

[68] See D. Currie, *The Pros and Cons of EMU* (Economist Intelligence Unit, 1997), p. 49.

growth as the primary objective of cohesion policy, and an expectation that the benefits of such growth will "trickle-down" to the Community's poorest members.

As has been seen, economic and social incohesion is an enduring characteristic in the EU, and may be anticipated to remain so in the future. The extent to which this matters is a question of considerable debate. It is a question which is approached most frequently from a perspective of political expediency. According to this conception, it matters only to the extent that uneven economic and social development, and an uneven distribution of the costs and benefits associated with European Union, threaten the political viability of the integration project. Such reasoning may go some way in explaining the Community's relatively greater preoccupation with the geographic aspects of cohesion. The growth of nationalism in the nineteenth century, and the splintering of empire which this induced, may be attributed in part to the phenomenon of uneven development and to the emergence of spatially concentrated, and separatist, pockets of "rich" and "poor".[69] While this integration-based logic may provide a rationale for Community cohesion policy which is politically robust, it implies a conception of citizenship which is undernourished in its equality dimension. Yet, the rise of the (social democratic) left in European politics notwithstanding, there is little in the Commission's current reform proposals, or in the on-going negotiations concerning national contributions to the Community budget, to suggest a radical re-assessment of the Community's role in tackling economic and social incohesion in the foreseeable future. It is one thing to talk of social citizenship. It is quite another, in a "culture of contentment",[70] to redefine the polity in such a way as to include among the "deserving poor" the barely visible citizens of distant places.

[69] See, especially, E. Gellner, *Nations and Nationalism* (Oxford, Blackwell, 1983).
[70] J.K. Galbraith, *Culture of Contentment* (Sinclair Stevenson, 1992).

PART FOUR

Prospects

8

The Euro and European Legal Order

PAUL BEAUMONT and NEIL WALKER

1. Introduction

T HE aim of this concluding chapter is twofold. First and foremost, it
has a pragmatic purpose. It seeks to round out the analysis
provided in the preceding contributions by revisiting a number of
themes which are not only vital to the long-term health of the euro, and
indeed of the European Union (EU), but have also been the subject of interesting developments in the perinatal period of the euro during which this
book was sent to press. The themes selected are the application of the
convergence criteria which determine eligibility to join the euro-zone; the
security from political assault of the constitutional independence of the
European Central Bank (ECB); and the implications of the birth of the
euro for the uniformity or fragmentation of the legal and political order of
the EU. Of course, attempting to provide a definitive freeze-frame analysis
of a legal edifice as vibrantly new as the single currency is rather like
chasing shadows, and no doubt a few more twists will have occurred in an
increasingly complex tale by the time these words are read. Nevertheless,
we can but try to highlight key developments and anticipate emergent
trends.

The choice of these three themes also provides a useful illustrative
backdrop for a modest intervention into the broader theoretical debate
about developments in the legal order of the EU. It is widely recognised
that law has played a pivotal role in the emergence of the new transnational polity, and has faced problems and crafted solutions which in their
uniqueness reflect the unprecedented character of that polity.[1] To begin
with, unlike the state—the main unit of the traditional post-Westphalian
world order—the European Community (EC) was established as a
"Community based on law". That is to say, whereas the legal "constitution" of the state typically built upon the foundations of a pre-existing

---

[1] See, for example, J.H.H. Weiler, "The Transformation of Europe" (1991) 100 *Yale Law Journal*, pp.2403–83.

political or cultural community, the EC lacked any pre-legal identity.
Rather, it entered the institutional mosaic of the 1950s world order as a
pure creature of law

In turn, the new European polity has confronted difficulties in the
forging of its constitutional and substantive law which are rooted in its
"nonstate"[2] character. Constitutionally, the key dynamic has been provided
by the "dual structure"[3] of the institutional order of the EU. On the one
hand, the legal-constitutional structure of the EU, notably through the
early development by the European Court of Justice (ECJ) of the doctrines
of supremacy and direct effect, has been bold in its fashioning and robust
in its defence of a uniform "supranational" order. On the other hand, until
recently the balance of power within the political constitution of the EU
remained with the states. Major decision-making conformed to an "inter-
governmental" logic, with each member state retaining an effective power
of veto. Yet there was a crucial nexus between these apparently divergent
constitutional processes. The development and sustenance of a legal
constitution which asserted the priority of European law over domestic
legal orders was made possible because of—not in spite of—the pro-state
bias of political decision-making. Put simply, the states could afford a
strong supranational legal order because they continued to control the law-
making process. However, since the passage of the Single European Act,
with the gradual shift of the terms of political decision-making away from
the state veto and towards qualified majority voting (QMV), member
states have become more sceptical about the supranational legal order. The
constitutional primacy of the treaty framework and of the ECJ as its
authoritative interpreter have become less readily accepted and more
frequently challenged.

Many of the difficulties associated with the efficacy and legitimacy of
the corpus of substantive EC law are also distinctive. Unlike domestic law,
substantive EC law is primarily economic in focus.[4] Unlike domestic
economic law, moreover, the economic law of the EC is primarily of a
regulatory character. The EU lacks the tools, resources and authority of
the classical dirigiste state. It cannot rely upon public ownership, planning
or centralised administration as its infrastructure of legal control. Rather,
exaggerating a trend which is also discernible at the state level, the
economic law of the EU operates through a framework of rules which seek

---

[2] W. Streeck and P. C. Schmitter, "From National Corporation to Transnational
Pluralism: Organized Interests in the Single European Market" (1991) 19 *Politics and
Society*, pp.133–164, at 152.

[3] J.H.H. Weiler, "The Community System: The Dual Character of Supranationalism", 1
Yearbook of European Law, pp.268–306.

[4] See, for example, C. Joerges, "The Europeanization of Economic and Monetary Policy"
in R. Dehousse (ed.), *Europe after Maastricht: An Ever Closer Union?* (Munchen, Beck,
1994) pp.29–62.

to control or influence the manner in which institutionally distinct private and public enterprises conduct their operations.[5] Furthermore, in developing this indirect regulatory regime, the EU typically has to seek to resolve two dilemmas simultaneously. First, it has to achieve a workable balance between state and market. Its legal interventions must respect the operation and discipline of markets, yet also acknowledge and address both the possibility of market failure and the need to qualify market objectives in pursuit of public goods. Secondly, in so doing EU law has to be mindful of the proper balance of public authority between the national level and its own supranational level. It cannot be the only, or even necessarily the dominant, hand on the governmental tiller within the EU

In pondering these various tensions in the development of the European legal order, the difficulties associated with the euro my be treated as a "metaphor"[6] for the difficulties associated with the EU more generally. The three themes chosen for extended treatment in this chapter match the three levels of analysis of the problematic distinctiveness of EU law. The terms and contextual application of the convergence criteria address the dual regulatory problem of finding an accommodation between public authority and market, and between different levels of public authority. Scepticism towards the constitutional independence of the ECB reflects broader concerns about the legitimacy and status of the constitutional text. And the challenge to the basic unity of the European legal order raises in a very acute fashion the question of the continuing relevance of the EC's foundational claim to be an entity based upon the normative authority and instrumental capacities of *law* rather than any other medium of power.

More generally, the three illustrative examples serve to emphasise that the relationship between part and whole—between the legal dimension of European Union and European Union as a broader social and political project—is one of dynamic cause and effect. We should not simply see law as a normative support lending authority to the EU and as an instrumental resource concerned with the technical achievement of it objectives. That law was so central to the initial design of the EC does not mean that it can be relied upon indefinitely as the motor of European integration. Law is no reified entity standing outside of the social and political processes of the EU.[7] It is also a product of these processes, and where, as in the context of

---

[5] See for example, G. Majone, "The Rise of the Regulatory State in Europe", (1994) 17 *West European Politics*, pp.77–101.

[6] For a broader treatment of the metaphorical significance of EMU, see F. Snyder, "EMU —Metaphor for European Union? Institutions, Rules and Types of Regulation" in R. Dehousse (ed) *supra* n. 4, pp.63–99.

[7] For a cogent critique of the still widespread assumption of much legal analysis of the EU that law and integration are symbiotically linked, see J. Shaw, "European Union Legal Studies in Crisis? Towards a New Dynamic", 16 *Oxford Journal of Legal Studies*, pp.321–53; "Introduction" in J. Shaw and G.More (eds.) *New Legal Dynamics of European Union*, (Oxford, Clarendon, 1995), pp.1–14.

such a significant shift in scale and direction of the European project as Economic and Monetary Union (EMU), its instrumental capacity and normative authority meet new obstacles and new forms of resistance, the long-term standing of law as a technical and symbolic resource within the EU may be affected. Just as it is no exaggeration to suggest that the fate of the euro depends in significant measure upon the adequacy of its legal regulation, so too the prospects for law *in general* as a steering mechanism for the next generation of supranational development will be affected by how it responds to the multi-faceted challenge of currency integration.

2. Applying the Convergence Criteria[8]

The political drive of the Maastricht Treaty, agreed in 1991 but not in force until November 1993,[9] was to create a single currency no later than 1 January 1999 under the control of an independent central bank modelled on the Bundesbank. This was intended to deliver low inflation, a stable currency, and provide the most tangible evidence of the everyday relevance of the EU for its over three hundred million citizens. However the member states of Northern Europe, particularly Germany and the Netherlands, did not want to sacrifice their strong currencies and low inflation for the sake of visible signs of European Union. Membership of the euro-zone, there-fore, would have to be made subject to member states' controlling their economies in a way that made them fit to be part of it. The euro-zone would be unsustainable if the economic divergences between the countries making up the zone were too great.

Thus the framers of the Maastricht Treaty were faced with the classic double dilemma of European economic law discussed in the introduction. In the first place, since something had to be done to ensure that the member states participating in the single currency had economies which would not undermine the currency and the goal of price stability, various macro-economic thresholds for membership would have to be set and applied at the supranational level. Yet this strategy had an inherently paradoxical quality. The concern to preserve national economic self-interest in the shift to a single currency actually encouraged a stricter regime of central control. In a scenario of impeccable economic logic but precarious political legitimacy, the dangers to individual states of a collec-tive solution could only be answered by making that central solution stronger rather than weaker. In the second place, the establishment of macro-economic thresholds inevitably, and properly, involved reference to

---

[8] See also Chs. 1 and 4 *supra* by John Usher and Ian Harden.

[9] In large part because of the Danish "No" in the 1992 referendum and the challenge in the German Constitutional Court to its lawfulness; see *Brunner* v. *The European Union Treaty* [1994] 1 CMLR 57.

measures which were beyond the direct control or easy manipulation of national governments. But while some degree of autonomous market discipline was necessary, it raised in acute form the question of the proper balance of state versus market in the crafting of economic law. After all, what remained fundamentally a political process could not defer completely to the hidden hand of economic forces.

It was in the light of these concerns that the Maastricht Treaty and its associated Protocols established economic targets, known as the convergence criteria, which had to be fulfilled before a member state could join the zone. And it was in the light of these same concerns that between 1991 and May 1998 much speculation arose as to how hard member states would work to meet the convergence criteria; how strictly they would be interpreted; and whether strategic *political* visions, whether of a European Union moving forward together, or, conversely, of a fragmented Europe in which individual states can pick and choose their speed and areas of integration,[10] would prevail over economic and legal discipline to the extent that any state which wanted to join the euro-zone could do so, and any which wanted to stay out could do so.

In May 1998 the Heads of Government met in the Council to decide which states had fulfilled the convergence criteria and therefore qualified to be in the first wave of the single currency commencing on 1 January 1999.[11] The first and last convergence criteria presented a problem only for Greece.[12] The average rate of inflation in the year ending January 1998 for the three best performing member states (Austria, France and Ireland) was 1.2 per cent; the reference value, therefore, was 2.7 per cent and fourteen of the member states had inflation below that level. The average long-term interest rates in the three countries which performed the best on inflation was 5.8 per cent; the reference value, therefore, was 7.8 per cent and

---

[10] It is noteworthy that the two polar opposite visions of the European legal order – Europe as uniformity and Europe *a la carte* – tend to display greatest disregard for the complexities of the existing legal template of integration. The models which are placed at intermediate points on the integration/differentiation continuum, including multi-speed Europe, Europe of concentric circles and Europe of sector-by-sector flexible integration, tend to be more easily compatible with existing legal arrangements and tendencies. For discussion of the political underpinnings and legal ramifications of these general models, see, for example, N. Walker, "Sovereignty and Differentiated Integration in the European Union", (1998) 4(4) *European Law Journal*, pp.355–88, 362–69.

[11] See Art. 121(4) (ex 109j(4)) EC. The special composition of the Council reflects the fundamental importance of the decision as does the procedure leading up to it whereby the Commission made a recommendation on which states had qualified to join the euro, after both the Commission and the EMI had reported on whether the convergence criteria had been fulfilled, then the Council, in the composition of the economic and finance ministers, made a recommendation to the Council meeting in the composition of the Heads of Government and finally the European Parliament was consulted before the Heads of Government made their decision.

[12] At the relevant date it had inflation of 5.2% and long-term interest rates of 9.8%.

fourteen of the member states had long-term interest rates below that level.

When it came to the second criterion of avoiding an excessive government deficit the Treaty clearly allowed the political institutions much discretion in deciding what this meant. To begin with, Article 2 of the Protocol on the Convergence Criteria provides that this criterion is met if at the time of the examination of the member state by the Council it is not subject to a Council decision under Article 104(6) (ex 104c(6)) EC that an excessive deficit exists. That Article gives the Council significant scope in that it acts by a qualified majority on a recommendation from the Commission, and therefore does not need unanimity to amend the recommendation as it would were it a proposal from the Commission,[13] after making "an overall assessment" of whether an excessive deficit exists.

In making its recommendation, the Commission uses as a starting point the reference values stipulated in the Protocol on the excessive deficit procedure (i.e. 3 per cent for the ratio of the planned or actual government deficit to gross domestic product at market prices (the deficit ratio) and 60 per cent for the ratio of government debt to gross domestic product at market prices (the debt ratio)). However, Article 104(2) (ex 104c(2)) EC grants the Commission considerable discretion in allowing states to exceed the reference values and still be regarded as not having an excessive deficit. In relation to the deficit ratio a figure above 3 per cent can be condoned if:

> either the ratio has declined substantially and continuously and reached a level that comes close to the reference value; or, alternatively, the excess over the reference value is only exceptional and temporary and the ratio remains close to the reference value.

In relation to the debt ratio a figure above 60 per cent can be condoned if the ratio is "sufficiently diminishing and approaching the reference value at a satisfactory pace".

An early warning that the Commission intended to take advantage of the flexibility given to it by the Treaty was the decision in 1995 not to recommend a finding that Ireland had an excessive deficit even though it still had a debt ratio of 93.1 per cent.[14] By the time of the Council Decision of 3 May 1998[15] all the member states had achieved the deficit ratio target but only four (Finland, France, Luxembourg and the UK) had achieved the debt ratio target. Nonetheless, the Commission were able to recommend that all the other states apart from Greece did not have an excessive deficit in terms of Article 104(2) (ex 104c(2)) because the ratio was sufficiently diminishing and approaching the reference value at a satisfactory pace.

---

[13] See Art. 250(1) (ex 189a(1)) EC.

[14] See p.655 of Weatherill and Beaumont, *EC Law* (Harmondsworth, Penguin, 1995, 2nd ed.). See also the new 3rd edition in 1999 entitled *EU Law* at p. 771.

[15] Decision 98/317 OJ 1998 L139/30.

This recommendation seems at odds with the facts in three cases: Germany's debt ratio rose in 1997 and was above 60 per cent; Italy's debt ratio had reduced from 123 per cent in 1994 to 121.6 per cent in 1997; and Belgium's debt ratio had reduced from 142 per cent in 1994 to 122.2 per cent in 1997. The Italian reduction of 1.4 per cent in three years is surely not a sufficient diminishing in the debt and at that rate of improvement it would not reach the reference value of 60 per cent for nearly 135 years. It is incredulous to regard that figure as a "satisfactory pace"!

Clearly, reflecting the pressure to qualify economic orthodoxy in accordance with political imperatives, it was untenable that Germany should not be part of the euro at its foundation. In turn, once the rules are bent to accommodate one political preference it becomes harder to resist other political arguments against rigid application of the legal norms. It may also be that the Commission felt the debt ratio was the least important of the convergence criteria and that a state bringing high levels of debt into the euro-zone is unlikely to destabilise the euro if that state has, and will maintain, a low deficit or even a surplus on the annual budget.[16] So the legal rules were bent to allow the states into the euro-zone which were founder members of the European Economic Community in the 1950s.

The last convergence criterion relates to exchange rate stability. Again the Treaty provides the political institutions with a significant degree of interpretative latitude.[17] Article 121(1) (ex 109j(1)) EC sets out the exchange rate criterion in the third indent and then adds a significant rider in the fourth indent. The third indent requires states aspiring to join the euro-zone to observe:

> the normal fluctuation margins provided for by the exchange-rate mechanism of the European Monetary System, for at least two years, without devaluing against the currency of any other Member State.

It does not expressly require the state to be a member of the exchange-rate mechanism (ERM) of the European Monetary System (EMS), just to

---

[16] The lack of importance of the debt ratio to monetary policy was stated by Sir Nigel Wicks, then a member of the EMI, in his evidence to the House of Lords Select Committee on the European Communities, see Q 112 in *The European Central Bank: will it work?*, Session 1997–98, 24th Report (hereinafter *The European Central Bank: will it work?*). He did not think the debt ratios of themselves affected monetary conditions but rather the criterion was included to reinforce the no-bail out provisions in the Treaty (Art. 103 (ex 104b) EC). The guarantee that states within the euro-zone will continue to run a broadly balancing budget over the medium term is the Stability and Growth Pact, discussed *infra* and by A. Scott and I. Harden in Chs. 2 and 4 *supra*.

[17] The fact that the convergence criteria were not automatic and were subject to political evaluation was recognised by the German Constitutional Court in its judgment of 31 March 1998, 2 BvR 1877/97 and 2 BvR 50/98, deciding that it was lawful under the German Constitution for Germany to join the euro-zone. For an analysis of this case see M. Everson in Ch. 6 *supra*.

respect the normal fluctuation margins of that mechanism for two years. The rider in the fourth indent is a reference to the member state's "participation in the exchange-rate mechanism of the European Monetary System". So an aspiring member of the euro-zone has to have been in the ERM prior to the decision to admit it to the euro-zone but it does not need to have been in it for two years. A further complication is that the third indent must be read in the light of Article 3 of the Protocol on the Convergence Criteria which says what it shall mean; i.e.:

> that a Member State has respected the normal fluctuation margins provided for by the exchange-rate mechanism of the European Monetary System without severe tensions for at least the last two years before the examination. In particular, the Member State shall not have devalued its currency's bilateral central rate against any other Member State's currency on its own initiative for the same period.[18]

Thus a member state is able to devalue the currency, despite what it says in the Treaty, and still qualify provided it does not do so "on its own initiative".

In the context of the decision as to which states would join the euro in January 1999 the Commission struck an ambivalent note in its treatment of what constitutes the normal fluctuation margins. In its Report on Progress Towards Convergence it used the normal fluctuation margin at the time the Maastricht Treaty was agreed, namely plus or minus 2.25 per cent around each currency's central rate against the median currency in the ERM grid.[19] Yet in the Recommendation of the same day, it recognised that the widening of the margins of fluctuation to plus or minus fifteen per cent "modified the framework" for assessing exchange rate stability.[20] The Report also indicates that the Commission was prepared to tolerate fluctuations of more than plus or minus 2.25 per cent[21] and that the fact that Italy and Finland had not been in the ERM for the full two years of the review period (March 1996 to February 1998) was not a barrier to their entry to the euro-zone.

The final Council Decision[22] of the Heads of Government does not

[18] This is an extraordinary piece of drafting given that the text in the EC Treaty and in the Protocol were agreed as part of the Maastricht Treaty. Why did the draftsmen create two texts at the same time and say that one will mean what the other says? If there is a rational explanation it eludes the authors.

[19] The Commission Convergence Report of 25 March 1998, 1.2. See the discussion by J. Usher in Ch. 1 *supra*.

[20] The Commission Recommendation of 25 March 1998, recital 8.

[21] Spain, France, Portugal were said to have "almost always traded within" the plus or minus 2.25% fluctuation during the review period (see 1.3.4., 1.3.5, and 1.3.11), Finland, since it joined in October 1996, "most of the time traded within" the plus or minus 2.25% fluctuation (see 1.3.12.) and, most interestingly, Ireland was accepted although it traded beyond its plus or minus 2.25% margin "for an extended period of time" (see 1.3.6.).

[22] Decision 98/317 OJ 1998 L139/30.

mention the "normal fluctuation margins" at all, far less adjudicate on whether it is to be regarded as 2.25 per cent or 15 per cent. Instead it applies the rest of the formula from the Protocol on Convergence Criteria; that the particular currency "has not been subject to severe tensions" and that the country "has not devalued, on its own initiative, the . . . bilateral central rate against any other Member State's currency". The Council Decision's approach to states which were not in the ERM for the full two years, Finland and Italy, is to say that the criterion mentioned in the third indent of Article 121(1) (ex 109j(1)) EC is satisfied because the currency "has displayed sufficient stability in the last two years". The Decision explicitly confirms that both the Finnish marka and the Italian lira "appreciated vis-a-vis the ERM currencies" during the first part of the two year review period, prior to the entry of those currencies into the ERM. One can see here the careful hand of the legal functionary in crafting the political decisions in accordance with the text of the convergence criteria, though a pedant might have expected them specifically to state that the appreciation of the currencies during that period did not go beyond the normal fluctuation margins of the ERM.[23]

The treatment of Sweden is noteworthy because the Swedish Government was politically disinclined to join the euro in January 1999 but, unlike Denmark and the UK, did not have an opt-out. The Commission Report indicates that during the review period the Swedish currency was not part of the ERM and that the Swedish krona "has fluctuated against the ERM currencies" and therefore does not fulfil the exchange rate criterion. However the Report does not attempt to give figures as to how wide the fluctuation of the Swedish currency was against the ERM currencies and instead talks about nominal effective exchange rates.[24] The Council Decision states that Sweden does not fulfil the convergence criterion mentioned in the third indent of Article 121(1) (ex 109j(1)) EC on the basis of the following statement:

> the currency of Sweden has never participated in the ERM; in the two years under review, the Swedish krona (SEK) fluctuated against the ERM currencies

---

[23] The "normal fluctuation margins" is a key part of the test laid down by Art. 3 of the Protocol on the Convergence Criteria so it is arguable that the lawyers, and the Council, erred in ignoring it. The detailed information on the Finnish and Italian currencies is available in the Commission's Convergence Report of 25 March 1998 (see 5.2.2.) and this shows that the Council were deliberately avoiding referring to normal fluctuation margins because they did not want to explicitly decide on the debate between plus or minus 2.25% or plus or minus 15% as the "normal" figure. At their most diverse moments during the period before joining the ERM Italy's currency was 8% below its future central rate against the median currency and Finland's currency was 4.2% below its future central rate against the median currency.

[24] See 5.2.3. of the Report which shows that Sweden's nominal effective exchange rate had a variation of as much as 5% and that its exchange rate with the German mark followed a similar trend but with "larger amplitude". The lack of figures from the Commission was surely an attempt to force the Council's hand into deciding that the exchange rate criterion had not been met.

reflecting among others [sic] the absence of an exchange rate target.

Clearly the rider in the fourth indent about participation in the ERM would have provided a basis for the Council simply to say that complete non-participation in the ERM is a barrier to membership of the euro-zone. However, the Council chose to go further and make statements about fluctuation and exchange rate targets. Why did it not stick to its formula about severe tensions and the absence of unilateral devaluation which it used for all the other states who did get to join the euro-zone? No evidence is given that the Swedish currency traded outside plus or minus fifteen per cent fluctuation margins with any ERM currency. It is hard to resist the conclusion that the terms of the decision reflect a determination to dress up a political decision in the cloak of economically-corroborated legal neutrality. Yet the fact remains that the exclusion of Sweden from the euro-zone in January 1999 shows that membership of that zone is voluntary. Quite simply, Sweden chose to remain outside the zone and was able to make that choice happen by not participating in the ERM and by not giving the degree of independence to its national central bank required by the EC Treaty.[25]

The only state which wanted to join the euro-zone but which was excluded was Greece. Why was it not permitted to join the party? First, it failed to meet all the convergence criteria, not just one. Arguably, while some rule-bending is possible, blatant disregard for legal rules and economic realities is too much even for the most euro-fanatical of politicians. Secondly, and perhaps more pertinently, it is a small, peripheral economy that joined the Community only in the 1980s and, unlike Portugal, which is in the same category, it did not force its way into the euro-zone club by complying with all the rules. However, even Greece was offered warm words by the politicians of the Council in order to encourage it in its economic endeavours to achieve the convergence criteria by 2001.[26]

Of course all the convergence criteria and their interpretation still have relevance for states like Greece who want to join the euro-zone; possibly,

[25] See Arts. 108 and 109 (ex 107 and 108) EC. National Central Banks must be independent and the Governors of National Central Banks must be appointed for at least five years, see Art. 14 of the Protocol on the Statute of the ESCB. This is to ensure that the Governing Council of the ECB, which takes the crucial decisions on money supply and interest rates, is made up of persons independent of the governments of member states. The composition of the Governing Council is the Executive Board of 6 members and the 11 Governors of National Central Banks in the euro-zone. By and large simple majority prevails in the Governing Council, see Art. 12 of the Protocol on the ESCB.

[26] In May 1998 the Council made a statement on Greek Convergence stating that: "The Council notes the substantial progress achieved by Greece towards meeting the convergence criteria. The Greek Government's determination to pursue its policies of fiscal consolidation and structural adjustment with a view to joining Stage 3 of EMU by 1 January 2001 is welcomed. At that time Greece's progress will be judged in the same way as that of the Member States which will join EMU on 1 January 1999."

Denmark, Sweden and the UK who may yet decide that they want to join; and states still to join the Union which may in time seek to join the euro-zone. The Council's message to future aspirants to the euro-zone is that some participation in the ERM is necessary, even if not for two years, and that if the participation is relatively short perhaps the state will have more chance of being admitted to the euro-zone if it had an exchange rate target with the euro before joining the ERM.

The implications for policy in the UK are interesting. The Bank of England currently eschews exchange rate targets and the UK has no intention, at the time of writing, of joining ERM Mark II.[27] Given that a referendum[28] on joining the single currency is highly unlikely until after the next general election (and therefore will probably not be held until late 2001 or 2002 at the earliest) it may be that unless the UK joins the ERM before the referendum or the Bank of England adopts an exchange rate target with the euro, the UK would, on a cautious reading of the legal runes, have to wait for over a year after the referendum to establish a long enough membership of the ERM before being able to join the euro-zone. However, the politicians may find a way of squaring the legal circle. It could be decided that minimal participation in the ERM is enough to satisfy the fourth indent and that keeping sterling within plus or minus fifteen per cent of the euro

[27] The British Prime Minister, Tony Blair, in an answer to the Leader of the Opposition in Parliament on Wednesday 24 February 1999 denied that the government had any intention of taking the UK into ERM II, explicitly making the point that other states had not been disqualified from joining the euro even though their membership of the Exchange Rate Mechanism had been less than two years (HC Debs., 24 February 1999, cols. 383–84).Treasury sources also made it clear that the government did not intend to ask the Bank of England to have an exchange rate target with the euro, see *The Times*, 25 February 1999. ERM II was established by the Resolution of the European Council on the establishment of an exchange-rate mechanism in the third stage of economic and monetary union of 16 June 1997, OJ 1997 C236/5.

[28] As we were finalising this chapter the UK Prime Minister made a statement to the House of Commons on Tuesday 23 February 1999 launching the *Outline National Changeover Plan* (London, HM Treasury, 1999) available on the web at http://www.euro.gov.uk/oncop.pdf. In chs. 1.4 and 2.4 of the *Plan* the following carefully crafted words appear: "Barring some fundamental and unforeseen change in economic circumstances, making a decision, during this Parliament, to join is not realistic. But preparations should be made in this Parliament so that, should the economic tests be met, a decision to join a successful single currency can be made early in the next Parliament. Without preparation, it is not a practical option. The British people should be in a position to exercise genuine choice."

[29] Para. 2.1. of the Resolution of the European Council, n. 27 supra, establishes that the ERM Mark II, which began on 1 January 1999 with a membership of Denmark, Greece and the euro-zone, has "one standard fluctuation band of plus or minus 15 per cent" around the currency's central rate against the euro. Although para. 2.4. allows for states to negotiate a narrower band with the euro-zone if they so wish, para. 2.5. explicitly states that: "The standard and narrower bands shall not prejudice the interpretation of the third indent of Article [121(1) (ex 109j(1))] of the Treaty." This last point leaves the Council free to put its own gloss on the interpretation of the third indent.

for two years prior to the examination is enough[29] to satisfy the third indent. Therefore, on this hypothesis, the UK could join the euro-zone very quickly after the referendum, perhaps in time for the withdrawal of the validity of national bank notes in the euro-zone on 1 July 2002.

In fact, however, the UK Government on 23 February 1999 announced a timetable for UK entry to the euro[30] which would be compatible with two-year membership of the ERM Mark II before joining, but which scrupulously avoids any mention of joining another ERM. The political ghosts of the UK's ignominious exit from ERM I still haunt Westminster and it is not surprising that the Government is not yet ready to say it will join another ERM. The government's timetable for joining the euro refers to a period of four months from its decision after the general election to recommend joining the euro until a referendum can be held, and then a further twenty-four to thirty months from the date of the referendum before the UK can join the euro. The reasons given for this long transitional period relate to the time it will take for retail banks and large retailers to change their systems and train their staff for adoption of the euro (up to thirty-six months), for the Royal Mint to produce sufficient coins (up to thirty months), and for some government departments to change their technology and staff (up to four years).[31] Due to the very long time needed for public sector changes, the Government has authorised preparations to begin ahead of the result of the referendum to reduce the four-year period post-referendum to at most thirty months.[32] Finally, the Government envisages a period of between two and six months when both the euro notes and coins and sterling would be in circulation before the latter is withdrawn. So even on a best case analysis of a summer 2001 UK general election, followed by a referendum in October 2001, it will be October 2003 before the UK joins the euro.

The question still arises, how long will the UK be required to be a member of ERM II before it can join the euro in 2003? Of the two scenarios outlined above, of at least a year or just a few months, which is the more likely? Our analysis of this particular area of European economic law-in-context suggests the latter. The mixture of "soft law",[33] executive discretion, alternative standards and informal and non-binding "jurisprudence" which characterises the text and application of the convergence criteria, suggests that the use of law in this way as such an overt tool of economic policy is highly susceptible to politically-motivated challenge and exceptionalism. Arguably, this is not just the inevitably precarious outcome of seeking to resolve the double dilemma of European economic

[30] See the *National Changeover Plan* , *supra* n. 28.

[31] *Ibid.* at Ch. 3.

[32] *Ibid.* Ch.5.

[33] On the centrality of soft law, albeit in an increasingly "juridicized" form, to the regulation of EMU generally, see Snyder, n. 6 *supra*.

law. It also tells us something more general about the evolution of legal form and technique within and beyond the EU. What we observe in the transparent use of law in pursuit of a particular economic orthodoxy is evidence of a wider process of "instrumentalisation"[34] of law, which involves, *inter alia*, the increasing "de-differentiation"[35] of legal method from other forms of policy implementation. It is unsurprising that this development, which tests the resilience of a more normative image of law as the repository of shared meanings and values, should leave already highly "instrumentalised" law vulnerable to the challenge of other forms of instrumental rationality, including the barely disguised political instrumentality of those member states who want to join the club on precisely their own terms.

3. The Constitutional Independence of the Central Bank

As John Usher demonstrated in the first chapter of this book, the creation of the euro is one of the most blatant examples of the leading politicians in Europe regarding themselves as being above the legal constitution of the EU. The ECJ may regard the EC Treaty as the constitutional charter of the European Union[36] but the Heads of Government meeting in the European Council were quite prepared to change the name of the single currency from the "ECU" to the "euro" without amending the Treaty. Even when the opportunity presented itself to do so in the Amsterdam Treaty the politicians were so frightened of reopening the provisions on economic and monetary union that not only did they fail to change "ECU" to "euro" but they retained the co-operation procedure, in this area alone, when otherwise it could have been consigned to history and the legislative procedures of the EU rationalised and improved with significant benefits in transparency.

At the time of the first appointment in 1998 all the members of the Executive Board were appointed for periods of between four and eight years in accordance with the rule in Article 50 of the Protocol on the Statute of the European System of Central Banks (ESCB) on the initial appointment of the Executive Board. Interestingly the only member of the Executive Board which that provision requires to be appointed for the full eight years is the President. It was this binding legal requirement that was

---

[34] See for example, R. Cotterrell, "Law's Community: Legal Theory and the Image of Legality", (1992) 19 *Journal of Law and Society,* pp. 405–22.

[35] See for example, M. Galanter, "Law Abounding: Legalisation around the North Atlantic", (1992) 55 *Modern Law Review*, pp.1–24, at 18.

[36] See Case 294/83 *Les Verts* v. *European Parliament* [1986] ECR 1339; Case C–2/Imm *Zwartveld* [1990] ECR I–3365; and Opinion 1/91 *Opinion on the draft agreement on a European Economic Area* [1991] ECR I–6079.

at the root of one of the greatest controversies surrounding the launch of the euro. France wanted the Governor of the French Central Bank, M Jean-Claude Trichet, to become the President of the ECB and Germany[37] and the Netherlands wanted Dr Wim Duisenberg, the Dutchman who was the President of the European Monetary Institute (EMI), the transitional body set up to prepare the way for the ECB to become its first President. For France the battle was not about the way in which the ECB should be managed but rather a traditional EU issue of national virility or "jobs for the boys". As Brussels got the Commission and Council, France insisted that Strasbourg should keep the plenary sessions of the European Parliament no matter how much it hampers the effectiveness of the MEPs and subjects them to needless and expensive travel. Likewise, as Germany had been awarded the seat of the ECB in Frankfurt, France should have the honour of one of its citizens being the first President of the Bank rather than a person who could be caricatured as a former poodle of the Bundesbank.

One of the rich ironies of European politics is that the UK held the Presidency of the Council of the EU during the first six months of 1998. Nothing very tangible was achieved apart from some indifferent cartoon style drawings decorating the walls of the Council's building in Brussels—the breathtakingly boring, Justus Lipsius Building—and the decisions surrounding the launch of the euro in May 1998. In the former context the new Labour Government was able to parade the end of UK semi-detached European diplomacy with some cool Britannia, and in the latter context Tony Blair strode the stage of Europe playing the disinterested honest broker who could find the third way between eight years for M Trichet and eight years for Dr Duisenberg. An eleventh hour deal was done. Legal niceties would be observed and Dr Duisenberg would be appointed for eight years. However, the French price was high. This proud man was to be compelled to go on record in front of the Heads of Government saying that he would resign some time during his eight year appointment, probably about half way through. The other Heads of Government were in turn to limit the discretion of their successors by informally agreeing that when Dr Duisenberg retired M Trichet would be appointed for a full eight-year term. Dr Duisenberg stated to the assembled Heads of Government that in view of his age he would "not want to serve the full term" of eight years. He made it clear he would not resign before the withdrawal of national notes from circulation on 1 July 2002. Curiously, however, Dr Duisenberg also observed that "in the future the decision to resign will be my decision

---

[37] Germany and the Netherlands have long been close allies in monetary policy and this was cemented by the decision to maintain 2.25% fluctuation margins between the mark and the guilder at the time when the ERM increased the margins to plus or minus 15%. It is notable that Dr Duisenberg was at the time the head of the Netherlands Central Bank and therefore effectively compelled to follow every move that the Bundesbank made.

alone" and therefore he could insist on his legal right to serve the full eight years, or at least substantially more than the three and a half years he has already committed himself to.[38] Thus the political deal could come unstuck if Dr Duisenberg decides to serve the full eight year term as President. This possibility, which Dr Duisenberg refused to discount in subsequent utterances around the time of the launch of the euro, really would be a test of the independence of the ECB. In such an eventuality the politicians would have no legal means of removing Dr Duisenberg from office and no way of curbing the independence of the ECB (short of Treaty amendment).

The one significant power which the Council does have, apart from the unlikely eventuality of agreeing an ERM between the euro and non-member states,[39] is its right to participate in the meetings of the Governing Council of the ECB.[40] This is the body which determines interest rates for the euro-zone and controls the money supply. The ECB hopes to keep a thick veil of secrecy over its deliberations. Minutes will not be published, unlike the monetary policy committee of the Bank of England. Thus the money markets will only know what the President of the ECB wants them to know about the reasons lying behind interest rate decisions.[41] The collegiate nature of the ECB decision-making is to be protected from scrutiny at the expense of transparency. This is a long, if questionably honourable, legal tradition in the EC as the same collegiality hides disagreements in the Commission and in the Court of Justice where public dissent is not allowed. If Dr Duisenberg were to carry on for more than four years would the representative of the Council attending the Governing Council of the Bank, especially if he or she happened to be French, start making the President's job very difficult by briefing against him using the inside knowledge gleaned from being present in the holy of holies? However far-fetched such a scenario is, and however unacceptably Machiavellian these consequences, it would nonetheless be a refreshing check on the cavalier attitude of the Council to the constitutional source of its legitimacy, the EC Treaty,

---

[38] The oral statement, as recorded on the EU's website – http://europa.eu.int/index-en-htm, contains this eloquent testimony to how embarrassed Dr Duisenberg must have been at having to appease the French and their allies: "I wish to emphasise that this is my decision and my decision alone and it is entirely of my own free will and mine alone and not under pressure from anyone that I have decided not to serve the full term." The fact that this was not his preferred option is also clear from his evidence to the House of Lords Select Committee on the European Communities on 24 February 1998 when he had said he would not accept appointment as President of the ECB if it was on condition that it would be "only for a limited period", see *The European Central Bank: will it work?*.

[39] See Art. 111 (ex 109) EC. See n.49 *infra*.

[40] See Art. 113(1) (ex 109b) EC.

[41] After each meeting of the Governing Council there will be a press conference and the release of the President of the ECB's introductory statement which will give a summary of the conclusions of the Governing Council, as for example after the meeting in Frankfurt on 4 February 1999. See the ECB website - http://www.ecb.int.

if Dr Duisenberg were to change his mind, now that he is no longer under duress, and prove the independence of the ECB by adhering to the constitution and serving the full eight-year term.

Although the controversy surrounding the appointment of Dr Duisenberg is an embarrassing example of petty nationalism in the EU, the two candidates for the job were both equally committed to the ECB's primary objective of price stability. On this occasion there was not a fight for the economic soul of the ECB and therefore the compromise struck, however shabby, should not have long-term implications for the stability of the euro. By the same token, the fact that such a serious threat to the independence of the ECB should have been made without a commensurably serious argument of principle being brought to bear, whether about macro-economic strategy or the proper constitutional balance between independence and democratic accountability,[42] raises even more profound questions about respect for the rule of law—even the highest manifestation of that law in a constitutional provision—amongst the political elite of the EU.

It was a safe bet that the deal would be immune from successful legal challenge.[43] Non-privileged applicants would not have standing to bring an action in the Court of First Instance (CFI), none of the member states would bring an action in the Court of Justice because they agreed to the deal in the shape of their Heads of Governments, and the Council made the deal. The ECB would hardly create a constitutional crisis at the beginning of its life before it had established the confidence of the markets. So the Council only had to fear possible action from the Commission and the European Parliament. Doubtless there were collective sighs of relief when the two months' time limit expired without either of them launching an action in the Court of Justice.

Changing the name of the single currency is essentially a trivial matter

---

[42] There clearly are important questions about the democratic accountability of the new EMU regime which have not yet been satisfactorily answered in law or in practice. One aspect of this is the question of transparency, considered in the text *supra*. Another aspect is the adequacy of the conditions and procedures for dialogue between the economic institutions and the democratic institutions, as considered by M. Everson in Ch. 6 *supra*. A third aspect, whose relevance is inescapable when considering the adequacy of accountability within all new areas of EU institution-building, concerns the adequacy or otherwise of the representative quality of existing democratic institutions of the EU, on which new structures have no alternative but to build. On the long shadow cast by the existing "democratic deficit", see R. Elgie, "Democratic Accountability and Central Bank Independence: Historical and Contemporary, National and European Perspectives", (1998) 21 *West European Politics*, 53–76. Of course, none of these considerations would justify blatant disregard of the constitutional provisions concerning the security of tenure of the President of the ECB. What is more, even if proper constitutional form was observed, it is hard to imagine how a measure so crude as reduction in the President's tenure could ever be viewed as a coherent and satisfactory answer to the complex problem of democratic accountability.

[43] For some discussion of this issue see P. Craig, Ch. 5 *supra*.

and perhaps reflects the fact that the EU has far too much detail in its constitution which would be better left to more flexible secondary provisions. The Treaty drafters should have referred to a generic term like "the european single currency" rather than a name like the "ECU". Manipulating the period of office of the President of the Central Bank is more serious. The eight-year term was a carefully chosen period to ensure stability and to remove political influence by making the term long enough that it could be made non-renewable.[44] By trying to compel the candidate to waive his entitlement to a reasonably long period of office the politicians were changing the constitutional balance. There is now no guarantee that future candidates will not be forced to do likewise, leading to a series of short term appointments which could destabilise the ECB.

Thus this example also makes the point that the political scepticism, even hostility, which has begun to be generated against the legal constitution of the EU since the move towards qualified majoritarianism may have a cumulative effect, and efforts to side-step or contradict the fundamental text may become normalised and casualised. Of course, the language of constitutional convention might be invoked to dignify such a systematic departure from the clear constitutional text, and constitutional realists would remind us that every constitutional order generates its own conventions, and that the EU itself is no stranger to such devices.[45] Yet we should surely be wary to accept this convenient dilution of constitutional integrity. Departures by way of convention from the constitutional text are most easily defended in the context of constitutional orders in which formal amendment is difficult and infrequent, and where constitutional norms, *including* a limited subset of non-legal conventional norms, tend to be highly resilient. The increasingly frequent invocation of the Inter Governmental Conference and the increasingly rapid substantive and structural transformation of the EU constitutional order suggest that this defence is not available in the European context. Informal executive renegotiation of the constitutional order in the short intervals between the iterative operation of the formal treaty amendment mechanism, itself run as a closed-shop by national executives, hardly contributes to the solemnity and the legitimacy of the supranational constitutional order. Indeed, it lends added vigour to the potentially corrosive argument, still very much alive, that by dint of its roots, structure, vision and authority, the EU lacks

---

[44] By way of contrast members of the Commission have five-year mandates which can be renewed and members of the Court of Justice and Court of First Instance have six-year mandates which can be renewed. The judges are protected from too much political interference at reappointment by the collegiate nature of their judgments. They never have to expose their opinion in public in the way that the President of the ECB has to in accounting to the European Parliament.

[45] Most notably with the Luxembourg Compromise, and, more recently, in the Ioannina Compromise of 1994, subsequently reduced to law in the form of a Council Decision (OJ 1994 C105/1, amended by OJ 1995 C1/1).

the credentials to establish itself as an entity for whom full constitutional recognition is appropriate and deserving.[46]

4. The Euro and a Fragmented Legal Order

The irrevocable fixing of the exchange rates between the eleven member states of the EU participating in the first wave of the single currency took place on 1 January 1999 following upon the adoption by Ecofin of Council Regulation 2866/98 of 31 December 1998 on the conversion rates between the euro and the currencies of the member states adopting the euro.[47] The euro notes and coins will start to circulate in the euro-zone on 1 January 2002 and by 1 July 2002 the national banknotes and coins in the euro-zone countries will be withdrawn from circulation.[48] So the euro was born on 1 January 1999 for eleven of the fifteen member states of the EU. The Governing Council of the ECB now controls interest rates, money supply and exchange rate policy for the eleven states in the euro-zone.[49] However, although its birth was vitally important to the financial markets and currency traders it rather passed the citizen of Europe by. Cashless transactions can be conducted in the euro[50] and the Commission recommends

[46] See for example, the seminal debate in the pages of the *European Law Journal*, (1995) 1(3). D. Grimm, "Does Europe need a Constitution?"; J. Habermas, "Reply to Grimm"; J.H.H. Weiler, "Demos, Telos, Ethos and the Maastricht Decision. See also N. Walker, "European Constitutionalism and European Integration", (1996) *Public Law* pp.266–90; R. Bellamy, V. Bufachi and D. Castiglione (eds.) *Democracy and Constitutional Culture in the Union of Europe* (Edinburgh, Lothian Foundation, 1995); M. Everson, "Beyond the *Bundesverfassungsgericht*: On the Necessary Cunning of Constitutional Reasoning", (1998) 4(4) *European Law Journal*, pp.389–410.

[47] OJ 1998 L359/1 which entered into force on 1 January 1999.

[48] See Arts. 10–16 of Regulation 974/98 of 3 May 1998 on the introduction of the euro, OJ 1998 L139/1.

[49] See Art. 12 of the Protocol on the ESCB. The Council can create a new ERM with non-member states by unanimity among the eleven members of the euro-zone (see Art. 111(1), ex 109(1) EC) but this is unlikely for the foreseeable future. The Council can also formulate by qualified majority vote among the eleven members of the euro-zone "general orientations for exchange rate policy" (see Art. 111(2), ex 109(2) EC) but the Luxembourg European Council of 13 December 1997 decided that such guidelines would be restricted to "exceptional circumstances" like a "clear misalignment" of exchange rates with non-EU currencies and "should always respect the independence of the ESCB and be consistent with the primary objective of the ESCB to maintain price stability". In any case "guidelines" are not binding and the ECB could choose not to follow them. The same Luxembourg European Council Resolution also stated that "the harmonious economic development of the Community in Stage 3 of EMU [single currency phase] will call for continuous and fruitful dialogue between the Council and the ECB." This is a recognition that although monetary policy is in the hands of the ECB, economic policy remains with the member states of the euro-zone and to a much lesser extent with the Council, see Ch. 4 *supra* by I. Harden.

[50] See Regulation 974/98 of 3 May 1998 on the introduction of the euro, OJ 1998 L139/1, esp. Art. 8.

dual pricing of goods in the local currency and in the euro,[51] but the average citizen is still using the familiar local currency of francs, marks, lira, etc. to pay for their transactions and even when they move within the euro-zone still incur the charges involved in changing currency. It will be the latter half of 2002, when the euro coins and banknotes are brought in and the national banknotes and coins are withdrawn, before all transactions will be conducted in the euro. At this point currency conversion, and the associated costs, will not be necessary and people will identify with the euro. This may have profound implications for a sense of European citizenship or European identity.

What European entity will the euro enable people to identify with? If no further progress is made before 2002 it will be the truncated eleven member euro-zone, not the EU. The European integration project has always cherished the idea of developing the *acquis communautaire* for all member states. However, arguably the most profound development of the Union to date, at least in terms of its day-to-day impact upon the average citizen's life, will go ahead in 2002 with only some members of the Union. Perhaps variable geometry or differentiated integration is now inevitable and the Union is set to evolve in a more fragmented way[52] but this will have

[51] See Commission Recommendation of 23 April 1998 concerning dual display of prices and other monetary amounts (98/287/EC), OJ 1998 L130/26, discussed by J. Usher in Ch. 1 *supra*. Not surprisingly dual pricing was already very evident in the restaurants of Brussels, with some notable exceptions, by February 1999. Given the percentage of the clientele who work in the Community institutions there or who are visiting those institutions for meetings, it is little wonder that they are sensitive to pleasing the Commission and other eurocrats. The lack of complete compliance with the recommendation in Brussels and the tiny amount of purchases being made in euros in France, see *The Times* 18 February 1999, show that the psychological change to using the euro is still in its infancy.

[52] Even the Community institutions may favour fragmentation in certain circumstance. The Opinion of the Council Legal Service on the Legal Consequences of the Treaty of Amsterdam on the revision of the Brussels Convention, Brussels 5 February 1999, JUR 25, JUSTCIV 3, states that once the Treaty of Amsterdam enters into force the appropriate legal basis for the revision of the Brussels Convention is Arts. 65 and 67 EC, and therefore the instrument would be a regulation or a directive, rather than its current legal basis of Art. 293 (ex 220) EC. This view is advanced notwithstanding the fact that the choice of Arts. 65 and 67 EC definitely precludes Denmark (it has a complete opt out from Title IV of the EC Treaty) from participating and may exclude the UK and Ireland (which have a flexible opt out from Title IV of the EC Treaty which permits those states to opt in to particular measures if they wish). Both legal bases require unanimity and the legal protection for the Community citizen is greater under Art. 293 (ex 220) EC because the 1971 Protocol to the Brussels Convention permits any appellate court in a contracting state to refer cases to the European Court of Justice for a preliminary ruling whereas a Community regulation or directive adopted under Title IV of the EC Treaty can only be referred to the European Court for a preliminary ruling by a court against whose decisions there is no judicial remedy (Art. 68(1) EC). It is likely that the Commission Legal Service will support the view taken by the Council Legal Service. So much for the importance of keeping the whole of the European Union together, for enhancing judicial protection of European citizens and for developing the *acquis communautaire*!

the consequence of people having a weak sense of which Europe, or which *Europes*, they belong to. However the degree of fragmentation could yet be minimised.

As we have seen above[53] Greece is keen to join the euro-zone and hopes to have achieved the convergence criteria by the time of the next review in the year 2000 so that it can join the euro-zone on 1 January 2001, well before the introduction of euro notes and coins. The Labour Government elected in the UK in 1997 shifted Government policy from a wait-and-see approach, steeped in constitutional scepticism, to a commitment in principle to join the euro which is free from sovereignty objections but is guided by macro-economic consideration, in particular having the UK business cycle running more in parallel with that of the euro-zone.[54] It now seems likely that if the Labour Party win the next general election in the UK in 2001-2 they will subsequently launch a referendum on the UK adopting the euro. However, they have hardly begun to persuade public opinion that it would be a good option to join the euro-zone.[55] Although in late February 1999 a poll suggested that opinion was almost evenly divided on whether the UK should join the euro, earlier surveys had consistently suggested a more hostile attitude.[56] Much work remains to be done to overturn the largely hostile propaganda of the UK press[57] but, as argued above, it is still conceivable that the UK will join the euro-zone some time

[53] See n.26 *supra*.

[54] See Ch. 3 *supra* by A. Darling. The *Outline National Changeover Plan* (London, HM Treasury, 1999) reiterates the Chancellor of the Exchequer's October 1997 statement that there is "no constitutional bar to British membership of EMU" and repeats the five economic tests which have to be met before any decision to join can be taken: "These are: whether the UK economy has achieved sustainable convergence with the economies of the single currency; whether there is sufficient flexibility in the UK economy to adapt to change and other unexpected economic events [code for could the UK economy cope with an asymmetric economic shock]; whether joining the single currency would create better conditions for businesses to make long-term decisions to invest in the UK; the impact membership would have on the UK financial services industry; and ultimately whether joining the single currency would be good for employment [code for whether the ECB will avoid running such a tight monetary policy that it becomes deflationary]." (Ch. 2.3).

[55] Indeed, given the strong campaign by the Scottish National Party, in particular by its leader Alex Salmond, in favour of early entry to the euro, the ironic possibility is opened up that a project developed in part better to secure *European* political identity could in fact contribute to the fracturing of *British* political identity.

[56] In *The Times*, 27 February 1999, 46% indicated in favour, 45% against. On the other hand, an opinion poll in *The Guardian* on 11 February 1999 showed that 52% were against the euro, 36% for and the rest undecided and this was the narrowest gap between those in favour and those against in a series of *Guardian* polls. Scottish opinion was recorded as being evenly divided, 40% for, 40% against, see *The Herald* 18 February 1999.

[57] A summary of the coverage of the euro in UK national newspapers between May 1998 and January 1999 showed a significant preponderance of unfavourable articles about the euro with only the *Financial Times*, *The Guardian* and *The Independent* with a majority of stories in favour, see *The Times*, 12 February 1999.

in 2003.[58] The Prime Minister's statement to the House of Commons on 23 February 1999, and more particularly his responses to questions and his intonation, indicated a much stronger commitment to the euro and a sign that he will encourage a cross-party campaign in favour of UK membership of the euro. Of course, if the Conservative Party were to win the next UK general election it has ruled out the possibility of the UK joining the euro during the lifetime of the next Parliament (i.e. for a further four or five years).[59] As a third possibility, should a coalition between Labour and the Liberal Democrats be the outcome of the next UK general election, then a referendum on the single currency becomes even more likely given the Liberal Democrats' pro-euro stance.

In May 1998 Sweden clearly did not want to be a part of the euro-zone but public policy could change in that country, particularly if its Finnish neighbour is seen to benefit from its membership of the euro-zone. Already at the beginning of 1999 it seems that public opinion is moving in favour of the euro.[59a] Several of the major political parties are in favour, including the Conservatives (Moderates), Christian Democrats and Liberals, but crucially the Social Democrats are as yet undecided. The question of membership of the euro-zone could be determined at the next Swedish general election, at the latest in the year 2002, or by a referendum on the issue. It is still possible that Sweden, like the UK, could join the euro-zone by 2002 or 2003, not long after the euro banknotes come into circulation in the euro-zone. Denmark has an opt-out which it exercised prior to the May 1998 decision on who should join the first wave of the euro. However, public opinion has shifted since then and an opinion poll in February 1999 showed a majority in favour of Denmark joining the euro and only about a third against with around a fifth don't knows.[60] Given that most of the political parties are in favour of the euro in Denmark it now seems quite likely that there will be a referendum by the year 2000 on Denmark joining the euro-zone. It is therefore possible, if not probable, that Denmark, will join the euro-zone by the year 2002 when the currency is fully launched.

The enlargement process is moving slowly so any new member states are unlikely to come into the EU until after 2002, when the euro begins its

---

[58] See the discussion of this matter supra at n.27 *et seq*. The UK's participation or lack of it in the ERM Mark II may be a significant factor. Dr Duisenberg is on record (see *The European Central Bank: will it work?*) as saying that the UK should be in the ERM Mark II for 18 months before joining the euro-zone but it is the Council, not the ECB, which decides on whether states can join the euro.

[59] However, some very senior Conservatives like the former Prime Minister, Edward Heath, the former Deputy Prime Minister, Michael Heseltine, and the former Chancellor of the Exchequer, Kenneth Clarke, will join a campaign for the euro in alliance with the Liberal Democrats and the Labour Party.

[59a] See *Dagens Nyheter*, 23 March 1999, recording an opinion poll in which 38% were in favour of Swedish membership of the euro and 37% against.

[60] See *Berlingske Tidende*, February 1999. This does not appear to be a rogue poll.

visible life. In any case, several central and eastern European countries will struggle to meet the convergence criteria and therefore their membership of the euro-zone may, at least in some cases, be postponed beyond their membership of the EU. Yet, on the basis of the above survey, it is becoming increasingly plausible that for the fifteen current member states of the EU the variable geometry associated with the euro will be short-lived. By 2002 or 2003 the whole of the Union may be united in monetary union and the identity created by the euro will be that of the Union as a whole and not some smaller sub-group. The dreams of visionaries like Jacques Delors may yet be realised.

However this new found enthusiasm for the euro is based on the first few weeks of its existence and may be evidence of a honeymoon period. The euro may not be tested for some time, perhaps not until after all fifteen member states have joined. As we have seen in this book there are some limitations on the mechanisms available within the EU to cope with the strains of fitting one monetary policy into a large number of different economies. The EC Treaty does provide mechanisms for controlling excessive government deficits and a regime of sanctions comes into being from the beginning of the single currency for the member states which are part of the euro-zone.[61] A member state which persistently fails to follow the recommendations of the Council to correct an excessive deficit may be given a time limit to comply.[62] If the state fails to comply then the Council, by a two-thirds majority not counting the representative of the state concerned,[63] can require the member state to make a non-interest bearing deposit of an appropriate size with the Community until the excessive deficit has, in the view of the Council, been corrected, and/or the Council can impose fines of an appropriate size.[64] Germany and some other member states were anxious to put some more flesh on the bones of these Treaty provisions to help to ensure fiscal rectitude by all the member states in the euro-zone and yet to allow some modest fiscal leeway for states facing an economic crisis. High level discussions took place and the importance of the negotiations was highlighted by the fact that it was at European Council level that final approval was given in 1997 to the "Stability and Growth Pact" (SGP).

This package comprises hard law[65] and soft law.[66] In order to help

[61] See Arts. 104(11), 116(3) and 122(3) (ex 104c(11), 109e(3) and 109k(3)) EC.

[62] See Art. 104(9) (ex 104c(9)) EC.

[63] See Art. 104(13) (ex 104c(13)) EC. The votes are weighted using the numbers in Art. 205(2) (ex 148(2)) EC.

[64] See Art. 104(11) (ex 104c(11)) EC.

[65] Regulation 1466/97 of 7 July 1997 on the strengthening of the surveillance of budgetary positions and the surveillance and co-ordination of economic policies, OJ 1997 L209/1 and Regulation 1467/97 of 7 July 1997 on speeding up and clarifying the implementation of the excessive deficit procedure, OJ 1997 L209/6.

[66] Resolution of the European Council on the Stability and Growth Pact of 17 June 1997, OJ 1997 C236/1.

member states within the euro-zone cope with asymmetric economic shocks[67] or localised economic downturns it permits them to exceed a deficit of three per cent of Gross Domestic Product (GDP) in a severe recession. If there is an annual fall of real GDP of at least two per cent then the strong presumption is that the member state can increase its borrowings beyond three per cent of GDP[68]. An annual fall of real GDP of between three-quarters of one per cent[69] and two per cent will be regarded as a severe recession, and therefore permit the state to exceed a deficit of three per cent of GDP, only "in the light of further supporting evidence, in particular on the abruptness of the downturn or on the accumulated loss of output relative to past trends".[70] If a member state in the euro-zone's deficit exceeds three per cent when that country is not in a severe recession then it will be required to pay a deposit to the Commission of up to half of one per cent of GDP and if it continues to run excessive deficits for two years the deposit will, as a rule, be converted into a fine.[71]

Although the SGP contains the "medium-term objective for the budgetary position of close to balance or in surplus"[72] it can be criticised for not creating enough incentives for euro-zone states to maintain a surplus in the good years to balance the inevitable deficits in the bad years, thus forcing an over-reliance on the mechanisms for policing excessive deficits.[73] And while the Pact allows states within the euro-zone to borrow beyond three per cent of GDP this may not be a sufficient remedy for an affected state in a severe recession, particularly if the majority of the euro-zone is not affected by the downturn, perhaps due to an asymmetric economic shock. The ECB may decide not to adjust interest rates[74] and the

---

[67] An "asymmetric economic shock" is one which effects part of the euro-zone but not the rest e.g. if the world market in cork were to collapse the effects on the Portuguese economy would be major but the impact on the other euro-zone economies would be negligible. See further A. Scott in Ch. 2 *supra*. Normal economic downturns should not be a problem. Dr Duisenberg in his evidence to the House of Lords Select Committee (see *The European Central Bank: will it work?*) noted that in the Netherlands over the last fifty years the "maximum cyclically-caused variation in the public deficit had never exceeded 2 percentage points of GDP". See also the statistics cited by A. Scott in ch. 2 *supra*, n.19.

[68] See Art. 2 of Reg. 1467/97.

[69] This minimum threshold is part of soft law not hard law, see para. 7 under the "Member States" of the European Council Resolution, note 66 *supra*.

[70] See Art. 2(3) of Regulation 1467/97.

[71] See Arts. 11–16 of Regulation 1467/97.

[72] See Art. 3(2) of Regulation 1466/97.

[73] See *The European Central Bank; will it work?*; Eichengreen and Wyplosz, "The Stability Pact: More than a Minor Nuisance?", (1998) 26 *Economic Policy* 65–114; and, more generally on the Stability and Growth Pact, Chs. 4 and 2 *supra* by I. Harden and A. Scott.

[74] The ECB regards price stability, its primary objective, as meaning between 0 and 2% inflation in the euro-zone (see the evidence by Dr Duisenberg in *The European CentralBank:*

value of the euro may be unaffected on world markets. In these circumstances the state affected might have high borrowings and high taxes to pay for the increased public expenditure, which is almost inevitable in a recession due to more people requiring unemployment and welfare benefits and fewer people paying taxes, a strong currency making exports difficult,[75] but little or none of the hoped for labour migration to other parts of the euro-zone. Of course, the state might be in receipt of cohesion funds and some or all of its regions might qualify for structural funds, but the scale of these funds is such that they are unlikely to be sufficient to help the state get out of the economic crisis.[76] The Community's competence in funding poverty alleviation programmes is questionable and the scale of resources that could be devoted so pitiful[77] that it is highly unlikely to be able to

will it work? and his speech on 25 January 1999 at the Frankfurt Chamber of Commerce and Industry, see *Monetary policy in the euro areas*). As the latter speech by Dr Duisenberg shows, the Governing Council are trying to achieve price stability by having an inflation target and by having a target for limiting growth in the money supply. Hopefully it will be willing to reduce interest rates to help economic growth and higher employment whenever it believes it can do so without pushing inflation beyond 2% rather than always trying to drive inflation to as close to zero as possible. Such a policy will help a general downturn in the euro-zone but will give little assistance to a relatively small economy within the zone which is facing severe recession while other economies are relatively buoyant because the ECB will have to set interest rates to cope with inflationary pressures in the latter economies. The fact that the President of the Council and a member of the Commission are present at the Governing Council of the European Central Bank and can submit motions to the Governing Council (see Art. 113(3) (ex 109b) EC) enables the Community institutions to engage in a "constructive dialogue" (see Ch. 6 *supra* by M. Everson) with the ECB while it is formulating its interest rate policies. The opportunity exists to persuade the Governing Council of the ECB to give appropriate weight to achieving high unemployment and sustainable growth as part of the ECB's duty to "support the general economic policies in the Community with a view to contributing to the achievement of the objectives of the Community as laid down in Article 2" (see Art. 105(1) EC). This constructive dialogue prior to decision making by the ECB and the *ex-post facto* reporting and questioning in the European Parliament (see Art. 113(3) (ex 109b(3)) EC) provide constitutionally entrenched procedures to create the appropriate degree of accountability for the ECB consistent with its independence. Some commentators think the ECB may end up giving "the goal of high employment virtual parity with that of price stability" (see R.J. Goebel, "European Economic and Monetary Union: Will the Emu ever fly?", (1998) 4 *Columbia Journal of European Law* 249, 300). However the ECB is tied by the constitution of the European Union to give price stability formal primacy over all other objectives. This can be contrasted with the more flexible solution in the United States which allows Congress to set goals for the Federal Reserve Board (*ibid*, pp.291–99). The House of Lords Select Committee thought the greatest danger to the euro lay in member states not proceeding fast enough with structural reforms to free up their labour, product and financial markets (see para. 131 of *The European Central Bank: will it work?*).

[75] The strength of the euro vis-a-vis other currencies may not be such a major factor because most of the trade will be within the euro-zone. Dr Duisenberg reckons that the share of exports in GDP of the euro-zone states, excluding intra-euro zone trade, will be around 10% (a figure similar to that for both the United States and Japan), see *The European Central Bank: will it work?*, para. 92.

[76] See Ch. 7 *supra* by J. Scott and S. Vousden.   [77] *Ibid.*

placate social unrest from Union citizens in the affected state who blame their country's membership of the euro on their predicament. With little or no prospect of fiscal transfers from other member states it is difficult to see how such a state could recover.[78] So the Delors vision may yet turn into a nightmare, at least for one or more of the member states.

Thus, in conclusion, we may note that the challenge of variable geometry[79] to the foundational legal identity of the Union arises at one or both of two stages. There is, first, the contemporary challenge, which appears to be receding, with all four states outwith the euro-zone moving towards full membership, however slowly and unsurely. If this prediction is correct, the current trajectory is consistent with the operation of a multi-speed Europe in which all members move at different speeds towards the same ultimate destination, and thus the fundamental unity of the legal order is preserved.

Yet it is beginning to appear that a second wave of challenge will in due course tax the fundamental unity of the European legal order much more keenly. Clearly, even if the fifteen do fall obediently into line, the long-term sustainability of the single currency will depend upon whether the EU has the political legitimacy to withstand and the regulatory tools to address the economic difficulties which the maintenance of the single currency will inevitably visit upon certain states and regions from time to time, not least states and regions from outside of the present fifteen which will start from a position of significant disadvantage. In an echo of the paradox which attended the development and early application of the convergence criteria, and indeed a number of other major institutional debates and developments throughout the history of the EU,[80] the Union's response to criticisms as to the adequacy of its institutional design and to misgivings as to the extent of its political authority may be to ask for *more* powers. Thus the integra-

---

[78] In his evidence to the House of Lords Select Committee on the European Communities the Commissioner responsible for EMU, Mr de Silguy, thought there was no prospect of an increase in the Community budget to enable resources to be transferred to states in the euro-zone which are facing severe economic difficulties (see *The European Central Bank: will it work?*, para.89). The scale of the EU budget is far too small in relation to the size of the EU economy to provide for meaningful fiscal transfers. Dr Duisenberg has noted that the US Federal budget is around 30% of US GDP whereas the EU budget is 1.27% of EU GDP, see his evidence in *The European Central Bank: will it work?*. For further discussion of this problem see Chs. 2 and 7 *supra* by A. Scott and by J. Scott and S. Vousden.

[79] For discussion of present trends and prospects as regards differentiated integration, with particular reference to the post-Amsterdam situation, see for example, J. Shaw, "The Treaty of Amsterdam: the challenges of flexibility and legitimacy", (1998) 4(1) *European Law Journal*; G. Gaja, "How Flexible is Flexibility under the Amsterdam Treaty?", (1998) 35 *Common Market Law Review* pp.855–70; H. Kortenberg, "Closer Co-operation in the Treaty of Amsterdam," (1998) 35 *Common Market Law Review* pp.833–54; N. Walker, *supra* n.10.

[80] One thinks, for example, of the protracted debates over the desirability of majority voting in the Council, or the "deepening versus widening debate".

tionist utopia of a comprehensive co-ordination of all dimensions of economic governance may clash head-on with the nationalist dystopia of the final loss of economic and political sovereignty, with seemingly little scope left for a compromise solution. Then, more than ever, the dual significance of law in the EU—as both cause and effect—will be highlighted. Not only will the resolution of the fundamental debate about economic co-ordination depend in part upon the authority and versatility of the legal instruments then available, but it will also have significant implications for the very nature and potential of the legal order (or orders) of the EU in the new millennium.[81]

---

[81] Thus, if neither law nor politics can prevent the movement towards a more fragmented legal order, that resulting legal order will face new, or at least intensified problems concerning boundary disputes between different European jurisdictions, co-ordination within an increasingly complex jigsaw of political institutions, and democratic accountability along increasingly blurred lines of representation and responsibility; and will be required to do so without whatever "legitimacy credit" attaches to European law on account of its unbroken institutional continuity with the founding claim of the uniformity of supranational law. For fuller discussion, see N. Walker, *supra*, n10, pp.375–88.

Index